Novels and Hormones

Novels and Hormones

The Mystery of the Sexuality of Victorian Women

Lawrence B Mohr

ISBN: 1536930520
ISBN 13: 9781536930528

The Grandison Press
Portland, Oregon
2016

Acknowledgments

I owe a huge debt of gratitude to Professor Karen Lystra. Her careful critique of the manuscript steered me away from errors and led to a tighter whole. At earlier stages, I received valuable comments from Rick Mohr, Bill Broder, Lezlee Crawford, and Alexandra, whose last name is lost in my poorly organized notes. Moral support was critically important to me in this undertaking; I deeply prize the support I received from Bill and Gloria Broder, Tonia Short Rose, Nancy Rosenfeld, and my wife, my children, and my step-children. Lastly, the editing skills of Nina Catanese and Beth Skony were a terrific help in moving toward readability. Shortcomings remain, I'm sure, for which I alone am responsible.

Table of Contents

I

The mystery is introduced

There is one widespread image of women in the Victorian age that seems peculiar. In fact, it seems dubious. This image would have us believe that the women of that era were totally sexless, that is, straitlaced, prudish, repressed, ignorant, and, therefore, incredibly naive. It is easy to accept that authorities such as the church, state, parents, and the older generation in general might have tried to force them into that mold, but it is hard to believe that they succeeded – except, perhaps, so far as to drive their sexual behavior underground even more than usual. Yet, the image is a strong and persistent one. Just consider this smattering of quotes from scholars on the subject:

> Victorian Britain is mainly remembered for two things: sexual prudishness and long novels. (Professor Eric Clarke in a 1998 book review.)[1]
> Evidence seemed to indicate that Victorians stumbled about in the pre-Freudian darkness, victims of a sexual repression so thoroughgoing that it severed entirely the mind from the body. (Professor Sarah Stage in a 1975 book review.)[2]
> Acton's book was undoubtedly one of the most widely quoted sexual-advice books in the English-speaking world. The book summed up the medical literature on women's sexuality by saying that "the majority of

1 Clarke 1998, p. 260.

2 Stage 1975, p. 480.

> women (happily for them) are not very much troubled with sexual feelings of any kind." (Professor Carl Degler in a 1974 article.)[3]
>
> There are also memorable absurdities of etiquette, like that recommended by Lady Gough in 1863: "The perfect hostess will see to it that the works of male and female authors be properly separated on her bookshelves. Their proximity, unless they happen to be married, should not be tolerated." (Professor F. Barry Smith in a 1977 chapter.)[4]
>
> As every schoolgirl knows, the nineteenth century was afraid of sex, particularly when it manifested itself in women. . . . Women's alleged lack of passion was epitomized, too, in the story of the English mother who was asked by her daughter before her marriage how she ought to behave on her wedding night. "Lie still and think of the Empire," the mother advised. (Professor Carl Degler in the same 1974 article.)[5]

Surely, the picture painted by these quotes is too far-fetched to believe. True, they wore long skirts in those days, but long skirts can be lifted. Should we not presume that they often were? On the other hand, the Victorian age is not that far in our past. Seniors alive today can tell you simply from having interacted with their grandmothers that the Victorians adhered to a different moral code. The stereotype, in other words, has been handed down through real people. And then there are the novels. I recall the 1993 movie *Indecent Proposal*. It begins with a contemporary married couple naked in bed making passionate love. In the Victorian novels, married couples never make love. The only way we know that they have sex is through the sudden appearance of births and children. In addition to what has come down through real people, the persistent, living stereotype is due prominently to the major novels and now the many movies that have been based on them. But is the portrayal in the novels an accurate one?

To be honest, several of the passages quoted above, particularly those from the historian Carl Degler, were given as straw men; the authors soon went on to say that the traditional view needed to be modified: nineteenth-century women

3 Degler 1974, p. 1467.

4 Smith, F. Barry 1977, p. 182.

5 Degler, 1974, p. 1467.

actually behaved a lot more like twentieth-century women than has generally been thought. But what is their evidence for this? In fact, what is the evidence for the older, more common view? Crucially, which view is correct? I say "crucially" because it would seem to be important for our grasp of what is often called "human nature" to learn whether the near obliteration of sexuality is a possibility.

Accordingly, our interest in this book will be primarily in the following questions: Could there possibly have been an age in which the women of a large and growing social class – the middle class – had almost no sex? Is it possible that there was a time when the married women had sex only when needed to produce children and the young, unmarried women had no sexual experience at all – no reading of sexual materials, no sexual conversation of any sort, and not even any sexual thoughts?

There are those who would answer, "Yes, not only could there have been such a period but there was, namely, the age loosely bracketed as the Victorian Period in Britain and America." We will see that many who hold this view are scholars who have spent years studying the period. But we will also see that many people would take the opposite view. Some of these are also scholars, but in addition there are ordinary folks who consider that Victorian women were nevertheless women, having the normal complement of sexual hormones and opportunities. Sexual inclinations have always found a means of expressing themselves and always will. The Victorians were no different.

Queen Victoria reigned in Britain from 1837 to 1901, but the term "Victorian" is often used more loosely. Here, it will be advantageous to consider the whole nineteenth century and a bit of the beginning of the twentieth because it is that span of time that is so different in overt sexual policy from the starkly more liberal periods coming just before and just afterwards. I shall try to be fairly precise in the use of these terms, but often "Victorian" will be employed loosely to refer to this whole period in which women, supposedly, were more than usually sexually repressed.

Milling about at a cocktail party, I posed the following question to two well-educated strangers about thirty years of age, one a man, one a woman: What's your guess regarding the sexuality score of middle-class Victorian women on a scale of 0 to 5? On this scale, zero equals very repressed and ignorant, with no sexual thoughts or behaviors except when married – for the purpose of reproduction – and the attitude that even the tiniest sexual liberty is both sinful and dangerous. At the other end, 5 equals very aware, knowledgeable, amorous, and ready and willing to take chances if it could be done discreetly. They both immediately answered "5." Why? Probably because they did not really know much about the Victorian period and assumed that hormones are hormones. On the other hand, most folks who have read a lot of the classic Victorian authors – Dickens, Eliot, Hardy, and so on – would probably have answered something like 0 or 1. Academic experts would have a more guarded view. They would probably say that most of the available literature and documentation by far would indeed place the answer close to zero, but, they would add, there is some contrary evidence and, in sum, there is not enough information to really be sure. Too bad! We would like to know the answer.

It happens that we are in an extremely difficult position here. The problem we face in trying to solve "the mystery," as I will call it, will not yield to ordinary methods. What we would like to have is hard evidence demonstrating either that Victorian women were totally repressed or that they were sexually quite interested and active. Certainly, for example, if there were an abundance of descriptions of marital sexual bliss and pre-marital sexual liaisons in the letters and diaries of the age, then the issue would be settled. We would be quite certain that hormones prevailed. (I use the term "hormones" throughout this book in the informal, colloquial sense to stand for natural, biological sexual inclinations and urges.) Nobody would be claiming that Victorian women were radically sexually repressed. That is the way we would like historical questions to be resolved.

But what if there were no positive evidence at all in the diaries and letters? If you were one of those who wished to make the claim of "sexually quite interested and active," you would be in a difficult spot. You would have zero evidence to support your position. But does that mean that those who wished to claim radical repression – sexuality at a bare minimum – must be correct? Not at all. Just because a record of widespread sexual activity does not appear in letters and diaries, we cannot necessarily conclude that such activity did not take place. Perhaps it did indeed take place, and quite commonly, but without generating a record.

There are therefore two critical issues here that must be confronted. One is whether appropriate historical documents do exist to support a claim of abundant sexual activity. The other is whether the activity could have been common without generating the expected record.

Start with the first issue: Do we have the documentation that we need to demonstrate widespread sexual activity? No, we do not, and this is surprising because the nineteenth century was full to the brim with writing. There are volumes upon published volumes of edited letters and also endless collections of diaries and letters that have been examined but not published. If there is no trace of sexual indulgence in all of this, then a preliminary conclusion must be that there was no sex.

Scholars have diligently combed through the documents and have found scant evidence of the expected achievements of sex hormones among middle-class women of the period. There is a smattering of published letters and diaries from the American side of the Atlantic, and we will examine those in a special light in Chapter VI, but they are too few to treat quantitatively and too unusual to be considered representative of the population as a whole. Researchers have commented on the lack of hard information concerning Victorian sexuality in all of this rich historical material.

> Any systematic knowledge of the sexual habits of women is a relatively recent historical acquisition, confined to the surveys of women made in the 1920s and 1930s and culminating in the well-known Kinsey report. Until recently no even slightly comparable body of evidence for nineteenth-century women was known to exist. (Professor Degler again in 1974.)[6]
>
> As others before him, the late Humphrey House once remarked upon the paucity of our knowledge concerning sexual behavior in Victorian England. For House, the extreme reticence of the Victorians magnified the value of every fragment of evidence pertaining to sexual behavior

6 Degler 1974, pp. 1479-80.

> that scholars uncovered. (Professor Peter Cominos in an article from 1963.)[7]
>
> Advice literature was ample, accessible, and undeniably enjoyable. The actual sexual behavior of Victorian women and men remained obscure. (Professor Sarah Stage in 1975.)[8]
>
> Indeed, when one begins to look for evidence for the stereotype, its insubstantiality becomes worrying. . . . We know almost nothing about actual sexual practices. (Professor F. Barry Smith in the 1977 chapter.)[9]

Ordinarily, this staggering silence would go far toward reinforcing the stereotype of repression, the presumption being that if, in this important area, people commonly behaved in a certain way, a great many of them would somehow be sure to have left a record. However, if in a particular, special historical instance there were good reason to believe that the documentation would be absent *even if the behavior were present*, then doubt and uncertainty would justifiably arise. This brings us to the second issue noted above, the question whether sexual activity could have been common without generating the expected record.

As it happens, unfortunately, we do know for sure – and this will be treated later in detail – that the social policies, the training of young people in the middle class, and the norms of publication and polite speech in the Victorian era strictly forbade and quite effectively restricted the public airing of sexual experiences and possibly prevented even their private recording. Public shame, sharp critical disapproval, and financial jeopardy discouraged authors from writing about sex. Child-rearing practices commonly hid from girls and young women all knowledge that there was such a thing in the world as sexuality. All reference to sexual topics was strictly forbidden in polite speech, especially if women were present. Yes, most diaries and letters are supposed to be private, but it is readily believable that Victorians would avoid sexual topics even there for fear that their scribblings might somehow be exposed to uninvited eyes. Therefore, the silence on these topics in the writings of the period cannot be

7 Cominos 1963 p. 18.

8 Stage 1975, pp. 480-1.

9 Smith, F. Barry 1977, pp. 183, 188.

used to show that Victorian women must have been severely sexually repressed. Whatever they may have done sexually – and for all we know at this point in the story it may have been quite a lot – it was not the sort of thing that people wrote about.

But at the same time, this very silence makes it impossible for my two cocktail party respondents to make a clear case for rule by sex hormones. Their side would love some good documentation of sexual goings-on, but it apparently does not exist. The letters and diaries provide no evidence that the women of the period had sexual urges or, if they did, that they indulged them. Still, we have to allow that my respondents might have been correct. It is possible that both pre-marital sexual experience and married sexual enthusiasm were fairly common while necessarily being hidden totally from view because of the social norms.

Thus, the enforced lack of documentation bothers both sides while not demolishing either one. It makes the case for the victory of hormones hard to defend because of the lack of positive evidence but keeps it alive by showing that this absence of a record is completely understandable. At the same time, the silence strongly suggests that there was little or no sex, but since people would not write about sex even if it were common, we cannot be sure.

In the exploration of subsequent chapters, these bothersome norms against any allusion to sexuality will complicate the analysis but will not frustrate it completely. For the analyst, the strong norms of reticence are regrettable – but then again, without them the Victorian era would not have been quite what it was.

Because of the lack of satisfactory documentation, our central question – complete repression versus common but unrecorded sexual activity – is highly unlikely ever to be answered with absolute certainty. At the moment, the academic community across several disciplines is divided. There is, however, a lot of good material – varying widely in source and type – that can well be considered as evidence to aid in the solution of the mystery. The bits and pieces need to be looked at closely, challenged, and then laid out all together so that one can judge the weight of both sides. I will access these fragments of evidence. They are taken from the advice literature, some letters and diaries that do exist, some vital statistics, some academic reasoning, the nineteenth-century novels, the record of sexuality in earlier and later periods, and, most beguilingly, the Mosher survey, a long-hidden questionnaire on sexual topics that was answered by forty-five Victorian women. One chapter of this opus is devoted in full to the Mosher survey and several others are devoted to it in part. Although this combination of sources does not produce the certainty that would come from abundant contemporary written evidence of sexual activity, it does yield an answer that in my estimation has a high probability of being correct. As one might suspect from the fact that there is disagreement and a good deal to be said for the arguments on both sides, the answer, though definite, is not as simple as are the two opposing positions that have dominated the discussion up to now.

This book is by no means a historical treatise on Victorianism. One of its two principal aims, however, in addition to solving the mystery, is to provide the reader with insight into the key social, psychological, and political aspects of Victorianism that influenced the sexuality of Victorian women and that render it understandable in what turns out to be its critical diversity.

We turn first to the so-called "advice literature." It happens that those writings of the period that bore heavily on how women *should* behave – moral treatises, sermons (it was a very religious age), expert opinion, laws, and so on – were apparently so strong and unified that their general thrust was unmistakably in the category of public policy. Almost by definition, most people adhere to public policy. Whatever the advice, if it was public policy, women would have been under intense pressure to conform. The pressure does not necessarily mean that they *did* conform – certainly not all of them, at any rate – but it does raise the likelihood substantially of widespread obedience. Chapter II gives the flavor of what the advice literature had to say.

II

Victorian women are told who they are and how they must behave

If middle-class Victorian women were sexless, it is highly unlikely that this phenomenon occurred spontaneously. The pull of natural interest and desire is too strong for that. It is much more likely that they were influenced by intense, thoroughgoing socialization. If so, documentation of salient aspects of the socialization will help us judge how far it might actually have gone toward controlling behavior. It is difficult to grasp the events in a different culture while steeped in one's own. If we try to analyze personal behavior in a historical period, we are apt to go wrong without, for example, some knowledge of the social norms and pressures of the time. It is these pressures that we will be concerned with documenting here. Otherwise, our experience of the society of today might lead us to a snap judgment that would too easily give the victory to hormones in our assessment of the central question.

The Evangelical Christian advice literature

To characterize Victorian socialization in regard to sexuality as intense and thoroughgoing is to make use of strong terminology, but not too strong for the advice literature of the late eighteenth and early nineteenth centuries. It was radical and it was laid on heavily. Modern readers will find it amusing on one level but disturbing, perhaps, on another. Some will gag upon reading a few of the passages soon to be reviewed. But apparently, and this is partly to be shown in later chapters, the young, middle-class Victorian woman on both sides of the Atlantic took this moralizing seriously. She was being defined and for the most part she accepted the definition. She had little choice! In England, she generally had no basis in her training from childhood through adolescence for critical judgment of any sort or independence of thought. She had sex hormones, but those precisely were what the advice literature and other socialization strategies were designed either to deny or to overcome, both in Britain and America.

In the first part of this chapter, I will convey the gist of the Evangelical Christian advice literature of the period. I condense and paraphrase at times and use direct quotes at others, all of the material being taken from writers considered by recent scholars to have been among the most widely read of those who preached and wrote in this vein during the time in question. In the second part of the chapter, we will turn to the medical advice literature that took the theme over from the Evangelicals in the latter half of the nineteenth century.

It helps, before we start, to understand that this Evangelical surge of heavy-handed morality was in large part an extreme reaction to an extreme reaction to an extreme prior morality.

The earliest of these three sets of events was the relatively short-lived Puritan ascendance after the English Parliament beheaded King Charles I in 1649. From then until 1660, when Charles II was installed and the Restoration period began, the Puritans held the supreme political power, part of the time through their majority in Parliament and part of the time through the reign of Oliver Cromwell, their political and military leader, and his son, Richard. The religious views of the Puritans were extreme – what we would now call fundamentalist. They felt that essentially every nook and cranny of life must be governed by biblical principles, and they imposed their ideas of private and public morality on the populace.[1] They banned most pleasures, such as gambling, the theater, and Christmas and Easter celebrations (but, curiously enough, not the opera). The traditionally free-wheeling aristocracy was effectively bottled up. Though the aristocracy was not abolished, as some desired, it was as though

1 See the colorful descriptions of both the Puritan period and the Restoration in the *History of English Literature* by the Frenchman Hyppolyte Taine, Vol. II, pp. 132-272.

bound and gagged for years. Aristocrats seethed and smarted under the intense restrictions. Gloom and doom was spread as well over the laboring classes, whose habits of carouse and sexual permissiveness came under the disapproving eye of Big Brother in both government and the pulpit.

In 1660, Richard Cromwell was deposed by internal enemies dissatisfied with his reign, and a brief period of confusion and struggle, both political and military, ensued. Charles II made known his willingness to resume the throne and, after being installed as rightful monarch that year, was crowned in 1661.

The stopper then came out of the bottle. The Restoration period has the distinction of being, in combination, the most lewd, bawdy, filthy, violent, and cruel span of years in English history. Although the extremes of violence abated in the early 1700s, the influence of the Restoration in both literature and sexual mores was felt for a hundred and fifty years afterwards in both Britain and the colonies, displaced finally by Victorian morality only in the nineteenth century. Virtue of any kind was derided as Puritanism. Large segments of the aristocracy became bloodthirsty, brutal, vicious, and decadent. The hero of the age was the Earl of Rochester. His pleasures were in lawlessness, in debauching women – including gutter girls, innocent virgins, and middle- and upper-class wives – in fighting, drinking incessantly, and writing lewd songs and filthy pamphlets. Take, as an example, the opening stanza from his "A Satyr [Satire] on Charles II," which cost him one of many banishments from the court. The language would kill a Victorian; even many moderns will be shocked to get an inkling of the lewdness that was broadly tolerated in the late seventeenth century:

> In th' isle of Britain, long since famous grown
> For breeding the best cunts in Christendom,
> There reigns, and oh! long may he reign and thrive,
> The easiest King and best-bred man alive.
> Him no ambition moves to get renown
> Like the French fool, that wanders up and down
> Starving his people, hazarding his crown.

Peace is his aim, his gentleness is such,
And love he loves, for he loves fucking much.

Rochester ended in poverty at age thirty-three as a quack astrologer and procurer of abortion drugs, his mind and body destroyed by a life of vice, degradation, alcoholism, and excess.[2] The torch was passed to gangs of upper-class youths who terrorized the streets of London until 1712. The last and worst of them called itself the Mohocks. They assaulted both men and women. The men they often disfigured by breaking their noses, cutting off a hand, or pressing out an eye. A large bounty was finally put on their heads, and the institution came to an end.[3]

In the upper class, it was succeeded by another institution, referred to as "Fashion." A large portion of the aristocracy was conspicuously to be witnessed throughout almost the whole of the eighteenth century parading their values by appearing in public places scantily dressed and flaunting their sexuality. The cruelty and violence, however, were dropped. Pressure toward a more decent morality was exerted by leading writers, especially the highly influential, attractive, sometimes whimsical essays of Joseph Addison (1672-1719) in the second decade.[4] Fashion and its sexual tone continued to prevail in the upper classes, but now there were limits. Men could and did visit prostitutes and have unhidden liaisons with working-class women without fear of even the mildest censure, but it was a different story within their own class. The sexual code governing those relations was in reality quite loose, permissive – so much so that by the end of the century numerous gentlemen in high position warned that the crime of adultery was becoming ever more common[5] – but actual behavior under this permissive code had to be private and undiscovered. Both men and women could and did indulge freely as long as it was done discreetly. Public exposure could be costly for men in terms of social disapproval and ruinous lawsuits. A woman might have several lovers and be quietly assumed by her

2 Taine 1900, Vol II, pp. 143-144.

3 Taine 1900, Vol II, p. 277.

4 Taine 1900, Vol II, pp. 327-359.

5 Wilson 2007, p. 34.

associates to be so conducting herself, but allowing one indiscretion to rise to public consciousness would ruin her for life, cutting her off from essentially all respectable social contact. There was no forgiveness.[6] Thus, there developed a social code based in hypocrisy.

In the lower classes, the legacy of the Restoration was more free-wheeling, less guarded. A highly influential book of the period was *Aristotle's Compleat Master Piece*, originally published in 1694 and running to at least forty-three editions by 1800. Its authorship was always anonymous, and it would seem to have been originally written and progressively updated by several hands. Why they dragged Aristotle into it I will never know, but it is certain that the great Greek philosopher had nothing whatever to do with this opus. Some considered it to be subversive and deliberately arousing;[7] to me, it seems more to construe as a fact that there is pleasure in sex and to present this circumstance to the general public along with a thousand other distantly related and considerably drier "facts," a very substantial proportion of which may now be seen to have been wildly incorrect.

For example, the modern historian Ben Wilson rephrases and quotes from the *Master Piece* as follows: (From here, and throughout the remainder of the book, I will quote frequently from sources written in the eighteenth and nineteenth centuries. The reader will encounter examples of spelling, grammar, capitalization, and punctuation – including inconsistencies in all of the above – that are strange, even bizarre, to the modern eye. I have left the quoted text as it appeared in the original rather than attempt to modernize the written culture.)

> Celibacy was [explained to be] dangerous for teenage girls, for they would suffer from the chlorosis or the "green sickness" – respiratory problems, hysteria, loss of appetite or "an unnatural desire of feeding on chalk, coals, stones, tobacco-pipes, sealing wax, and other things of an hurtful and improper nature."[8]

6 Trudgill 1976, pp. 147-174; Wilson 2007, p. 156.

7 Wilson 2007, p. 46.

8 Wilson 2007, p. 45.

In the main, it is a fairly dry, medical sort of text emphasizing pregnancy, childbirth, and midwifery, but its early pages and scattered additional passages describe the sexual organs and the sex act itself with a cheerful gusto, as well as passing judgment pro or con upon numerous other aspects of sexuality.[9] For Victorians, this would have been pornography and very few would have seen it. Nothing even close to the frankness of these descriptions was available to the general Victorian or post-Victorian reader until the publication of Marie Stopes's startling book, *Married Love* in 1918.[10] Some further excerpts from the *Master Piece* give the flavor of its contents:

> I will show that Nature need not be ashamed of her work; give a particular description of the parts or organs of generation in man, and afterwards in woman; and then show the use of these parts in the act of coition; and how positively Nature has adapted them to the end for which He has ordained them.
>
> The organ of generation in man, Nature has placed obvious to the sight, and is called the Yard; and because hanging without the belly, is called the Penis, a pendendo.
>
> And nature has so ordered it, that when the nerves are filled with animal spirits, then the Yard is distended and becomes erect; when flux of the spirit ceases, then the blood and the remaining spirits are absorbed or sucked up by the veins, and so the Penis becomes limber and flaggy.
>
> The fourth is the Glands [glans], which is at the end of the Penis, . . . and by it moving up and down in the act of copulation brings pleasure both to the man and woman.

---

9 Anonymous 1752

10 Stopes 1918.

And thus man's nobler parts we see,
For such the parts of generation be;
And they that carefully survey will find
Each part is fitted for the use design'd.
The purest blood, we find, if well we heed,
Is in the testicles turn'd into seed.
Which by most proper channels is transmitted
Into the place by Nature for it fitted;
With highest sense of pleasure to excite
In amorous combatants the more delight.
For Nature does in this work design
Profit and pleasure in one act to join.

The next thing is the clitoris, which both stirs up lust, and gives delight in copulation; for without this, the fair sex neither desire nuptial embraces, nor have pleasure in them, nor conceive by them; and according to the greatness or smallness of this part, they are more or less fond of men's embraces; so that it may properly be styled the seat of lust.

The use and action of the clitoris in women, is like that of the penis or yard in men, that is erection; its extreme end being like that of the glands in the man, the seat of the greatest pleasure of the act of copulation, so is this the clitoris in women, and therefore called the sweetness of love, and the fury of venery.

But when they are married, and those desires satisfied by their husband, these distempers vanish, and their beauty returns more gay and lively than before. And this strong inclination of theirs may be known by their eager gazing at men, and affecting their company, which sufficiently demonstrates that Nature excites them to desire coition. Nor is this the case with virgins only, but the same may be observed in young widows who cannot be satisfied without that due benevolence which they were wont to receive from their husbands.

> Why is this action [coition] good in those who use it lawfully and moderately? Because, say Avicen and Const, it eases and lightens the body, clears the mind, comforts the head and senses, and expels the melancholy.

Wilson goes on to record that:

> "Want of chastity in girls was common." Peter Gaskell, who studied urban life, wrote in the 1830s that in the previous century premarital sex was "almost universal" in the countryside: "Many of the sports of the period, amongst the young of both sexes, were obviously intended to facilitate and give opportunities to familiarities of the closest kind." Sex was common with young couples, but there was "a tacit understanding . . . that marriage would result." Demographic study suggests that 40 percent of marriages among the lower orders occurred when the bride was already pregnant.[11]

A chronicler of the period with first-hand knowledge to whom we are greatly indebted was Francis Place, born in London in 1771. Later in life he recalled "the ignorance, the immorality, the grossness, the obscenity the drunkenness, the dirtiness, and depravity of the middling and even of the better sort of tradesmen, the artisans, and the journeymen tradesmen of London in the days of my youth."[12] Wilson informs us that, "Girls of Francis Place's age were told that they should seize the initiative and get the pleasure that was their right."[13]

It did not help moral matters in the laboring classes that gin was discovered in 1684. By 1743, over fourteen million gallons were consumed annually in England, or about 2.2 gallons per person of population. There were over nine thousand shops selling cheap gin in London alone and, by 1811, fifty thousand public houses in England, Scotland, and Wales; one house in every forty was a

11 Wilson 2007, p. 78.

12 Wilson 2007, p. 74.

13 Wilson 2007, p. 78.

licensed premises.[14] It was frequently advertised that one could get drunk for a penny, dead drunk for two pence. A well-known depiction of the resulting human depravity and destruction is William Hogarth's engraving, "Gin Lane." It is apparently not an exaggeration. Hyppolyte Taine, the French historian of English literature, recorded in 1900 that during the riots of Lord George Gordon in 1780, "Barrels of gin were staved in and made rivers in the streets. Children and women on their knees drank themselves to death. Some became mad, others fell down besotted, and the burning and falling houses killed them, and buried them under their ruins."[15] Where drinking led, sex naturally followed. Francis Place described his father as being proficient at "Drinking, Whoring, Gambling, Fishing, and Fighting." Women commonly sold themselves for gin, often to drunken comrades.[16]

The fruits of adultery in this period cannot be well measured with hard data, but a good index of the prevalence of premarital sexual indulgence is the "prebridal" pregnancy rate. This is derived by matching the date of a marriage with the date of a subsequent birth to the bridal couple, considering the pregnancy to have been "prebridal" if the birth occurred less than some time after the wedding, usually eight or eight and a half months. This rate surged as the eighteenth century progressed. In England, using the eight-and-a-half-months criterion, the prebridal pregnancy rate grew from about 16% of first births in the 1600s, which included the Puritan period, to over 40% of first births during 1750-1800. In America, the comparable rate grew from about 11% before 1701 to over 33% during 1761-1800.[17] Caution is necessary because these figures are derived from scattered regional and local data rather than nationally collected statistics, but they are considered on evidence to be at least approximately representative.

In all of this, there is scant evidence of immorality in the middle class. Small wonder, for in the early part of the eighteenth century, there hardly was a middle class. Class level is notoriously difficult to define with precision and

14 *Canadian Content*. 2006; Wilson 2007, p. 244.

15 Taine 1900, Vol II, p. 274.

16 Wilson 2007, pp. 74, 77, 257, 259.

17 Smith and Hindus 1975, pp.561-570; Smith, Daniel Scott 1973 p. 323.

to general satisfaction. However, we can say roughly that those in the middle class were persons who occupied a certain range of posts and positions. In 1700, there was only small need for those positions. It was the dynamic progress of the industrial revolution over the eighteenth and nineteenth centuries along with the rapid growth of trade due to empire that produced a huge middle class and made it dominant. There was, of course, a multiplication of shopkeepers, lawyers, and entrepreneurs, but primarily the century saw the entrance and spread of moderately large organizations. There were the manufacturing organizations themselves, but in addition there grew up banks, insurance companies, shipping companies, railways, and merchant houses. Cities grew exponentially, and with them a population of engineers, managers, accountants, and professionals in all of the newly required fields such as health, public safety, water supply, and so on. By the first few decades of the nineteenth century, there was indeed a middle class, a class almost always concerned with respectability, as we shall see, and in lock-step with the growth of this class came the advance of the new morality. A strong, negative reaction to sexual license both above them and below was felt by this growing middle class, stimulated or at least reinforced in substantial part by Evangelical preaching and writing. The rise of Evangelicalism in the eighteenth century, with its forceful literature in books and from the pulpit, had a continuing influence on nineteenth-century ideology regarding women until the role was taken over by moralizing physicians in the latter half of the Victorian period.[18]

The authors of the reforming tracts and sermons were interested in getting middle-class women to behave in particular ways. To do so, they had to impress upon them that the effects of the counseled behavior were important, and therefore that the women themselves were important. Thomas Branagan was an Irish-American abolitionist, but he also became interested in the status of women. Writing in 1828, he asked and answered: "What is a real virtuous and pious female, adorned with personal beauty and intellectual acquirements? She is no less than the glory of man, the ornament of nature, the favorite of Heaven, and the daughter of Jehova himself."[19]

18 Cott 1978, pp. 221-228.

19 Branagan 1828, p. 1.

However, it was a hard sell in the nineteenth century because by most common yardsticks middle-class women were not important at all. They could not vote. Only a few ever held significant public office. With a few exceptions, such as by writing or by teaching children, they earned no money. The "higher" professions – clergy, law, medicine – were essentially closed to them. Education such as their brothers received was rarely obtainable. Until 1882, they had no rights to any property they brought to a marriage; indeed, they themselves were the property, pure and simple, of their husbands. The seducer of a married woman not only committed a sexual crime, but could be and often was sued in civil court for damage to the husband's property. An 1857 law in Britain made it reasonably practical for a man to obtain a divorce; the same status was not granted to women until 1923.[20]

Branagan, aggrandizing the value of the fair sex, felt called upon to deplore "the ridiculous partiality of mothers in particular, and parents in general, to their male, in preference to their female children. One would suppose . . . that they did not believe in the immateriality of the souls of females; but that they were created and put into this world merely for the sensual convenience of men and for their domestic accommodation, and, of course, that men are of decided and transcendent superiority to women."[21] His purpose was to cloak himself in the mantle of advocacy by asserting the rightful importance of women, but his reporting of this blatantly unequal treatment in the parental home shows that, in the meanwhile, their concrete position was one of inferiority and relative unimportance.

In this situation, the moral reformers emphasized the role of women as mothers and thus as the formers and shapers of the character of the next generation.[22] Branagan expresses himself as being ". . . deeply sensible of your great importance and respectability in society, and convinced that on your intellectual improvement and prosperity, nay the very existence of society depends."[23]

To my mind, the Branagan of these passages, for all his undoubted good intentions, was setting them up. What further sort of advocacy

20 The laws in America varied by state but primarily followed the British pattern.

21 Branagan 1828, p. 132.

22 Fordyce 1766, pp. 34-39; Gisborne 1797, p. 12.

23 Branagan 1828, p. 220.

would we logically expect to follow from his protestations of the equality – or at least near-equality – of women and men? Naturally, it would be that women should become lawyers, doctors, professors, members of Parliament or Congress, merchants, and captains of industry. Not at all! It quickly becomes clear that to Branagan, as to the other Evangelicals of the period, not inferior actually meant superior in the moral arena but inferior, indeed, in all others. His concrete advice, when he gets down to it, rehearses a common refrain: dress modestly, resist the love of being admired, avoid character assassination directed at your friends, avoid libertines – repulse them with your virtue, do not allow sensual liberties between the times of engagement and marriage, choose your husband from among "prudent, discreet, and honorable persons of our sex."[24] This is not the kind of advice one would give to a budding doctor, lawyer, or banker.

Her Christian duty.

Who, then, is the Victorian woman, and what must she do and not do? First and foremost, she is a true Christian with the duty both to personify the religion in her daily world and to influence others, especially her children and her husband, toward honoring and practicing it. Professor Barbara Welter, influential historian of the station of women in the nineteenth century, summed up this aspect as follows:

> Religion or piety was the core of woman's virtue, the source of her strength.[25]
>
> She would be another, better Eve, working in cooperation with the Redeemer, bringing the world back "from its revolt and sin."[26]
>
> From her home woman performed her great task of bringing men back to God.[27]

24 Branagan 1828, pp. 220-258.

25 Welter 1966, p. 152.

26 Welter 1966, p. 152.

27 Welter 1966, p. 162.

Like Branagan, the English clergyman Thomas Gisborne was active in the abolition of the slave trade, and, also like Branagan, he became interested in the roles and duties of women. Unlike Branagan, however, he was clear in his position that the social hierarchy, including the subordinate station of women, was divinely imposed. We will see this unfold clearly as the discussion continues. Speaking of mothers as teachers and formers of character, he wrote in 1797:

> The chief solicitude, therefore, of everyone who is called to fulfil the duties of tuition ought to be this: to engage the understanding and the affections of the pupil in favor of piety and virtue, by unfolding the truth, the importance, and the inherent excellence of the Christian religion.[28]

John Gregory, considered primarily as a moralist, was a Scottish physician, medical ethicist, and professor of mathematics and moral and natural philosophy. A few decades before Gisborne, he wrote:

> Besides, men consider your religion as one of their principal securities for that female virtue in which they are most interested.[29]

In this passage from Gregory's most famous work, *A Father's Legacy to His Daughters,* we have the woman's religion serving not just to raise the moral conduct of men, but to give men the peace of mind that was all too likely to be unsettled in the waning days of the age of cuckoldry.

Professor Welter shows us that Caleb Atwater, Esq., well-known Ohio archeologist, historian, politician, and advocate of equality of education for women, writing in *The Ladies' Repository,* saw the hand of the Lord in female piety (whereas the reader might see in Caleb Atwater the ingrained male chauvinism that thoroughly predominated in the nineteenth century):

---

28 Gisborne 1797, p. 42.

29 Gregory 1774, pp. 10-11.

> Religion is exactly what a woman needs, for it gives her that dignity that best suits her dependence.[30]

Atwater brings to the top of our consciousness the brute fact that women were economically dependent, initially on their fathers and then on their husbands – no matter how great a fortune they may have brought to the marriage. Welter goes on to say, "The marriage night was the single great event of a woman's life, when she bestowed her greatest treasure upon her husband, and from that time on was completely dependent on him, an empty vessel, without legal or emotional existence of her own."[31]

If they did not marry, their situation could become dire after a father's death. They may have received a modest bequest, but otherwise they must generally hope to find a home as the dependent of a living relative, such as the inheriting brother. In many cases they got neither of these. Citing others, Professor Welter continues:

> "She feels herself weak and timid. She needs a protector," declared George Burnap, in his lectures on *The Sphere and Duties of Woman*. . . . Or put even more strongly by Mrs. Sandford: "A really sensible woman feels her dependence. She does what she can, but she is conscious of inferiority, and therefore grateful for support."[32]

In the middle class, this debasing dependence would make the dignity that Caleb Atwater speaks of difficult to come by. In his view, nevertheless, it could be found in religion. Perhaps so, particularly if men were less than zealous in contrast, but the Evangelicals did not stop there. They continued beyond bare religion to try to lift women into an unbelievably exalted and therefore dignified moral position. This is Thomas Branagan:

30 Welter 1966, p. 153.

31 Welter 1966, pp. 154-155.

32 Welter 1966, p. 159.

> Finally, remember you were created for the special purpose of being the temples of the Holy Ghost here on earth, and the celebrators of the glorious praises of the Holy Trinity hereafter in heaven; therefore, let your conduct correspond with your high vocation.[33]

One can assume that the churchmen among those cited were sincere in their encouragement of moral reform. At the same time, we should recognize that it was to the advantage of the church for women to adopt these behaviors – and the ones soon to be reviewed – and to encourage their husbands in the same direction. It meant more church attendance and donations as well as greater status for the clerical professions. In the following chapter, we will examine whether other groups in the system had similar or perhaps opposite interests, including as a relevant group the women themselves.

Her deportment.

Christian duty entails specialized rules of conduct. Let us move now to what the Evangelical advice literature had to say about how women should conduct themselves in general. Here, a first principle is modesty. In what follows, I will frequently add emphasis to the word "but." This is to point out that the style is often hypocritical. What comes after the BUT will show that what came before was not really to be encouraged.

Modesty was important in the teachings of Gisborne. A wife should not hide her good sense, BUT she should not use it to pontificate on worldly matters. That would be immodest. He ingeniously condemns masquerades and masked balls in the perspective of a virtuous woman because they encourage immodesty by allowing her to avoid the shame that would otherwise come with openness.[34]

James Fordyce constructed an entire sermon on dressing modestly. He was a Scottish Presbyterian minister of the late eighteenth century, a forceful and popular preacher who was influential on many topics but best known for his *Sermons to Young Women,* published in 1766. As well as dressing modestly, he emphasized: "She loves the shade." "There is nothing so engaging as bashful

33 Branagan 1828, p. 258.

34 Gisborne 1797, pp. 135-160, 246-267.

beauty." (Note that the merit of modesty lies not only in that it is virtuous, but that it is engaging.) "At any rate, the majesty of the sex is sure to suffer by being seen too frequently, and too familiarly." (It was extremely common in the nineteenth century, both in novels and in other literature, to refer to women as "the sex.") "Discreet reserve in a woman, like the distance kept by royal personages, contributes to maintain the proper reverence." Dancing? Some authorities say no but Fordyce allows that it is good exercise and promotes health, good humor, and social spirit. BUT it must be done with temperance and prudence. Certainly, it is not to be pursued in public assemblies, which will dissipate that lovely bashfulness, but only in private among family, close relatives, and good friends.[35] Fordyce continues,

> For my part, I would heartily wish to see the female world more accomplished than it is; BUT I do not wish to see it abound with metaphysicians, historians, speculative philosophers, or Learned Ladies of any kind. I should be afraid lest the sex should lose in softness what they gained in force; and lest a pursuit of such elevation should interfere a little with the plain duties and humble virtues of life.[36]

He went on to recommend reading and study for those women who are inclined toward such interests, but he cautions us to bear in mind that men and women were designed for different spheres. Clearly, "War, commerce, politics, exercises of strength and dexterity, abstract philosophy, and all the abstruser sciences, are most properly the province of men." For women, he recommended history, biography, books of voyages and travels, and geography. BUT such studies must be pursued only to prudent lengths. "For should they push their application so far as to hurt their more tender health, to hinder those family duties for which the sex are chiefly intended, or to impair those softer graces that give them their highest luster; nothing, I think, can be more apparent than that, in such

35 Fordyce 1766, pp. 43-107, 235-238.

36 Fordyce 1766, pp. 201-202.

cases, they would relinquish their just sphere, for one much less amiable, and much less beneficial."[37]

The moralist John Gregory in 1774 urged women to modesty, to blushing, and to silence for the most part in company. The virtuous woman will dress with delicacy and judgment: "The finest bosom in nature is not so fine as what imagination forms." In dancing, it is ease and grace that must be displayed, not mirth. Wit, he advises, can be a dangerous talent. Humor is acceptable, of course, BUT women must be careful how they indulge it. Be cautious in displaying your good sense. If you have any learning, keep it a secret, especially from men. Don't worry about being considered prudish; better that than disgusting. For the sake of modesty, "If you love him, let me advise you never to discover to him the full extent of your love, no not although you marry him."[38]

The quoted advice in this last sentence is a mixture of modesty and strategy. It would have interesting consequences. We must keep in mind that the era upon which we focus was the epitome of a romantic age. Love was incredibly important (even though marriage for love was all too often subordinated to marriage for status and money). Sex was taboo as a topic in conversing and writing, but love was everywhere. The love itself was felt to be undying and the lover all-sacrificing. The climax of a standard novel of the period was arriving – at long last – at the realization of love and intention to marry. Yet, the Evangelicals would make a young woman so modest, bashful, and delicate that she should not be able to confess a love that she strongly felt and which, in her heart, was certain to be forever. Given the place of love in this romantic era, we would expect the heroines of nineteenth-century novels to avow their love as the high point of their existence, but then there was the advice literature with its tireless emphasis on modesty. In view of that pounding refrain, we would expect young Victorian women to have been so thoroughly habituated to and characterized by modesty as to keep their consuming love sadly, but necessarily, locked inside. If women of our inquiry were indeed modest to that extent in real life – just imagine it for a moment – then the taking and permitting of sexual liberties would be next to impossible. We will look at the novels in a later

37 Fordyce 1766, pp. 271-284.

38 Gregory 1774, pp. 14-26, 39.

chapter and make a point of exploring how the novelists, at any rate, portrayed life in terms of the tension between fulfilling, exhilarating love on one hand and the Goddess of Modesty on the other.

Her duty toward men.

As noted, one aspect of a woman's embodiment of Christianity was her influence over men for the good. The Evangelicals gave this facet substantial emphasis. Gisborne, for example, considered that the effect of the female character is most important for three reasons, including, "In forming and improving the general manners, dispositions, and conduct of the other sex, by society and example."[39] James Fordyce agreed:

> The least degree of refinement or candor will dispose us to regard them in a far higher point of light. They were manifestly intended to be the mothers and formers of a rational and immortal offspring; to be a kind of softer companions, who, by nameless delightful sympathies and endearments, might improve our pleasures and soothe our pains; to lighten the load of domestic cares, and thereby leave us more at leisure for rougher labours, or severer studies; and finally, to spread a certain grace and embellishment over human life.[40]

This suggests that there was also quite another side impressed upon the nineteenth-century's True Woman in her relations with men, and that was her particular duty toward her husband. The first duty of a married woman, Gisborne taught, is to improve or maintain the good character and religious attention of her husband by her virtue, affection, and modesty.[41]

From Welter's 1966 survey of American women's magazines of the Victorian period:

39 Gisborne 1797, p. 12.

40 Fordyce 1766, pp.207-208.

41 Gisborne 1797, p. 240.

> Samuel Miller preached a sermon on women: "How interesting and important are the duties devolved on females as wives . . . the counselor and friend of the husband; who makes it her daily study to lighten his cares, to soothe his sorrows, and to augment his joys; who, like a guardian angel, watches over his interests, warns him against dangers, comforts him under trials; and by her pious, assiduous, and attractive deportment, constantly endeavors to render him more virtuous, more useful, more honourable, and more happy." A woman's whole interest should be focused on her husband. . . . "She should consider nothing as trivial which could win a smile of approbation from him."[42]

Gisborne in 1797 cited passages in the Bible that explicitly enjoined women to be obedient and submissive to their husbands in all things. These charges are not just arbitrary, he explained. It is plain that somebody has to be in command or else there would be constant disagreement and confusion. Clearly, it should be the man because the important work is devolved on him and he has been given the physical and mental equipment to deal with it.[43] Further, the virtuous wife should realize that her husband, out in the world (where the laboring classes and the aristocracy were much in evidence), is subject to all sorts of wicked example and temptation.

> Is she desirous of his society? Would she confirm him in domestic habits? Would she fortify him against being lured into the haunts of luxury, riot, and profaneness? Let her conduct shew that home is dear to herself in his absence, still dearer when he is present. Let her unaffected mildness, her ingenuous tenderness, place before his mind a forcible contrast to the violence, the artifice, the unfeeling selfishness which he witnesses in his commerce with the world. Let the cheerful tranquility of domestic pleasures stand in the place of trifling and turbulent festivity abroad. Let his house, as far as her activities can be effectual, be

42 Welter 1966, p. 170.

43 Gisborne 1797, pp. 230-238.

> the abode of happiness; and he will have little temptation to bewilder himself in seeking for happiness under another roof.[44]

James Fordyce, in his opus of 1766, urged that a major part of Christian meekness for women is to be in subjection to their husbands. Does your husband seem to prefer the company of others to yours? It may well be your own fault. He continued:

> Not that I would justify the men in any thing wrong on their part. But had you behaved to them with a more respectful observance, and a more equal tenderness; studying their humours, overlooking their mistakes, submitting to their opinions in matters indifferent, passing by little instances of unevenness, caprice, or passion, giving soft answers to hasty words, complaining as seldom as possible, and making it your daily care to relieve their anxieties, to enliven the hour of dullness, and call up the ideas of felicity: had you pursued this conduct, I doubt not but you would have maintained their esteem, so far as to have secured every degree of influence that could conduce to their virtue, or your mutual satisfaction; and your house might at this day have been the abode of domestic bliss.[45]

The historian B. Welter went on to cite a work originally published in 1837:

> Mrs. Gilman's perfect wife in *Recollections of a Southern Matron* realizes that "the three golden threads with which domestic happiness is woven" are "to repress a harsh answer, to confess a fault, and to stop (right or wrong) in the midst of self-defense, in gentle submission."[46]

In this last, dismaying passage, we see that Victorian male chauvinism was not confined to males. In fact, examples of this mindset in women appear over and over again in the novels. Indeed, a woman's duty toward her husband was apparently so

44 Gisborne 1797 pp. 331-332.

45 Fordyce 1766, pp. 264-265.

46 Welter 1966, p. 161.

consuming that she essentially had no other. The prevailing Victorian orientation, as reported by the suffragette Frances Power Cobbe, was that "The wife's true relation to her husband" is that her "whole life and being, her soul, body, time, property, thought, and care, ought to be given to her husband; that nothing short of such absorption in him and his interests makes her a true wife."[47]

The modern reader is highly likely to react negatively to this urging of women to be so extremely solicitous of their husbands. There is no indication, however, that the Victorians found it to be offensive. The rules were commonly observed. But there is also another aspect that deserves notice. Any woman who is so sweet, so submissive, and so virtuous is in danger of being *boring* to a normal middle-class husband, especially if, as was usually the case, she hardly had the education to permit her to carry on an interesting conversation. In this respect, even many Victorians were apparently troubled. The sociologist Peter Cominos wrote in 1963:

> There was, according to the "Saturday Review" of January 1867, a "growing disinclination to marry . . . among rich men no less than poor." As early as 1845, the "Quarterly Review" described how education stereotyped the character of English wives making them so dull and insipid as to deter men from marriage. . . . The "Saturday Review" faced the truth that "bored husbands" were by no means rare. . . . In 1869 the "Quarterly Review" recognized the problem of enticing young men into marriage. "The more admirable the wives," meaning the closer they resembled the model of the ideal type, the womanly woman, "the more profoundly bored the husbands."[48]

The Evangelical moralizing covered so far – and there is more to come – may seem ponderous to modern readers. As it happens, there is also a piece of evidence that it struck even some young women of the period as overdone. In Jane Austen's *Pride and Prejudice*, there is a scene in which the Bennets were visited by their cousin, Mr. Collins. The latter is a conservative, dim,

47 Cobbe 1869, pp. 18-19, cited in Cominos 1973, p. 161.

48 Cominos 1963, p. 253.

dull, self-important cleric who is asked one evening to read aloud to the four Bennet sisters. He is first handed a novel but protests that he never interests himself in such materials. He then chooses a book of the sermons of none other than our friend James Fordyce. The young ladies can hardly believe it. After he performs three pages "with very monotonous solemnity," one of the girls rather rudely interrupts and addresses her mother on a completely foreign, social topic! She is quickly silenced by her two elder sisters, but Mr. Collins puts the book away with a comment on "how little young ladies are interested by books of a serious stamp, though written solely for their benefit."[49]

It is not at all certain that the chosen sermon was on the subject of the behavior of women, but it is clear that, whatever it was, the Bennet sisters found it tedious. That, however, does not mean that they rejected the advice offered by Fordyce and others on the conduct of women. In *Pride and Prejudice*, that conduct was exemplary – with one exception: Lydia Bennet was found to have broken the rules by running off with an officer. The family was immediately thrown into crisis. The consequences of such behavior could be devastating, ruinous, not only for Lydia but for her sisters – for the whole family and forever. We see here, dramatically, a critical segment of the code by which middle-class Victorians apparently lived. In other words, the morality was internalized in spite of the sanctimonious tone in which it was often delivered.

What she should approach and avoid.

Observing Christian doctrine and living always under the guiding principle of modesty would seem, when fleshed out as it was, to be enough to steer female conduct into the desired channels. However, the Evangelicals were also micro-managers. They found it important to give more specific guidance on what to do and what not to do in terms of the social context of the times. How to select a husband, for example, was significant. In addition, they ran through most of the popular amusements and activities of the day and passed on each of them – thumbs up or thumbs down, mostly the latter.

49 Austen 2000, (Ch. 14) p. 71.

Fordyce calls parents "barbarous wretches" who would force a daughter to marry a man she could not love. To the daughter he says, "There your submission must stop." BUT he then continues to address the topic for ten pages in which he feels he proves conclusively that the parents are better evaluators in such matters than the daughter and that she, therefore, should rationally submit to their superior judgment.[50]

Recall Gisborne's teaching that it must necessarily be the husband who commands in the household. For that portentous reason, he cautions women on the great importance of the decision regarding whom to marry. He concludes: "If a woman marries a person without having sufficient reason to be satisfied, from actual knowledge of his character, that the commands of the Scriptures will decide his conduct, the fault surely is her own."[51] One can be sure that Gisborne was aware that there would be substantially fewer marriages if this dictum were scrupulously observed. It seems he felt that putting pressure on women in this direction would result in their showing that they cared about such criteria and by that means would put pressure on young men, in turn, to maintain a positive moral reputation – and go to church.

Balls and similar entertainments are to be avoided because they incite showing off and competitiveness and they expose the young woman to "undesirable and improper acquaintance among the other sex." The theater, also, must be shunned as it inevitably influences morals. The English stage, Gisborne concludes, has improved since Charles II, but it is still abominable.[52]

There was mixed advice in regard to reading. Welter points to the following:

> The female was dangerously addicted to novels, according to the literature of the period. She should avoid them, since they interfered with "serious piety." If she simply couldn't help herself and read them anyway, she should choose edifying ones from lists of morally acceptable authors. She should study history since it "showed the depravity of the

50 Fordyce 1766, pp. 189-200.

51 Gisborne 1797, p. 232.

52 Gisborne 1797, pp. 161-183.

> human heart and the evil nature of sin." On the whole, "religious biography was best."[53]

The instruction of Fordyce on this topic was that, except for the immensely popular author Samuel Richardson, novels and plays were not improving and not safe.[54] The exception for Richardson is quaint. These sermons of Fordyce were published in 1766. Recall that his sermons were mentioned in *Pride and Prejudice*, published in 1813, so that his teachings were still very much alive by then. By the time Victoria ascended the throne in 1837, however, it would have been impossible for an Evangelical minister to recommend Richardson to young ladies. The latter's best known novel was *Pamela* (1740). In it, a young and wealthy landowner, Mr. B., takes on Pamela, who is even younger, as a servant. There then ensue a few hundred pages in which Mr. B. tries relentlessly to seduce her and she, knowing perfectly well what he wants, just as stubbornly manages to escape and avoid his persistent advances. He even poses as a woman and jumps into her bed. He never lets up. She is in the weaker power position, but somehow her virtue manages repeatedly to triumph. In the end, he marries her.

The novel was meant to convey a moral message; its subtitle is *Virtue Rewarded*. However, it was written at a time, as we have seen, when masters commonly bedded their female servants who, if the literature of the period is to be believed, were often not unwilling. Hardly anybody other than such leading heroines, it seems, was unwilling. Fordyce could recommend this superb and influential early novel because the moral lesson was uplifting. At the same time, the unconcealed sexual undercurrent was not scandalous. As a recognized part of the culture of the time, it was acceptable. By the 1840s, however, a time when books were commonly read aloud in the family circle, no novel could be published with passages that might bring a blush to the maiden cheek. *Pamela* was out; it would have bred a roaring flame.

Aside from avoiding novels, Fordyce cautioned against going to places of entertainment and even against sprightly conversation. Certainly, he allows, the latter is natural and, indeed, a part of youth. BUT it can also be dangerous.

---

53 Welter 1966, pp. 165-166.

54 Fordyce 1766, pp. 144-157.

Therefore, the maiden should find her partners in conversation among pious older women.[55]

With all of these avenues of diversion and entertainment compellingly discouraged, one might fear that not only the husband but the virtuous woman herself might be bored. Gisborne did not think so. It goes without saying, he felt, that married women had no need to be bored for they have the duties of mother and housewife to occupy their time. As for single women, they should read, but not romances. In addition, they should help manage the house, take care of sick relations, cheer old folks, look into the wants and distresses of female inhabitants of the neighborhood, promote useful institutions for mothers and children, and "give delight in the affectionate intercourse of domestic society."[56]

Among objects to avoid, the most dangerous of all was men. Professor Welter reviews much of this advice, and I give two examples here from her text, one an instance of rather mild coaching – quaint in retrospect – and the other a good example of the Evangelical tactic of persuasion through terror:

> Mrs. Eliza Farrar, in *The Young Lady's Friend*, gave practical logistics to avoid trouble: "Sit not with another in a place that is too narrow; read not out of the same book; let not your eagerness to see anything induce you to place your head close to another person's."[57]
> Therefore all True Women were urged, in the strongest possible terms, to maintain their virtue, although men, being by nature more sensual than they, would try to assault it. . . . Woman, stronger and purer, must not give in and let man "take liberties incompatible with her delicacy." "If you do, . . . you will be left in silent sadness to bewail your credulity, imbecility, duplicity, and premature prostitution."[58]

It should be understood that, in both Britain and America, the consequences of known, illicit loss of virginity were probably more serious during this

---

55 Fordyce 1766, pp. 172-178.

56 Gisborne 1797, pp. 211-223.

57 Welter 1966, p. 155.

58 Welter 1966, p. 155.

period than at any other time in the history of these peoples. Such a woman was frequently driven out of her family. In Anthony Trollope's novel, *The Vicar of Bullhampton,* Cary Brattle, the miller's daughter, is seduced as an innocent young woman and cast out completely by her father. She becomes a prostitute in London. Certainly, the family in these cases felt a disgrace from which it might never recover. Its members could be totally shunned or dropped by their former friends and acquaintances.

The transgressing young woman herself – like Carry Brattle, Esther Barton (in Elizabeth Gaskell's first novel, *Mary Barton),* and many others, frequently was left with no option in life but prostitution. If there was a child, its future was either an early death or, at best, a miserable life begun with a destitute mother or in a harsh institution. There was no forgiveness. The sin could possibly be hidden, but even if it was, the woman herself usually felt that she was unsuitable ever to marry respectably – at least according to the major novels of the period.

As Sara Jethro starkly put it in Wilkie Collins's 1884 novel, *I Say No,* referring to a new suitor, "Have *I* any right to love? Could I disgrace an honorable man by allowing him to marry me? . . . A woman would have remembered what reasons I had for pitying the man who loved me, and for accepting any responsibility rather than associate his memory, before the world, with an unworthy passion for a degraded creature."[59] The morality imposed on middle-class women was enforced in large measure by the terror of the consequences of falling into this sin.

But there was one problem. The exact nature of the sin could hardly be communicated to young women because the moral code banished sex as a subject. "A book of advice to the newly married", Professor Welter tells us, "was titled *Whisper to a Bride.* As far as intimate information was concerned, there was no need to whisper, since the book contained none at all."[60] Instead, to plug this hole, we have all of the admonitions about modesty, novels, balls, the theater, bad company, and so forth, coupled with vague but terrible warnings against allowing men to get close and the example of women who descended into total, abject ruin because they did allow some

59 Collins 1995, Chapter 66. [look up]

60 Welter 1966, p. 158.

man to get close. Those things could be spoken. If she took them to heart, even in ignorance of the details, the young woman was probably safe, and so was the family.

Professor Welter continues:

> A "fallen woman" was a "fallen angel," unworthy of the celestial company of her sex. To contemplate the loss of purity brought tears; to be guilty of such a crime, in the women's magazines at least, brought madness or death. . . . The frequency with which derangement follows loss of virtue [in the magazines] suggests the exquisite sensibility of woman, and the possibility that . . . her intellect was geared to her hymen, not her brain.[61]

In view of the devastation that could easily be caused by this worst of all lapses, the Irish-American abolitionist Thomas Branagan had particularly harsh words for the men who were ultimately responsible:

> The thief who robs me of my purse robs me of trash which may easily be replaced with industry and economy: but the villain who robs the innocent defenseless virgin of her virtue, bereaves society of a gem that might become its brightest ornament, and its boast, namely, the virtuous mother of a respectable family; and lets loose, sends forth, constitutes and qualifies a pest, a curse, a disgrace to society, who will in future live to ensnare and enslave others, trample upon her own character, expose her constitution, murder her soul, and at last die the victim of a fearful and fatal disorder, and a tortured mind, cursing with her last breath the murderer of her body and soul. . . . And when you have entered the gates of death, and are approaching the mighty gulph, without bottom or shore, what horrors must seize your naked and forsaken soul, when the first object that faces you, with a grin of fury, in eternity, is the screeching ghost of the girl you have robbed of her

61 Welter 1966, pp. 154, 156.

> virtue and plundered of her life. She is eagerly waiting to pour on your guilty head the vengeance of Heaven and the wrath of eternity.[62]

If middle-class Victorian women obeyed all of this advice on Christian duty, modest deportment, forbidden activities, and absorption in their husbands, they might well have been reduced to nonentities – angelic nonentities, perhaps, but nonentities nevertheless. No streak of independence. No forcefulness of character. As it happens, the effects were probably not that extreme, but they were there. There is good evidence of a smaller but still substantial impact both in the novels and in the Mosher survey, to be treated in Chapters IV and V. A telling quantity of the socialization did filter into them and did have a notable effect upon their outlook. We have, then, a first hint that these women, while retaining a modicum of individuality, might well have been quite ignorant of sex, quite mindful of the appropriateness of modesty, and quite fearful of too close association with men. We will see in a moment how the medical advice literature of the latter part of the century contributed to solidifying this culture and, in the following chapter, how other social forces encouraged and reinforced it. We do not abandon the significance of hormones completely, but we take proper account of the case for the stereotype of repression.

First, however, we inaugurate the series of portraits, an intermittent perusal of the married lives and sexual adjustments of the women who responded to the Mosher survey. Dr. Mosher and her research will be described more fully in a chapter devoted to the survey, Chapter V. I would briefly anticipate that discussion here, by way of introduction, by noting that Dr. Clelia Mosher was a physician, primarily associated with Stanford University, who obtained responses to a survey on sexual attitudes and behavior from forty-five American women between 1892 and 1920. The women were middle to late Victorians. However, Dr. Mosher never analyzed the responses. After her death in 1940, the completed questionnaires lay utterly unnoticed by the world until they were discovered in the Stanford archives in 1974.

It is of great importance to note that, whereas I assign names to the women of the portraits, those names are entirely fictitious. I have no idea who in

62 Branagan 1828, pp. 20, 176.

particular they were, and neither, I am certain, does anybody else. Dr. Mosher no doubt promised them anonymity and kept her promise, which was entirely proper and is still standard practice in survey research.

Chapter V treats the Mosher women collectively, mostly in averages and other characterizations of the group of forty-five as a whole. These portraits present eighteen of them in a more individual and personal perspective in order to obtain a good sense not only of their own unique actions in regard to sexuality but of their attitudes – and where those attitudes came from in the age of Victoria. I chose these particular eighteen because the information available on them is relatively abundant. Dr. Mosher did not always administer the complete questionnaire, and the respondents did not always give very full answers, so that the information in a great many cases is too sketchy to serve as the basis for an expansive narrative portrait.

Interludes: Sexual Portraits of Eighteen American Victorian Women
First Interlude: Portraits 1 – 3

Portrait 1: Eleanor Girard.[63]

At the very end of this particular questionnaire, Dr. Mosher wrote the note: "Husband said she was cold blooded." One gets the feeling from the tone throughout the interview that Mrs. Girard told this to Dr. Mosher neither with embarrassment nor regret, just with resignation. She has had to resign herself to many circumstances – including, somewhere down the list, a tedious sex life.

We are somewhat at a disadvantage here because this is one of the many instances in which the respondent was not given the questionnaire to take home and fill out herself, at her leisure. Instead, Dr. Mosher interviewed the subject and filled in the blanks herself, often in the respondents own words but sometimes just giving the general idea of the answer. That is unfortunate because we get an additional feel for the character of the subject when we can see verbatim answers in the first person.

The lives of most people are characterized by ups and downs. We might say that they have lives of moderately good fortune. Some people, however, seem to be battered by an unremitting series of troubles. Mrs. Girard found herself to be in the latter category, a person who encountered many misfortunes, especially in connection with her children. However, she displayed no bitterness, anger, or resentment in the interview. Rather, as indicated above, it is resignation that shows through her recorded responses.

Eleanor Girard was born in 1834, married in 1857, and was interviewed for the Mosher project in 1895 at the age of sixty-one and having been married for thirty-eight years. Dr. Mosher was herself thirty-two years of age at that point – the same age as Mrs. Girard's one living child, a daughter. Before her marriage, Eleanor taught in a country school for two years, having apparently taken two years of preparation for a teaching career after high school. When she got married, she left her job. It is quite common throughout the Mosher

63 Mosher 1980. Blank No. 9, pp. 91-102.

interviews that the women did some sort of work, usually teaching, until they got married, whereupon they quit working abruptly and completely. Working wives were rare in those days.[64]

The Mosher protocols tell us almost nothing about childhoods. What we do know about the girlhood of Eleanor Girard is that she got her period when she was almost sixteen and that it did not settle down to regularity until she was twenty. She generally experienced menstrual pain in the mornings for the first three days of each period. Thus, here was an initial bother in connection with her organs of reproduction and potential pleasure.

Her husband, Tobin Girard, was a teacher and practicing physician. About four years after the marriage, he began taking morphine habitually. The habit continued for nine years, from 1861–1870, at which time he became "insane" and was apparently confined to an institution for two years. I say "apparently" confined to an institution because there is no direct information on this point, but we know that he was "insane" for two years and that, when he relapsed into morphine use about seven years later, he overcame it himself, "without going to asylum." Note that whereas I use the word "institution," the respondent used the word "asylum." In that era, and even in my own youth, one did not talk about people being "institutionalized," but rather about their being in "the insane asylum."

We do not know how Mrs. Girard coped with life in the late 1860s and especially in the early 1870s, during the two years of Girard's confinement, but we can guess that it would not have been easy.

The Girards had three children, all of them by choice rather than by accident. This is in a way remarkable because their primary method of birth control was male withdrawal at the point of orgasm. Besides being difficult and distressing for the man and frequently leaving the woman unsatisfied, as was the case with Mrs. Girard, it is generally not very effective in preventing pregnancies. Moreover, the potential difficulties attached to withdrawal were compounded in the case of the Girards because of a relatively high frequency of intercourse. They had sex at least twice a week as a rule, even during the pregnancies,

64 Smith 1973a, p. 41, gives the figure as 2.5%.

sometimes every night for a while, and upon a few occasions twice in the same night. Nevertheless, there were no accidental births.

All three children were daughters. The first was born in 1860, three plus years after the marriage. She was a healthy baby until Mrs. Girard most unfortunately contracted typhoid fever. She continued to nurse the child and she did herself recover from the disease, but the baby was never strong after that episode. She tragically died of scarlet fever and diphtheria at one year old.

They tried again a little more than a year afterward and had a second child in 1863. (As an aside, note that this was at the height of the Civil War, but neither in this interview nor in all but one of the Mosher response sets is there any mention of the war or its possible effect on the lives and marriages concerned.) The child survived and was apparently still alive at the time of the interview in 1895, but Mrs. Girard said nothing in the interview about the health or happiness of this daughter or whether she married and had children of her own. What she did choose to say about this second daughter suggests that the life of the latter may not have been a sunny one. She reported that this was a crying baby who had colic for three months. She also reported that she herself, Mrs. Girard, was constantly annoyed by a servant before the baby was born. Why would she make a point of this? Because in those days it was widely believed that such events during pregnancy could have a negative effect on the child. Mrs. Girard seemed to be implying some unspecified negative effect upon her daughter by offering a partial explanation for it – being constantly annoyed by the servant. In fact, in a section of the questionnaire dealing with the respondent's mother, Dr. Mosher asked her subjects to "note any prenatal influences before your birth," showing that the doctor herself harbored this same belief. Mrs. Girard also noted that her husband had been taking morphine for two years before this baby's birth, including at the time of conception, but that it was not yet a confirmed habit and so probably had no effect. This is all we know about the second child.

The third daughter of the Girards was born two years and eight months after the second, therefore in 1865 or 1866. Mrs. Girard said nothing this time about the possible effects of her husband's morphine addiction, which by then was presumably well established. The baby had large ankles and wrist joints and did not walk until she was nineteen months old. Early on, she had what was thought to be a slight fall on her knee, but the knee began to swell. Also, she had a protrusion on one side of her ribs. She "had measles, which did not come out well," and Dr. Mosher adds in parentheses here "rickets." Rickets is rare now in advanced societies, but it is still common in developing countries and was quite common in Britain and America in the nineteenth century. It is basically a softening of the bones in children, often leading to fractures and deformity. It does not result from measles, although it is possible that such infections can exacerbate the condition. Its cause is dietary – deficiencies of calcium, phosphorous, and vitamin D have been implicated – but this was not known in the nineteenth century. In this case, the child soon had to walk with a crutch and was constantly doctored. At age sixteen, she suffered running sores on her knee for an entire year. She finally died as a teenager – at nineteen – the diagnosis being tubercular meningitis, or tuberculosis of the brain. Tuberculosis does sometimes spread to the brain. It is possible for this to occur via the rupturing of spinal vertebrae – which might have been softened in this particular case by rickets – but there is no information on that possibility in the interview.

Thus, two of the Girards' three children died young. This is not a rare percentage for the nineteenth century. Eleanor's father, for example, was one of ten children, only two of whom survived to maturity. Still, all evidence indicates that the death of a child was as painful to mothers in the nineteenth century as it is today.

Mrs. Girard was in the minority of Mosher women who knew what sexual intercourse was before she got married. All we know about how she obtained this knowledge is that she was told by others. In any case, it did not help much.

The Girards regularly slept together in the same bed until their second child was born. After that time, their habit was to sleep apart. The reason given by Mrs. Girard is that because her husband was a doctor, he might bring contagious diseases home to the children. This suggests that the children slept in the same room as their mother. It also suggests that Dr. Girard did not spend much time with his children at all, or else there would have been ample opportunity other than at night to infect them.

When asked if she had a desire for intercourse, Mrs. Girard's recorded answer is "usually a nuisance. Never cared much for it." Perhaps she would have felt desire at times if only her husband had let her alone long enough for it to awaken spontaneously. It may be that for her, intercourse was just too frequent. If so, she would not have been alone among women. Note that Mrs. Girard was post-menopausal at the time of the interview, but Dr. Mosher asked this question about desire anyway. There was considerable disagreement among nineteenth-century physicians on whether post-menopausal women felt desire and took pleasure in sex, but we will see that there was disagreement regarding pre-menopausal women, as well! When asked if intercourse were agreeable to her, the recorded answer is "as a rule not." When asked if she always had a venereal orgasm, her answer was a simple "no," but Dr. Mosher then continued with the next question as if "sometimes" or "occasionally" had been implied, and not just "never." The follow-up question was: When you do, what is the effect immediately afterwards? And Mrs. Girard's answer was "fatigued." This response indicates that she did reach orgasm, if only very occasionally. Effect next day? "Felt worse next day." (She thinks her husband did also.) When asked if the true purpose of intercourse were pleasure, she said, "to men," and when asked if it were necessary to women, she answered "no."

Here is resignation. Mrs. Girard does not say that she hates it or that it drives her mad, but that it is a nuisance. It is something she doesn't care for, but she puts up with it. She was resigned in spite of the fact that intercourse was quite frequent, that there was usually withdrawal at the point of male orgasm, and that Mrs. Girard herself was usually left physically unfulfilled. The signs of a common syndrome are here, namely, that the man was generally ready for climax sooner than the woman. That needn't always spell disaster. There are ways of dealing with it. In this case, it is plain that the husband was not considerate enough or brave enough to help search out a way that might have worked for them. He just found his wife to be cold blooded. Indeed, it might well be that Mrs. Girard's own lack of interest was a factor, but it is impossible to say from this distance whether that lack of interest was the cause of the unsatisfactory sex or its effect. Nonetheless, such repeated lack of physical satisfaction, if not maddening, may very well have been wearing, wearying, or worse.

A final observation is that the ecstasy of occasional orgasm, which Mrs. Girard apparently did experience, was not in itself enough to change this one woman's outlook on sex from considering it a nuisance to be tolerated to feeling it as a joy of living. Occasional orgasm might well have this positive effect for many women. On the other hand, it could easily have a negative effect, as some Mosher women will testify, if the failures are what stand out rather than the occasional successes. From the experience of Mrs. Girard, whose uppermost responses to orgasm were "fatigued" and "felt worse next day," we get the idea that occasional orgasm neither added much nor detracted much within the context of her generally dispiriting life.

Portrait 2: Lucy Meadows[65]

Lucy and her husband, James Meadows, were both born in rural environments in the same year, 1860, and they both went to Cornell University. It is reasonable to assume that they met there and fell in love, although Lucy finished her Bachelor of Science degree and left Cornell in 1882 or 1883 and they did not get married until 1887. James continued his education and ultimately received a PhD. It was common at the time for couples to wait until the future husband was advanced and settled enough to be able to support a wife and family before they got married. James worked as a registrar in 1893, when Lucy filled out the questionnaire for Dr. Mosher, probably in Wisconsin, since Dr. Mosher began this research at the University of Wisconsin in 1892. Meanwhile, after college, Lucy worked at cataloguing books in libraries for four years before quitting her job and proceeding to the altar. By the time of the questionnaire in 1893, they had been married for six years and Lucy was thirty-three years old.

The questionnaire has several questions about the subject's mother, father, and grandparents. Lucy's maternal grandmother died of puerperal fever after giving birth to her sixth child at age thirty-two. Puerperal fever is a generalized blood infection, sometimes called septicemia or blood poisoning. It has always been extremely difficult to treat and was usually fatal in the nineteenth century. Unfortunately, it occurred so often as to make childbirth an extremely dangerous and worrisome event in that era. It figures significantly in our puzzling over our central question – whether repression or what I have informally called "hormones" prevailed with Victorian women – and will be treated at greater length in Chapter VI.

Lucy's father and her maternal grandfather were both ministers, although the latter also spent time as a lawyer and a banker. Lucy herself had a serious or earnest side, possibly connected with her attitude toward her religion, but she also seems to have been a basically happy person, having sailed through life to this point with few troubles in terms of education, health, mate choice, or children. Her only chronic health problem was hay fever. Her menstruation began at age fourteen, became regular almost immediately (with "rather copious flow"), and was always painless. One of the questions in the questionnaire

65 Mosher 1980, Blank No. 15, pp. 164-176

is "Habit of bowels; how often?" It was undoubtedly included because of Dr. Mosher's hypothesis that chronic constipation was one of four causes, all readily remediable, of debility during menstruation. Most of the Mosher women provided an answer to this question, contributing to a sense of unusual openness and candor in the responses, but Lucy left that one blank.

There was one noteworthy health issue. Both she and James suffered what was commonly then called "nervous prostration." It is hard to know exactly what she means by the term, which has near synonyms including breakdown, nervous breakdown, melancholia, and, more recently, depression. In Lucy's case, this occurred at about the time she was entering college and lasted for a year. In James's case, it happened three years before the date of the questionnaire and lasted three months, but Lucy explained that he really had only recently recovered completely. Nervous prostration by any of these names frequently incapacitates the sufferer in terms of carrying out his or her usual duties, but we do not know for sure whether it was quite that serious for either Lucy or James.

Lucy bore two children, both of them by choice rather than by accident. The first was a boy, four years old at the time of the survey, and the second a girl, who was probably only a month or two old at the time of the survey. It seems that Dr. Mosher dated the questionnaire when she handed it out, which was in January 1893, but Lucy recorded the birth date of her daughter as April 15, 1893, so that she took some time in filling out the form before returning it. At any rate, both children thrived. Lucy mentioned that her son was unusually sensitive to noise during his infancy, which, she says, was possibly due to her being much disturbed by noise in the apartment building where they lived before he was born.

When asked if she and her husband regularly shared a bed, Lucy answered, "Yes." They both preferred it, she explained, "Because of the companionship, rest, and pleasure which come with our being together."

Lucy was well aware of the meaning of the marital bed before the marriage itself took place. Her mother talked to her about menstruation and the physiology of childbirth when she was twelve. In college, as a science major, she studied physiology and was referred to textbooks that taught her something about what she calls "sexual connection." Additionally, a few months before the wedding, a "wise woman," a friend, gave her information about ways open to people at that time for preventing conception and about theories of sexual relations. She also recommended some books on the subject, which Lucy read. We do not know, most unfortunately, to which theories and books she was exposed by these means. What we do know is that, either through this exposure or by some other means, Lucy came to see the sexual relation as a spiritual experience more than a purely physical one. This view was shared by several other Mosher women, and we will see in the love letters of Chapter VI that it was more broadly shared, as well – in both Britain and America. It is a view that was advocated, surprisingly enough, in some corners of the medical advice literature of the period.

Nevertheless, in spite of this knowledge and the pleasure of sleeping together, Lucy and James did not consummate their marriage until a year after it took place. She did not say exactly why when she first mentioned this in her questionnaire responses, but later she indicated that the restraint came at some cost when she wrote, "There are sometimes long periods when we are not willing to incur even a slight risk of pregnancy, and then we deny ourselves the intercourse, feeling all the time that we are losing that which keeps us closest to each other." After that first year, they began having intercourse about once a week until Lucy conceived. They abstained during her pregnancies as well as when she was nursing her first child and when James suffered his nervous prostration. Lucy had no sexual desire during her pregnancies, and she felt very strongly that the sexual union must take place only when it was mutually desired. Otherwise, they allowed themselves two or three times a month, taking care to avoid those days when they thought that conception could take place.

Their sexual relations were clearly extremely important to them and, to Lucy at any rate, the importance was spiritual; it symbolically represented their union as well as strengthened it. She felt that both reproduction and pleasure could be counted as true purposes of intercourse. Lucy is one of the few Mosher women, however, for whom reproduction was not primary. It was secondary to "the desire of both husband and wife for this expression of their union." Intercourse for the sake of reproduction could never be right unless this mutual desire were also present. Sexual intercourse is not a necessity either for men or for women, she believed, in the same sense that food and drink are necessities. Whatever necessity there is "is a spiritual not a physical impulsion" and is the same for man and woman alike. "When it [intercourse] does not occur," Lucy says, she and James "spiritually miss it, rather than physically . . . because it is the highest, most sacred expression of our oneness."

When asked if she experienced desire for intercourse at times other than when pregnant, Lucy answered a clear yes, and, when further questioned concerning when this would usually occur in relation to "your menses," she specified the times, in general, as falling just after her periods and halfway between. The questions about desire were followed with, "Is intercourse agreeable to you or not?" Lucy's bold response would be noteworthy in any context but is especially comprehensible in light of her emphasis on the spiritual. She says, "It is agreeable when I wish it – would be unbearable if I did not." To this point, Lucy's responses and explanations would seem to be perfectly coherent simultaneously in spiritual and physical terms. The questions about orgasm, however, display the final ascendance of the spiritual, at least up to the time of the survey. When asked if she always had a venereal orgasm, she responded that she had had only one during her whole married life. Even that one was "not complete" and was occasioned not by intercourse but by her husband's being "very near" to her. One could make a good many plausible guesses regarding what she meant by "very near," but in the end we just do not know. To the questions about how she felt immediately after orgasm and the next day, she gave no answer at all. However, to the questions about how she felt when there had been intercourse without her reaching orgasm, she testified that after ten minutes to a half hour she felt "as usual" and that the next day there were no effects whatever.

Orgasm was not the be-all and end-all for Lucy Meadows. She essentially never reached orgasm, yet she loved her husband, regularly felt desire, and found sexual relations agreeable – in fact, she valued them extraordinarily highly. There could be many explanations, but from what we know, it appears that she was enabled to elude the usually corrosive effects of physiological frustration by her intense interpretation of intercourse as the spiritual expression of her oneness with her husband. Perhaps this outlook was right for Mrs. Meadows and would be just fine for their marriage in perpetuity. James loved her. There is no point in injecting other perspectives. On the other hand, Lucy and James had only been married for six years, and there was at least one occasion upon which something like an orgasm took place. James was apparently a most considerate husband. They valued togetherness. Perhaps they eventually worked that orgasm thing out.

Portrait 3: Maude Eldridge[66]

Mrs. Maude Eldridge was one of many Mosher women who emphasized the value of marital sex in enriching the quality of the relationship they enjoyed with their husbands. "Even if there are no children," she explained, "men love their wives more if they continue this relation." One gets the feeling that these women did not just happen to think of this connection on the spur of the moment when answering Dr. Mosher's questionnaire. It had occurred to them before, probably several times, and they articulated for the study a view or realization that had grown upon them, often in opposition to negative things that they had read or heard about the sexual relation.

This respondent had four children, all boys, and a fifth conception that terminated in a miscarriage between the first and second births. Like almost all of the Mosher women, surprising as it may seem at least to many men, she remembered almost every detail connected with the births of her children, including health and events that may have influenced the character of the child (according to the beliefs of the age), how long she nursed the baby, whether desire was felt during pregnancy, length of the labor, whether intercourse was held during pregnancy, whether the conception was by choice or accident, when the first post-natal menstruation occurred, and so forth. All of her boys were grown up and healthy at the time of the study. She reported that her first boy, for example, was very bright and active *because* she herself "was perfectly well, traveling and studying abroad up to the moment of his birth." (Emphasis mine.) Similarly, she related that she generally did not experience sexual desire during her pregnancies, but she did experience it before the birth of the third boy. However, she added, she could "not see that it [the desire] affected the character of this son. He is perfectly continent [meaning celibate] at twenty-five."

None of these births occurred by choice. The brand-new Mrs. Eldridge wanted to delay children for five years in order to study. However, the method of birth control that the Eldridges practiced during the early years was timing. Following the erroneous but common medical prescription of that time, they avoided intercourse just before, during, and after menstruation and permitted it two or three times a week for a two-week period in between, always taking the

66 Mosher 1980. Blank No. 41, pp. 410-417.

extra precaution of a douche immediately afterwards. This method, she tells us, worked for her mother, who was a physician, but it clearly "did not answer in my case." After the fifth conception, they made the decision to switch to the very new and unproven "French method," which was vulcanized rubber condom use, and this proved to be perfectly successful.

Mrs. Eldridge was born in 1862, received a B.L. degree from the University of California at the age of twenty, and got married immediately afterwards. The exact date of filling out the questionnaire is not specified in this case, but we can establish that it was 1913 by a reference to the age of her third son. Also, we learn that she began experiencing menopause at age fifty, or in the year 1912. Her youngest boy would have turned twenty-two in that year. Her health had always been quite good. She did have typhoid fever during her sophomore year of college, leaving her, she believed, with a problem of constipation for fifteen years, but she had no health problems otherwise. In fact, she said that she never had a headache in her life. Typhoid fever, a bacterial disease, was much more common then than now in the United States and Europe. It generally was contracted from food or especially water that had been contaminated by human waste – for example, by untreated or poorly treated sewage – or by personal contact with a human carrier. In spite of the typhoid, however, and in her fifties when she participated in the study, Mrs. Eldridge was energetic, vigorous, and clearly had a zest for life that was unusual for women of her age at that time.

The last eleven numbered Mosher questionnaires contain information only on the respondent herself. Therefore, not only do we know next to nothing about Maude Eldridge's parents and grandparents, but there is also very little about her husband. We do learn that he was also a graduate of the University of California. In addition, he was considerate, for example in not pressing the sexual relation when she was disinclined. From her use of the present tense a few times, we can infer that he was still living at the time of the study, at which point the Eldridges had been married for over thirty years. When asked if she generally slept with her husband, she indicated that she did because they found it comfortable and it kept the relationship close. "I believe people drift apart when they do not sleep together."

There are many indications in her responses that Mrs. Eldridge had been exposed to a good deal of negative information and opinion about sexual relations. It is just as clear, however, that this information did not determine her own reactions. The marital bedroom is a private sanctuary. In it, couples find their own way, there being, no doubt, about as many ways as there are couples. The details of adjustment, good or bad, almost never become shared knowledge, although parts of them are sometimes disclosed confidentially to a counselor, such as a physician or minister. Miss Maude got married, experienced the secrets of her unique bedroom, and developed her own outlook. It was not completely unaffected by prior information, but she was conscious of her own attitudinal and experiential independence. She had no premarital knowledge of the details. She received some notions from fellow pupils at school, but only vague ones. She actually asked questions of her physician mother, indicating that she had the idea that there was something shameful about child bearing, but her mother refused to instruct her, saying that she could read books about it when she was older.

One fact that Maude found out for herself was that she frequently experienced sexual desire. Moreover, to the question, "Is intercourse agreeable to you or not?" she answered "Yes." The way Dr. Mosher put her question about orgasm was most unfortunate. No social scientist of the present day would commit this error. She asked, "Do you always have a venereal orgasm?" Maude Eldridge, like a great many of the other Mosher women, answered "No," leaving us to try our best to tease out from other information whether that meant "Never," "Not always but usually," or something in between.

In this case, the indications are that she frequently reached orgasm. When asked about the immediate effects of orgasm, she answered, "No bad effect." In this answer, somewhat surprising for the present-day reader, she seems to imply that one might have expected a bad effect from what one had heard, but she experienced none. She went on to inject her belief that a reasonable frequency of intercourse conduces to health. As for the effects of orgasm the next day, she made a striking statement: "None – a general sense of well-being, contentment and regard for husband. This is true Doctor." This is as if to say, "I realize that one is supposed to feel some shame, or guilt, or harm, but I feel none of these things. For me, it only makes me feel good about myself and my marriage, Doctor, surprising as that may seem." How about the times when she does not reach orgasm? Here, she was philosophical, showing the maturity of her years and experience: "Every wife submits sometimes when perhaps she is not in the mood, but I can see no bad effect. It is as if it had not been. But my husband was absolutely considerate. I do not think I could endure a man who forced it." In other words, at times she was not in the mood and did not reach orgasm, but she took it in stride as she felt most women would do. At other times, she was more seriously disinclined. Then, if her husband had pressed the point, there might have been unpleasant consequences. But he was considerate; he did not press. Additionally, she considered that pleasure as well as reproduction is a true purpose of intercourse. Both women and men need this relation. "It makes more normal people."

As the questionnaire went on and Mrs. Eldridge settled into bringing out her true thoughts, she made two forceful statements. Regarding the sexual relation between husband and wife, she stated that, "The highest devotion is based upon it, a very beautiful thing, and I am glad nature gave it to us." This is an absolute revolt against some of the negative judgments she clearly had absorbed.

Then, she included her confident opinion that reasonable intercourse "makes married life the happiest state in the world on account of the spiritual union which results from it." Shall we presume that such a sentiment was peculiar to the nineteenth century? Why leap to such a conclusion? Given the privacy that still prevails in regard to these experiences and thoughts, there may be thousands of women – completely unsung women – who feel quite the same about marriage today.

The medical advice literature

The purpose here is to review relevant medical writings with a view toward assessing their impact on the middle-class women of the time. Two rather surprising characteristics will soon become apparent, however, and it is well to point them out at the beginning. The first is that the doctors moralize. We expect physicians, at least in their written contributions, to be scientific, objective. That was not strictly true in the nineteenth century, at least in writing about sexuality. Their observations often seem to be as much prescriptive as descriptive. They seem to defend an ideology, although it is not always the same ideology.

The second surprising characteristic is that most of these physicians do not appear to have the least idea of what it takes to establish and convey a scientific fact. They speak with the assumed authority of scientific learning and experience, but their pronouncements are often impressionistic, at best. Their conception of adequate evidence is rudimentary, uninformed. The nineteenth century was notable for great strides in science made on the basis of the scientific method, but that spirit seems not to have penetrated to the medical gentlemen (plus a few ladies) writing on sexuality. The experiments and discoveries of Michael Faraday and James Clerk Maxwell were in the general area of physics and therefore perhaps not seen as relevant. The careful work of Charles Darwin on evolution was perhaps too controversial to be influential. But there were the well-publicized advances in the field of disease by Robert Koch and Louis Pasteur, for example, which one might have expected to have an impact. Dr. Lydgate, a character in the widely read novel *Middlemarch,* shows that its author, George Eliot, for one, understood that medical generalizations needed to be made on the basis of the careful examination of a number of cases. The physicians whose work we are about to review did not share that understanding. The failing is too universal to be blameworthy. We must simply accept that, by this time and in this area of study, the scientific method had not yet gained a foothold. These doctors often simply wrote off the top of their heads or, worse yet, their hearts.

We will see, as well, that there were opposing points of view and conclusions. The doctors contradicted each other on the subjects of the sexuality of women and the consequences of sexual behavior in both men and women, although they did so without confronting one another's claims or constructing an argument for the preference of their own. Nevertheless, a quite unified general impression will emerge.

The conservatives.

The most widely cited authority on the sexuality of women is Dr. William Acton, a gynecologist and influential expert on the pervasiveness of prostitution in Great Britain throughout most of the nineteenth century. I say "widely cited" because almost anyone who writes anything on the sexuality of Victorian women these days will cite a particular few of Acton's phrases, which I will do as well, but Acton was also widely read in his own time. Here is what he said:

> I should say that the majority of women (happily for them) are not very much troubled with sexual feeling of any kind. What men are habitually, women are only exceptionally.
> There are many females who never feel any sexual excitement whatever. Others, again, immediately after each period, do become, to a limited degree, capable of experiencing it; but this capacity is often temporary, and may cease entirely until the next menstrual period. The best mothers, wives, and managers of households, know little or nothing of sexual indulgences. Love of home, children, and domestic duties, are the only passions they feel.
> As a general rule, a modest woman seldom desires any sexual gratification for herself. She submits to her husband, but only to please him; and, but for the desire of maternity, would far rather be relieved from his attentions. No nervous or feeble young man need, therefore, be deterred from marriage by any exaggerated notions of the duties required from him. The married woman has no wish to be treated on the footing of a mistress.[67]

Note that Acton does not say categorically that women experience no desire and have no sexual feelings. Intentionally or not, he was more clever than that. The *majority* are not troubled by desire, he says. The *best* wives and mothers feel passion only for their domestic duties, and so on. If he had claimed unconditionally that women have no sexual feelings, then any woman who experienced them herself might have thrown out his contention as an obvious error and therefore distrusted his word on all other matters as well. What he did instead, again intentionally or not, was provide a basis for shame and guilt. Some women who read or heard these expert views and who did frequently experience desire and pleasure in sex might very well feel that they were not normal.

---

67 Acton 1857, pp. 101-102. Cited in Marcus 1964, pp,31-32; Degler 1974, pp. 1467, 1478; Cominos 1963, pp. 231-232; Trudgill 1976, pp. 30-60.

Acton was not alone in his assessment of the sexuality of women. Other physicians wrote corroborative evaluations. The American obstetrician Dr. Theophilus Parvin, in a medical journal article of 1883, stated that he does "not believe one bride in a hundred, of delicate, educated, sensitive women, accepts matrimony from any desire for sexual gratification; when she thinks of this at all, it is with shrinking, or even with horror, rather than with desire."[68] New York pastor Augustus Kinsley Gardner asserted in 1856 that "sensuality is unusual in the sex."[69] The historian Ben Barker-Benfield cites ample evidence to substantiate the observation that, "Defining the absence of sexual desire in woman as normal, doctors came to see its presence as disease . . ."[70] We will soon see that other physicians took an opposing view on the question of whether women felt desire or took pleasure in sex. Significantly, however, neither side cited good evidence, or even any evidence, to support their assertions. They merely asserted.

In that connection, here is an aside: If writers such as Dr. Acton, Dr. Parvin, and Reverend Gardner had been married to wives who frequently experienced desire and took evident pleasure in their sexual relations, it is highly unlikely that the husbands would have written the lines you just read. Readers at the time, however, would see these writers simply as authorities and would be unaware of the role that personal experience might have played in their pronouncements. Such are the hazards of generalizing from case studies, anecdotes, personal experience, and other forms of severely restricted sampling.

The more important question, however, was the matter of advice – what to do with sexual desire if one did experience it. This issue was pertinent not only for those medical authorities who credited women with desire, but for all pertinent medical authorities because all credited men with desire. There were opposing views on this question of the proper response to desire, as well, but we will see that the difference was really a matter of degree. One detects the underlying persuasion common to all of these authorities that there was

68 Parvin, Theophilus. 1883, cited in Degler 1974, p, 1468.

69 Gardner, Augustus Kinsley. 1856, cited in Barker-Benfield 1973, p.348.

70 Barker-Benfield 1973, p. 348.

something bad or dangerous about sex. It was a behavior that needed to be approached with caution.

There were three basic reasons given for this belief in the potential dangers of sex, although all three were not necessarily important to each doctor who expressed an opinion. One was that sex could be bad for your health. More of that in a moment. A second was that sexual energy somehow represented a finite physiological force. Its use depleted the total store and could therefore weaken a person's capabilities, not only sexually but in other physical and mental endeavors as well. Elaborating a theory (or fairy tale) that had a great many nineteenth-century adherents, the American physician Dr. John Cowan, whose name will appear frequently in the following pages, stated that, "One of the products of the brain is a nervous fluid intended for the supply of the vital power inherent in the living body. When any special organ is greatly employed, this fluid is diverted from its ordinary channels to the organ exercised. If amativeness [he seems to mean acting out aspects of the disposition toward romantic love – in short, sexual indulgence] is greatly and constantly exercised, it can only be done at the expense of all the other organs."[71] Conversely, the nonuse of this supposed storehouse of potentialities conserved a valuable resource that contributed to well-being in a number of ways. For example, the widely read female American physician Dr. Alice Stockham, writing in 1911, put substantial emphasis on the idea that the "procreative elements" in men and women are absorbed when not used in coitus and confer benefits upon the individual's body.[72]

The third reason for the common Victorian belief that there is something dangerous about sex was more philosophical than physiological. There is abundant evidence, much of which we will come across in Chapters V and VI, that Victorians felt the importance of a certain series of similar, warring dualities: body versus mind, body versus soul, animal versus spiritual, appetite versus reason, and so on. Sensuality represented body, animal, appetite. To succumb to sensuality was to allow one's baser nature to prevail over one's higher, human gift. Reverend A. K. Gardner, for example, wrote that the sexual "passion may be restrained within proper limitations. He who indulges in lascivious thoughts

71 Cowan 1874, p. 97.

72 Stockham 1911, pp. 150-162.

may stimulate himself to frenzy; but if his mind were under proper control, he would find other employment for it, and his body, obedient to its potent sway, would not become master of the man."[73]

Dr. Acton – recall his dictum that women are not very much troubled with sexual feelings of any kind – provides a good example. He invoked the duality of appetite versus reason and also the notion that the use of one depletes the other. These powerful philosophical and physiological forces combine to reveal that sex can be perilous: "I have already alluded to the fact," he wrote in 1857, "that the intellectual qualities are usually in an inverse ratio to the sexual appetites. It would almost seem as if the two were incompatible; the exercise of the one annihilating the other. . . . All experience [Really? Whose experience?] tends to prove that if a man observes strict continence in thought as well as deed and is gifted with ordinary intelligence, he is more likely to distinguish himself in liberal pursuits than those who live incontinently, whether in the way of fornication or by committing marital excesses."[74] In other words, if you want to succeed in life, use your head rather than your genitals, because the more you exercise the latter the less you will be able to engage the former. (Note that Acton used the male gender here – and not just as a grammatical universal. Presumably, this particular reasoning does not apply to women, both because women have no sexual appetites to be bothered about and, anyway, are not concerned with distinguishing themselves in liberal pursuits.)

Reasons two and three, just elaborated, would have the psychological consequence at a minimum of making people apprehensive about sex. The warnings under reason one – sex can be hazardous for your health – would only have intensified that effect. Dr. John Cowan, for example, in his book of 1870, was the initiator of the highly influential Law of Continence. This was the moral edict, declared to be supported by medical fact, that unmarried individuals should indulge in no sexual behavior of any kind at any time and that married individuals should indulge in no sexual behavior except sexual intercourse in order to produce a child – preferably once and once only for each child. Reasons

73 Gardner, Augustus Kinsley 1870, cited in Barker-Benfield 1973, p. 344.

74 Acton, 1862 edition of Acton 1857, cited in Cominos 1963, pp. 36-37.

two and three are invoked in support of this law, but the genuinely frightening emphasis is reserved for reason one:

> The fact that the small brain, in which amativeness is located, is also the co-ordinating or harmonizing power of the muscular system, explains why sexual excesses are so soon followed by a weakening of the joints, and especially the joints of the knees, a softening of the muscles, a want of strength, and a motion of an unsteady, dragging nature, differing so noticeably from the springing, strong, elastic carriage of the continent individual.
>
> Noticeably in many ways do sexual excesses affect the brain. The faculty of memory is weakened and impaired, the person gradually lacking his usual power to remember men and things. The eyes are also affected; disordered vision is almost always a prompt indication of abused amativeness. The eyes are easily affected by night lights, and any ordinary effort strains and hurts them. The hearing is also in many cases impaired. Paralysis of the lower extremities occasionally results. Neuralgia [see Glossary below], affecting any part of the system, is among the frequent consequences. More than half the cases of epilepsy are unmistakably owing either to sexual or self-abuse [masturbation]. Falling of the womb, barrenness, abortion, and cancer of the womb or breast, are directly or indirectly caused by excessive indulgence in married life. Fickleness of temper, irresolution, and premature old age, are penalties that attach themselves indiscriminately to all who violate the laws of their organization.

The individual who leads a licentious life does, in part or in whole:

> Weaken his nervous system, and through that the digestive system is disorganized, the stomach, liver, kidneys, etc., are diseased, and dyspepsia, rheumatism, apoplexy, paralysis, and a score of other diseases, assert their sway.
>
> Weaken his lungs, and consumption appears.
>
> Disable his special senses – his sight, hearing and taste are affected.

> Disorganize his brain-tissue – memory is weakened, perceptive and reflective power is weakened, as seen in imbecility of plan and purpose, and indecision of thought and action; the moral sentiments are debased, the soul blighted, and love, religion and God cannot dwell within him.
> Arrests his growth, and brings on premature old age.
> Destroys his manhood, and the offspring propagated by him are sickly, scrofulous, deformed, and die prematurely
> And is, all in all, a blot and stain upon God's beautiful earth, a failure in this life and in the next a ______. [blank included in the original]

It is a common belief that a man and woman, because they are legally united in marriage, are privileged to the unbridled exercise of amativeness. This is wrong. . . . Excessive indulgence between the married produces as great and lasting evil effects as in the single man or woman, and is nothing more or less than legalized prostitution.

The exercise of abnormal amativeness is known in all its positive intensity by those newly married. The honeymoon is one nightly repetition of legalized prostitution, sinking the pure, high and holy into the low, debasing and animal. Think you, oh! new-made husband and wife, that in this you do right? – that in this you elevate your better natures? – that in this you find peace, strength and happiness? – that in this you grow into that pure and holy passion akin to God in its exercise – the passion of love? Do not, I pray you, deceive yourselves; for in this exercise of the sexual part of your nature you lower your standard of body and soul; and, as for love, *no man or woman can possibly love or be loved who lives other than a life of strict continence.* [Italics in the original.][75]

Masturbation was a particular obsession of nineteenth-century moralists, including medical practitioners. The Philadelphia physician Dr. George Napheys published a book in 1870 called *The Physical Life of Woman: Advice to the Maiden, Wife, and Mother.* It was extremely popular until well into the twentieth century and still commands fifty or sixty entries in a Google search. Of particular interest in this section is the fact that Dr. Napheys was commendably sensible. He

75 Cowan 1874, pp. 105-106, 119, 103-104.

avoided almost all pronouncing and generalizing on the basis of little or no evidence and, for the most part, escaped the temptation to allow ideology to cloud his views. When it came to masturbation, however, he lapsed into the familiar Victorian refrain. He says:

> [Experience provides a] warning to the mothers of America on this secret vice, which leads their daughters to the grave, the madhouse, or, worse yet, the brothel. . . . The results of the constant nervous excitement which this habit produces are bodily weakness, loss of memory, low spirits, distressing nervousness, a capricious appetite, dislike of company and of study, and, finally, paralysis, imbecility or insanity.[76]

Dr. John Roberton was a Scottish physician who seemed to have a propensity toward antagonizing his colleagues with controversial views. On the subject of masturbation, however, he provoked no quarrel. Instead, he provided this typical warning in 1812:

> From the commencement of the disgusting habit of self-pollution . . . there is seldom any desire for sexual intercourse . . . At length, there is induced a general lassitude, with a weariness, often approaching to pain, in the loins; the bowels become constipated, often in alarming degree, the face becomes pale and cadaverous, and the body in general flabby or emaciated, with coldness in the extremities. Then occurs trembling hands, dim eyes, confused indistinct hearing, if not entire deafness, frequent and violent headache, drowsiness, without the power to sleep, all attempts at which are interrupted by the most frightful dreams; and in this stage . . . the patient becomes terrified to go to bed, lest sudden death should be his fate; and, during the day is tired, fretful, terrified and discontented, he knows not for what; with violent palpitations of the heart; and although he seems sensible of the causes of his

76 Napheys 1876, p. 29.

> distresses, is unable to abandon his habits, particularly while in bed. A complete state of imbecility, both of body and mind, at length ensues.[77]

After Charles Goodyear's patenting of the vulcanization of rubber in 1844, the use of barrier methods of contraception such as the cervical cap and the condom began to become more popular, although it took many decades before they were very widely used. They did, however, occasion debate in the medical profession. As before, moral considerations were clearly important, but supposed connections with disease were also invoked. For example, in a twenty-nine-page pamphlet of 1879 entitled "The Moral and Physical Evils likely to Follow if Practices intended to Act as Checks to Population be not strongly Discouraged and Condemned," the author specified among the physical evils of contraception: "metritis, leucorrhoea, menorrhagia and hematocele, hysteralgia and hyperaesthesia of the genital organs, sterility, mania leading to suicide, and nymphomania."[78]

GLOSSARY

Neuralgia – Acute nerve pain
Dyspepsia – Indigestion
Apoplexy – Stroke
Metritis – Inflammation of the uterus
Leucorrhoea – White mucous vaginal discharge
Menorrhagia – Abnormally heavy or prolonged menstruation
Hematocele – Blood mass in the scrotum
Hysteralgia – Pain in the uterus
Hyperaesthesia – Abnormally increased, painful sensitivity
Nymphomania – Abnormally high sexual desire in a woman

For many physicians, the clear solution to the problem presented by these manifold, dire consequences of sexual indulgence and contraception was strict

77 Roberton, John 1812, cited in F. Barry Smith 1977, pp. 195-196.

78 Routh, C. H. F. 1879, cited in Trudgill 1976, p. 63.

obedience to Dr. John Cowan's Law of Continence: no sex except for reproduction.[79] As we will see in the next section, several physicians advocated a more permissive sexual regime, citing as reasons, for example, the need to keep marriages healthy and happy, but the ultra-conservative purists saw in this only a slippery slope: without the clear limitation prescribed by the intention to conceive a child, which they felt to be the one true purpose of sex, there was no telling where individuals would stop. There is still a bit of a problem with the efficacy of this view, however, in that as long as the wife were not pregnant, all sexual intercourse without contraceptive precautions could be seen as being for the purpose of conceiving a child. There could be quite a bit of it, and this would disturb most of the purists.

Dr. Cowan himself, the originator of the Law of Continence, did not believe that women were passionless even though he held strong conservative views on sexual restraint. He solved this remaining difficulty of apparently justified overindulgence through his own (mistaken) notions, and those of many colleagues, on the science of fertility. "It is necessary to a perfect sexual congress that the wife have a natural desire for such, which natural desire occurs *only* immediately after her 'monthly sickness.' At this time all healthy married women have such a desire; and if she earnestly express a wish for congress, and the husband accedes, a perfect union results."[80] In other words, there is no license for sexual indulgence at just any time when the wife happens not to be pregnant. One must wait for the day or two following the end of her period and then indulge only if she expresses "a wish for congress."

Several matters of interest to us are raised by this brief quote. It was apparently believed by many in the late nineteenth century that desire arose in a woman when she was likely to conceive and that this occurred during or just after the menstrual period.[81] The sensible Dr. George Napheys shows that he subscribed to this same very common and very tragic error in his concern that babies not come too soon to the newly wed – before they were really prepared: "We have said that a time about midway between the

79 F. Barry Smith 1977, p. 186, for example, mentions three eminent, titled medical men, Doctors Paget, Clark, and Allbutt, who advised strict continence except for procreation.

80 Cowan 1874, p. 105.

81 E. g., Cowan 1874, p. 170.

monthly recurring periods is best fitted for the consummation of marriage. As this is a season of sterility, it recommends itself on this account, in the interest of both the mother and offspring."[82] Dr. T. L. Nichols, an ultra-conservative adherent of Dr. Cowan's Law of Continence, falls into the same error, ascribing ovulation, and therefore the one interval permitted for intercourse, to the occasion of the menstrual flow.[83]

To those couples who meant to adhere to Dr. Cowan's Law of Continence, and who would therefore restrict sexual intercourse to the supposed fertile period around the time of menstruation, this would have the effect on average of permitting a large amount of sexual pleasure without enlarging the family. In fact, disappointment in the continued failure to conceive might well fill much of the time between trials. To those who were not inclined to the Law of Continence, however, the results could be not just tragic but both ironic and disastrous, ironic in that intercourse only at the midway point was often used as a means of contraception while it would have had just the opposite effect, and disastrous in that childbirth at this time was a grave threat to the life of the woman and large families frequently spelled economic devastation. If physicians had gathered some data instead of relying on impressions, preconceptions, and conservative ideology, they almost certainly would have avoided this most unfortunate error, but they did not. There is no indication that anybody even thought of it.

A second observation on the quote from Dr. Cowan is his belief in the "perfect sexual congress" and "perfect union." By this he means a union highly likely to result in a conception, and indeed the conception of a sunny, happy, well-endowed child. The belief connecting a joyful, loving occasion of conception with a well-endowed child was common at the time, as we will continue to see in dealing with the Mosher survey. Dr. Cowan's interest in the "perfect sexual congress" was not an interest in marital pleasure for its own sake, nor even in the health of a marriage that, on his advice, featured one copulation per kid, but rather an interest in an auspicious pregnancy, a flawless child, and, through these, the future of the race.[84]

---

82 Napheys 1876, p. 69.

83 Nichols, T. L. 1873, p. 118, 1853, p. 148.

84 Cowan 1874, pp. 170-172.

The liberals.

We are dealing with three issues here. The first is Victorian medical opinion on whether women in general experience desire or derive pleasure from sex. The second is opinion on whether sex is healthy or unhealthy. The third is a matter not of opinion but advice, namely, given the medical stance on the first two issues, what were Victorian women supposed to do about having sex? These issues are important for our inquiry because the Victorian age has been considered to be a period of extreme sexual repression for women partly on the basis of the medical literature's claiming that women were passionless, that sex tended to be bad for you, and therefore that sexual practice should be severely restricted.[85] If the medical authorities were actually divided rather than unified on those conclusions, the case that behavior was extremely repressed loses one prop, that is, if many doctors were recorded as finding that women derived pleasure from sex, that it was good for you, and that it was recommended, it is conceivable that both premarital and marital sex were more common than many now believe. Why? Because medical authorities tend to be influential. If more "liberal" views (if we may call them that) were current, one must admit the possibility that they affected attitudes and behavior.

I have used the term "repression" often enough to this point to give the idea that the Victorian period was special, even unique, in the emphasis placed on female virtue. That is not at all the case. Premarital sexual intercourse by women, for example, had been forbidden for centuries in the moral code of these societies. True, it is clear in such eighteenth-century novels as those of Fielding, Smollett, Richardson, and Burney that the prevailing sexual attitudes and behavior were loose. It is just as clear, however, that the loose behavior was not universal. The word "virtuous" was meaningful even in this most extreme period of license. In fact, the heroines of almost all of the novels of these authors were "virtuous" women. The standard was there. The Victorians did not invent female modesty and sexual restraint. In that eighteenth-century period and others, however, there was a general acknowledgment and acceptance of the fact that the standard was widely transgressed.

85 Degler 1974, p. 1479.

What is noteworthy is that the historically standard morality needs to be emphasized in regard to the Victorians precisely because it followed a period of substantial license. That is one of two prominent reasons why the term "repression" can be considered to have a special applicability to the period of our concern. The task of ensuring that the standard moral code was adhered to strictly rather than being extensively violated was made difficult by the need to reverse the momentum of the period of unusual license that preceded the Victorian era. The other reason why "repression" is particularly applicable in this context is that there are now revisionists, mainly encouraged by the Mosher survey, who urge that repression was no more effective in Victorian times than in the mid-twentieth century. Repression, explicitly, is now an issue.

The early explorations of the nineteenth-century medical advice literature found mainly the kinds of conservative positions quoted and referred to above.[86] Because of the discovery of the Mosher survey in the early 1970s, however, scholars began looking more broadly at what was written about sexuality by physicians in the Victorian period. They found views that did not harmonize very well with the conservative position on the three issues that opened this section.[87] As with the quotations from the conservative doctors, many of these other writings also went into multiple editions and sold tens of thousands of copies. Consider the following six examples, each published by a different reputable physician during the 1870s and 1880s.

> Passion is absolutely necessary in woman. Amativeness is created in the female head as universally as in the male. . . . That female passion exists, is as obvious as that the sun shines.[88]
>
> Conception is more assured when the two individuals who co-operate in it participate at the same time in the transports of which it is the fruit.[89]

86 Marcus 1966 was especially influential.

87 For an extensive overview of the liberal medical literature of the period, see Degler 1980, pp. 249-297.

88 Fowler, Orson S. 1870, cited in Degler 1974, p. 1469.

89 Napheys 1871, cited in Degler 1974. p. 1470.

> The sexual orgasm on the part of the female is just as normal as on the part of the male.[90]
> The creator has endowed men and women with passions, the suppression of which leads to pain, their gratification to pleasure, their satiety to disgust.[91]
> [It is her] duty to her husband, her children and herself, to heartily enjoy with her husband sexual intercourse, and to keep herself in such condition that she may enjoy it.[92]
> [The preparatory stage] may be reached by any means, bodily or mental, which, in the opposite sex, cause erection. Following upon this, then, is a stage of pleasurable excitement, gradually increasing and culminating in an acme of excitement, which may be called the stage of consummation, and the analogue of which in the male is emission.[93]
> Destroy the reciprocity of the union, and marriage is no longer an equal partnership, but a sensual usurpation on the one side and a loathing submission on the other.[94]

Thus, thinking first about desire and pleasure, middle-class women would get mixed messages from the medical community. One would think it important, therefore, to know which of the two sets of literature was more widely read by those upon whom we focus. Of course, very few unmarried women would ever be able to read such literature at all. As for married women, in one sense they would not really need the opinion of doctors to know whether they felt a desire for sex and enjoyed the experience. They would find out the answers for themselves, and we know from the Mosher survey and other sources that they did find out. However, they might well be curious and even nervous about how they fit in with the experience of most other women of their times. In truth, the important difference between the effects of the conservative and the liberal medical opinion regarding "passionlessness" is psychological: the conservatives

90 Trall, Russel T. 1879, cited in Fellman and Fellman 1981, p. 244.

91 Pierce, R. V. 1889, cited in Fellman and Fellman 1981, p. 243.

92 Hanchett, Henry G. 1889, cited in Fellman and Fellman, p. 244.

93 Van de Warker, Ely 1878, cited in Degler 1974, p. 1471.

94 Goodell, William 1887, cited in Degler 1974, p. 1473.

would lead married women to feel shame or guilt for experiencing desire or pleasure very often, whereas the liberals would lead such women to feel essentially normal and wholesome. As for which set was more widely read, we will see evidence in the chapter on the Mosher survey that the conservatives had the greater influence, at least to the extent of instilling the feeling that there was something bad or dangerous about sex.

To round matters out, one must also consider more pointedly the issues of health effects and behavioral advice. Was there medical opinion and advice contrary to the Law of Continence as there were judgments contrary to the doctrine of passionlessness? The answer is yes, there was such advice, as well as opinion regarding health effects, but not as contrary as one might expect from the six citations just reviewed.

The historians Anita Clair Fellman and Michael Fellman carried out an exhaustive review of the medical and related literature bearing on the issue of Victorian sexual advice. They found numerous medical writers whom we would class here as "liberals," physicians who stood clearly in opposition to such extreme views as Dr. Cowan's Law of Continence, which would limit married sex to a bare minimum. It is just as clear, however, that these liberal nineteenth-century authorities would have been deeply disturbed by completely unrestrained sexual indulgence or even just a regimen of daily sexual relations. Consider this series of excerpts from their 1981 article:

> [Quoting Dr. Elizabeth Blackwell, 1894:] It is this mental sentiment peculiar to human sex which is capable of a two-fold development. It may grow into a noble sympathy, self-sacrifice, reverence, and joy, which enlarge and intensify the nature through the gradual expansion of the inborn moral elements of sex. . . . It is the degradation of this mental power when running riot in unchecked licence that converts men and women into selfish and cruel devils – monsters quite without parallel in the brute creation.[95]
>
> [Drs.] John H. Kellogg [1889] and Russell T. Trall [1872] felt that by living naturally and correctly, humans could immediately reattune

95 Blackwell, Elizabeth 1894, quoted in Fellman and Fellman 1981, p. 247.

themselves to their instincts. Trall suggested that, through a stripping away of unnatural habits, one could return to a state of nature where the instincts would be sound and behavior naturally moderate. However, this ideal of the naturally sound individual was not generally shared by the other advisors; they presumed that rational control over the dangerous appetites, whether conceived of as instinctual or as the results of overcivilization, would always be necessary.[96]

Many advisors felt that one of the chief markers they could provide for their readers to aid them in charting a successful course through their sexual lives was that of suitable frequency of sexual intercourse. . . . Even those who regarded sex as a more continual part of marriage, perhaps even accepting the validity of birth control, felt it necessary to provide guidelines about frequency. [Quoting Dr. William A. Hammond, 1883:] "It is exceedingly difficult to lay down any rule in the matter which will be applicable for all men; indeed, the task would be insuperable, for all men are not alike, and what would be excess for one would be moderation for another." He did feel, however, that he could safely make a few mercantilist generalizations: "Twice a week is certainly excess for this majority of men, and will certainly lead to earlier than normal extinction of the sexual powers. Once a week is more generally applicable . . . If the individual desires to retain his ability to a green old age, he will not tax it too severely in his youth."[97]

In their efforts to balance control with correct expression, not just of sexuality but of all the appetites, the mainstream advisors inevitably settled upon the concept of moderation to describe the balancing principle they were seeking. [Quoting Dr. John Dye, 1882:] "It is a physiological fact that the moderate use of any function contributes to health, longevity, and enjoyment, while excessive indulgence is punished with physical ills."[98]

96 Fellman and Fellman 1981, p. 248.

97 Fellman and Fellman 1981, p. 249.

98 Fellman and Fellman 1981, p. 246.

> In sum, moderation was believed to be the royal road to good sexuality as it was to good health in general. Sexual moderation meant not total denial, but self-controlled expression in a most dangerous sector of life.[99]

The same basic message is conveyed much more colorfully in Dr. Samuel Solomon's *Guide to Health, or Advice to Both Sexes.* One might think of this gentleman as an early quack medicine practitioner, but the fact is that his book sold several hundred thousand copies, probably the largest-selling book of its age. A helpful distillation for our present purpose was provided by F. Barry Smith in a collection of articles on Victorian women published in 1977.

> Dr. Solomon, like Doctors Goss, Brodum, Ramsay, and others of their trade, fished both sides of the stream. He recommended male and female enjoyment in intercourse and noted that intercourse was "natural" and that orgasms made the participants happy and loving to each other. Yet he warned that "over-indulgence" created overexcitement of the physical organism, and that the excessive loss of seminal fluid occasioned by over-indulgence led to physical and mental exhaustion. So, while intercourse was "exstacy," "excessive venery" resulted in "lassitude, weakness, numbness, a feeble gait, headache, convulsions of all the senses, dimness of sight and dullness of hearing, an idiot look, a consumption of the lungs and back, and effeminacy." And because over-indulgence weakened the sensation of particular "extacies" it produced "a perpetual itch for pleasure," with inevitable debility. The remedy was to write for Dr. Solomon's "Cordial Balm of Gilead," apply muriatic quicksilver, and sleep on a hard mattress. Females had to be especially careful during sexual play because their blood, according to available medical opinion, was more "capillary and lymphatic" than that of males. This condition made them more excitable and insatiable than males and therefore more vulnerable to "exhaustion" and degeneration of their sexual organs. For ladies with this problem Dr. Solomon had

99 Fellman and Fellman 1981, p. 251.

> a "Special Cordial Balm of Gilead" at 10s. 6d. a bottle, obtainable at market towns throughout Great Britain.[100]

We see with these final excerpts summarizing the liberal perspective that mainstream medical opinion would not have made people feel free and easy about sex. On the contrary, the doctors' opinions and advice would have tended toward making married couples feel anxious about frequent sex and, if exposed to conservatives such as Dr. Acton, making women feel unnatural or guilty about desire and sexual gratification. Sex was to be avoided entirely by the unmarried – a responsibility laid upon parents by medical advice – and indulged in only sparingly by married couples. In addition, the Evangelical advice literature attempted to influence middle-class women toward being relentlessly modest, virtuous, obedient, and spiritual – "Angels in the House", as this combination of traits came to be known.[101] In all probability, this intense socialization had broad psychological effects. The question would be how broad and how deep, and the further question would be to what extent did the effects extend to influencing behavior?

There were several additional, reinforcing currents of socialization to which we will turn in Chapter III, after a second interlude for portraits based in the Mosher survey.

100 Smith, F. Barry 1977, pp. 194-195.

101 From *The Angel in the House*, a long poem by Coventry Patmore, first published in parts from 1854-1862.

Second Interlude: Portraits 4 – 6

Portrait 4: Adelaide Sanford/Shaw[102]

Adelaide's tale naturally divides itself into three chronological stages. The first of these includes background, life before marriage, marriage to Herbert Sanford, and, soon afterwards, the filling out of Dr. Mosher's questionnaire. We deal with that stage first.

The questionnaire asks only for minimal information about parents and grandparents and just a little more about the respondent's husband. In this case, we learn that Adelaide's father worked as a carpenter and a schoolteacher until age thirty-four, when, surprisingly to us moderns, he became a college professor. There is unfortunately no information about the level of his education. Mr. Sanford, her husband, received a Master's degree from Cornell University in 1878, worked as a "Practical Machinist" for seven years, and then, in 1886, he also became a college professor. Times have changed! Such routes to the professorship would be rare today. Adelaide herself was well educated, having received a Master of Science degree from Cornell University in 1882. The education became important to her later in life.

She did not complain about it at all, but Adelaide had her share of health problems. She mentioned catarrh (a word not in common usage anymore meaning an inflammation of the mucus membrane, so that copious mucus is produced, usually, but not always, from a cold), as well as tonsillitis, pneumonia, measles, small pox, whooping cough, bronchitis, grippe (now usually called the flu), and a bad case of diphtheria that left her with some paralysis. Apparently, the paralysis was not permanent. In addition, she reported a problem of flexion (bending) of the neck of the uterus, which may or may not have inhibited conception, and pretty severe and dependable menstrual pain, especially on the first day of her period.

When asked what she knew about marital sex before the marriage itself, she answered, "A great deal." She is one of the few who indicated having learned at least some things in talking to other children, but we do not know how much or

102 Mosher 1980. Blank No. 2, pp. 13-26.

exactly what. This was before the age of sixteen. After that, she says she learned from scientific books, mentioning Dr. Trall and "Dr. Wilder's *Tokology*." Her memory was a bit faulty there because Dr. Wilder did write a relevant book, as did Dr. Trall, but *Tokology*, which is also relevant, was written by the American physician Alice Stockham. It is probable that Adelaide had a pretty good idea of what to expect on her wedding night, but, as seems so often to have been the case, the knowledge (or lack of it) did not seem to have much effect on reactions to sexual practice after the first few days.

Adelaide was born in 1860, married at age thirty, and asked to fill out Dr. Mosher's questionnaire a year and a half after the wedding, in 1892. There had been no conceptions by this point in time. However, Herbert and Adelaide did have a fairly active sex life, with intercourse coming about once a week. She was conscious of feeling desire, usually just after her period, and her answer to the question as to whether intercourse was agreeable to her was a simple "Yes." "Do you always have a venereal orgasm?" "Generally, not always." She judged that intercourse was a necessity for the man and also for the woman, "if she be normal." Although she considered reproduction to be the primary object of the sexual relation, she felt that pleasure was also a true purpose. For birth control, they used a "rubber sheath for man," but she does not tell us whether they used it always or if they sometimes did not, and so invited a conception which, in any case, did not occur.

Adelaide's responses to Dr. Mosher's questions stand out from most of the others because they are almost all short. She gave simple, direct, often one-word answers and did not frequently go on to give more detail or insight, as so many of the others did. It is clear from these responses that her womanhood was being normally fulfilled by her sex life, but she seemed almost detached or impatient with the topic. It could have been just a matter of the mood she happened to be in on that day, but there are indications that it may have been something else. I am cheating here because I know more than has yet been divulged. Still, the signs are there once one knows to look for them.

For example, one of her longer responses was to the question about whether she and Herbert shared a bed. They did during the first year but not regularly afterwards. Why was that? "Because sleeping on my guard made me nervous and irritable. It made the necessary control on my husband's part, too hard." We see that, although the general sexual experience was physically satisfying, it may not have been what many of the other women called spiritually satisfying. She was on her guard lest it should happen too often. The "necessary control" on her husband's part was apparently not for fear of conception, but because her tolerance was limited. When asked about her husband's general health, the words she chose in her response make her seem just a bit critical: "Good, but not of vigorous make; lacks physical exuberance." Her reactions on the day following intercourse, whether or not she reached orgasm, were, "general weariness, often great nervousness." Finally, when asked what she thought would be an ideal habit with regard to intercourse, she said, "Twice a month . . . once a week too often for health in my case." What was the matter with her health? She did not say anything at all about current health problems – except the occurrence of weariness and nervousness on the days following intercourse. It can begin to seem as if her nervousness might have been connected to a stirring of dissatisfaction with her marriage and her weariness possibly connected to a dissatisfaction with her husband. That would be too bad. Sour marriages can be a severe, debilitating trial. Moreover, divorces were extremely rare and difficult to obtain in those years, both in Britain and America, and divorced women were seriously stigmatized.

The second chronological stage in Adelaide's saga comprised the eleven long years from the filling out of the questionnaire in 1892 until 1903. We have no specific information at all about that period, so the present paragraph will be short. However, we can surmise that the years were not pleasant ones, for in June of 1903, Adelaide and Herbert separated and soon after that they became divorced.

We know this because in 1913, ten years later, Adelaide wrote a free-style, narrative "supplement" to her questionnaire. Just how this came about we are not told. In 1892, Dr. Mosher was in Wisconsin, whereas in 1913 she was at Stanford University, half a continent away. We learn that Adelaide had also moved to the San Francisco Bay area, but not how her contact with Dr. Mosher was renewed. Somehow, however, Adelaide and Dr. Mosher did renew contact, and the supplement was a result.

There is no indication in the supplement that her marriage to Mr. Sanford ever produced children. At the beginning of the third stage, during 1903 and 1904, Adelaide was quite ill, no doubt largely because of the strain of the divorce. She spent some time in a sanitarium with "nerves" and lost a great deal of weight. But she recovered, rested, and began to work on sociological researches. These were interrupted in 1906 by the great San Francisco earthquake and fire, certainly one of the most destructive natural disasters in U.S. history. Adelaide tells us that she worked very hard during the relief period. Still, 1906 was not a completely grim year for her because of two events on the good side of the ledger. She published a statistical and sociological book and, at age forty-six, she remarried – to a "literary man," Benjamin Shaw.

In the 1913 supplement, she wrote that her health had been steadily improving ever since. She published two more books, one in 1908 and one in 1912. Her second husband, she says, was an unusually considerate man. "During the earlier months of marriage, intercourse was frequent – two or three times a week and as much desired by me as by him." Thus, we find a new, mature Adelaide, in love and experiencing desire two or three times a week at age forty-six, whereas at thirty-two she had found once a week to be "too often for health in my case." When her new husband was consumed with work, she said, he "has very little desire for intercourse. Whenever he stops work he at once becomes as passionate as before." Her change-of-life transition began three years after the second marriage, but it did not slow her down. She continued her researches and gained in strength. She rather proudly announced that, at fifty-three, she could walk fifteen miles without feeling it. Mrs. Shaw closed her update on the original questions with these words: "Although my *passionate* feeling has declined somewhat and the orgasm does not always occur, intercourse is still agreeable to me." (Emphasis in the original.).

Portrait 5: Mildred Conroy[103]

We learn from Mildred that her mother, at sixty-four, was subject to intense emotional excitement, for which morphine was sometimes administered, and melancholia, which Mildred would probably have labeled "depression" or perhaps "bipolar" had she been filling out Dr. Mosher's questionnaire today. Also, her mother's mother, a Roman Catholic, was a religious fanatic who had melancholia and died in a convent. There is no indication, however, that this family history extended to Mildred herself in any way.

Her father was a physician. Mildred obtained knowledge of the marital sexual relation from a good deal of reading in her father's library, and this was supplemented through her own experience as a student, earning a B.A. from Radcliffe College in 1891 with some coursework in Zoology and Physiology. Thus, she probably had a pretty good idea of what to expect in regard to the sexual side of marriage before the wedding itself.

The husband in this case, Merlin Conroy, received an M.P. degree from Syracuse University and is listed by Mildred as being both a teacher and an artist. We know very little more except that his relationship with his wife, judging by the intimate details provided, seems to have evolved into a good one. In fact, in responding to the question about knowledge of sexual physiology before marriage, Mildred added that, beyond the information she gleaned from books, she had not talked to anybody about the subject – except her husband. From all we know, that sort of discussion between Victorian husbands and wives was not at all common.

The Mosher questionnaire was filled out by Mildred in September of 1897. At that time, she was thirty years old, had been married only fifteen months, and had a four-month-old, healthy baby girl. Before the marriage, she had taught school for five years in Palo Alto, California. The Conroys did not use any sort of birth control, but there is evidence that they maintained a consciousness of the times of the monthly cycle when they thought she was most likely to conceive. As to the birth of the little girl, it was a difficult labor, leaving Mildred with general weakness and severe backaches, but these gradually diminished.

103 Mosher 1980. Blank No. 22, pp. 242-254.

It is uncertain whether Mildred absorbed the conservative perspective on marital sexual relations directly, as from reading or perhaps lectures or sermons, or if it was gathered indirectly from the tone and words, spoken and unspoken, of the people in her life. It is clear, however, that her orientation toward these matters at the time of her marriage owed much to the conservative view.

For example, she did not regularly share a bed with her husband. When asked why not, she gave three reasons. One was that the bed clothes took up so much room that one was uncomfortable with two in the bed. Come on! No doubt the abundant yardage in the male and female nightgowns of that era was more of a factor than the skimpy garments on the store shelves of today, but she is certainly the only Mosher respondent to make mention of that element. One can, after all, get rid of such encumbrances. She also for some reason considered it "more wholesome" for a person to sleep alone. Lastly, she frankly found this practice best in order to avoid the temptation of too frequent intercourse. She did not say explicitly who it was that might have been tempted, but it is clear that, until recently at any rate, it probably was not she.

Dr. Mosher's questionnaire includes this question about regularly sleeping with one's husband for most of her respondents, but for eight of the later-numbered cases, she substituted for this an entirely different question – one about the time of the first intercourse after marriage. This breaks a rule of modern questionnaire construction, which is to ask precisely the same questions of every respondent, but Dr. Mosher knew nothing of this. She was asking questions as best she knew how in order to obtain imprecisely defined information on a broad topic she considered to be important for her researches. In Mildred's questionnaire and no others, as it happens, both of these questions were included, so that we know not only about regularly sharing a bed but also when the first intercourse after the wedding occurred. It was ten days later. Why? There could be any number of explanations, and it would probably be of great help in understanding Mrs. Conroy if we knew the correct one, but there unfortunately is nothing else in the responses to hint at the reason. The conservative viewpoint might well have been a factor, but that is only one possibility.

Mildred is clear that before marriage she "thought reproduction was the only object and that once brought about, intercourse should cease." She was subscribing, in other words, to Dr. Cowan's Law of Continence – wittingly or unwittingly. As to desire, she declared that before the birth of the baby, she never "craved it" [intercourse] and often felt averse to it "even during the early months of our married life." She allows that intercourse was agreeable to her after it began but, "If too long continued it wearies me." She indicates a most interesting ambivalence in her own reactions due to the reality of her feelings on one hand and her preconceived notions on the other. She tells us that during the first six months of their intercourse she usually felt wearied and found the experience "distasteful afterwards; even when the act itself had been very pleasant." Why might it possibly have been distasteful even when pleasant? That seems almost contradictory. No doubt it had a great deal to do with having absorbed a negative attitude toward sex in the earlier years.

After those first ten days, their habit of intercourse was to average about twice a week until she was five months pregnant. After that, they abstained until after the baby was born in May of 1897. In June, they spent two weeks together in the Sierras, "during which intercourse occurred nearly every night." Her response to the question about orgasm was, "Never but once or twice." These were early days for the marriage, however, and some changes were developing, as we shall presently see. As to the effects of achieving and not achieving orgasm immediately afterwards and the next day, Mildred stated that she did not notice any. However, Dr. Mosher apparently discussed the matter with her further, for she included a note at this place in Mildred's questionnaire. She wrote that when Mildred "cares for" intercourse physically (she adopted Mildred's terminology here), she had a general sense of well-being and relaxation afterwards, but when she did not care for it, she was much more high strung and nervous.

Mildred Conroy would appear to have been an individual quite set in her outlook and unlikely to change much. Therefore, she would have been unlikely ever to have relished the sexual experience as a positive contribution to her life. It happens, however, that the sexual side of marriage itself, the birth of her baby, and those two weeks in the Sierras began to effect a transformation, certainly a transformation in outlook and possibly in physical response as well, although we will never know for sure about the latter. Mildred had the admirable flexibility to allow some deep-seated attitudes and opinions to alter, based on personal experience. Whereas before the birth of her child, for example, she never craved intercourse and felt averse to it, as we have seen, she recognized that "after the birth, I cared for it." Furthermore, during the two weeks in the mountains she "really enjoyed it" and "felt contented and physically at rest afterwards."

She changed her personal perspective on Dr. Cowan's Law of Continence as well. Before marriage, she clearly believed in it. Later, however, she found from her experience "that the habitual bodily expression of love has a deep psychological effect in making possible complete mental sympathy and perfecting the spiritual union" between husband and wife. She was philosophical about it. She believed that marital intercourse fulfilled two separate roles, giving it two distinct qualities. Husband and wife should enter upon intercourse for the purpose of reproduction "with deliberate design on both sides in time and circumstances most favorable physically and spiritually for the accomplishment of an immensely important act." It should be done "carefully and prayerfully." At other, more usual times, she would ideally have preferred intercourse to take place from four to six times per month when conception was least likely to occur, and she would have hoped that no accidental conception ever occurred – conception without proper intention and preparation. The purpose at these other times would simply be the expression of love between man and woman. She now considered this to be an important function of marital sex beyond procreation, and, "It would be a pity to limit it to once in two or three years." Thus, in her decorous, muted, but candid fashion, Mildred Conroy documented the evolution of her perspective. There was surely more to come, but it was probably not made known to Dr. Mosher – and certainly not to us more than a hundred years later.

Portrait 6: Sarah (Sally) Warren[104]

There is a particularly interesting response written by Sally Warren in the section of Dr. Mosher's questionnaire dealing with parents and grandparents, in this case her mother. The question asks how many miscarriages her mother may have had. Sally's answer is, "None so far as she [her mother] knows. Possibly one early abortion." The response indicates that respectable people in the United States did have abortions at the time, which is not new information, but it also indicates the openness with which the Mosher women voluntarily approached this task.

Sally married Richard Warren in 1887, seven years before filling out the questionnaire. There are substantial differences between them. She was then twenty-six, but he was only twenty-three. That was an early age for a man to get married, but she gave his occupation as manager of a manufacturing business, so perhaps he was financially established a little sooner than most. Richard did not attend college. Sally, on the other hand, earned a Bachelor's Degree in music from Syracuse University, probably in 1885, after which she taught school for two years prior to marriage. One can guess that music remained a part of her life – in those days, the resources of movies and television for entertainment were not available – but there unfortunately is no further mention of her music in the questionnaire.

One wonders whether the difference in education might have put a strain on the marriage. All indications are, however, that Sally both loved and admired her husband. Responding to the question about his origins, she said, "Descended from Pilgrim Fathers and Salem witches." Salem witches! Perhaps it is really true – from accused witches, anyway – but she seems to be writing it with a smile. Alluding to his build in a few places, she said "Unusually muscular," and, "Very robust, with magnificent frame and constitution." In speaking of their third child – the youngest, a little boy – she stated, "Everyone remarks his extreme good nature. He is like his father in this, and I was very happy beforehand." Here she not only attributed her son's personality to the inheritance of admirable traits from her husband, but also to her own frame of mind during the pregnancy. Similarly, Sally spoke of the eldest of their three healthy children

104 Mosher 1980. Blank No. 11, pp. 115-127.

as being "very sensitive; feelings easily hurt," and attributed it to her being unnaturally and morbidly sensitive herself during the months preceding the birth.

The second child was born a year and a half after the first and, like the first, was a girl. She was a "bottle baby." Sally was unable to nurse her because she came down with "malarial fever," which is just malaria, soon after the birth. That is, of course, an extremely serious illness which was and still can be very difficult to treat. It seems, however, that Sally either was misdiagnosed or successfully treated because she was apparently free of the disease at least for the five years that followed until the filling out of the questionnaire. Their third child was the boy with his father's good nature, as noted earlier.

The second child was an accident – "but not regretted" – and the third was conceived by choice but after a long period of trying unsuccessfully. Given these difficulties, what would have been their method of birth control? It apparently depended primarily on timing. Sally indicated that they felt the fertile period to be the two weeks "following menstruation." It is not clear whether she meant following the onset or the termination, but other passages indicate the former. During that period, say the first to the fourteenth day, they either refrained altogether or practiced withdrawal. Their method failed them in their intention of preventing the second baby, perhaps because she was conceived shortly after that two-week period, and it failed them also in their desire to have the third child earlier, perhaps because they concentrated their efforts to conceive too close to the time of menstruation. We see once more that when it came to the critical issue of birth control, nineteenth-century couples blundered about in the darkness of a small collection of well recommended but ineffective methods. In addition to timing and withdrawal, there were douches and suppositories of numerous descriptions, including hot water, tepid water, ice water, and carbonated water, as well as alcohol, sulphate of zinc, and bichloride.[105] All methods gave results that were convincing to some and discouraging or tragic to others. Barrier methods, such as the condom and the cervical cap, came along late in the century, but we will see that they were trusted only by a very few until around the time of the First World War.

105 Jacob 1981, p. 6.

On the question of what knowledge of sexual physiology she had before marriage, Sally answered, "None to speak of. Nothing at all definite in my mind." She recorded that she did not learn where babies came from until she was eighteen. These facts, however, did not seem to have the slightest effect upon her adjustment to marital sex. Sally and Richard regularly slept in the same bed, which she justified just a wee bit defensively in saying, "Yes, as I know no reason for not doing so, and preferred company at night." Their "habit of intercourse," as Dr. Mosher put it, was three or four times per month. This was clearly not too frequent for Mrs. Warren. She recorded that she felt desire about once a week, and when asked whether intercourse were agreeable to her, she responded, "Very seldom disagreeable. Usually very delightful." By now, we begin to see a pattern of cheerful honesty and firm independence in her often arresting responses.

She did not always achieve orgasm, but usually. As to the effect of orgasm immediately afterwards, she said, "Very sleepy and comfortable. No disgust, as I have often heard it described." It is clear, then, that she had come into contact with an important element of the conservative ideology, that which taught women "to regard the act of procreation as a necessary and rather repulsive duty."[106] It is just as clear, however, that, in her case, personal experience overcame the conservative teachings. On the effect next day, she answered, "Sometimes a little stupid." Here, she did not use the word "stupid" as we almost exclusively use it today – to mean lacking in intelligence or common sense – but in the older sense that relates to the term "stupor." The following is an almost identical usage from a novel by William Dean Howells, although referring not to marital sex but to a dinner party: "No, no, I'm just stupid from last night. One doesn't have such a good time for nothing."[107]

We can picture Sally wandering about on the morrow in a bit of a fog with the hint of a smile playing intermittently about her lips.

She felt that reproduction was the primary purpose of intercourse but that pleasure was also at least partially a purpose and that the sexual relation was necessary in some degree to both men and women. Are other reasons besides

106 Thomas 1959, p. 215.

107 Howells 1904, p. 76.

reproduction sufficient to warrant intercourse? Whereas most of the respondents who answered this question mentioned bonding, spiritual union, and similar matters, Sally answered that sometimes she "has taken it as a sedative." A sedative! Well, we recall her reaction of "sleepy and comfortable" and should not be too surprised.

The final question in the form is, "What, to you, would be an ideal habit?" and I record Sally's answer in full because it offers several items to think about: "Once a month," she says, "when both are well, and during the menstrual period, unless best to avoid conception, and in the daylight." Take the last phrase first – "in the daylight"! Certainly, this remark does not support the stereotype of repression. In fact, it might cause some today to think of Sally Warren as a "hot ticket." I do not think so. I think she was just a contented Victorian wife and mother with an upbeat personality. It must be said, in fact, that this phrase might not come out of the blue. It might indeed come, probably indirectly since Sally never mentioned him, from a surprising source – Dr. John Cowan, progenitor of the Law of Continence. Although Dr. Cowan was extremely conservative in restricting permissible intercourse to the purpose of procreation alone, he did not agree with Dr. Acton on the issues of female desire and pleasure. He would make the sex act, whose sole purpose must be the conception of a valued and healthy child, into a ritual of pleasure designed in part to have a positive prenatal effect. In the mistaken but apparently universal belief regarding the ability of certain prenatal events to influence the health and character of the unborn child, Dr. Cowan wrote:

> As mentioned on a former page, conception should occur immediately following the cessation of the menses or monthly courses, because at this time the egg is in its firmest and freshest state, and, when impregnated, is more likely at this time than later to develop a strong and healthy organism.
>
> Next in importance is the time of day that should be selected for sexual congress. As though there was something sinful and wrong in it, the hours of darkness are usually employed for this purpose. There is as little of reason used in this choice of hours, by the majority of mankind,

> as in the observance of any other department of the reproductive law. Now the best and only physiological time to generate a new life is in the broad light of a clear, bright day. Light implies health; darkness disease. Light is the source of life; darkness is the synonym of death. Let your New Life [Dr. Cowan's book is entitled *The Science of a New Life*] be a child of light rather than of darkness. Not only should the hour of darkness be avoided, but also dark, cloudy and rainy days. *Only a clear, bright day, when the sun is shining, should be employed in which to generate the New Life*. [Emphasis in the original.][108]

In this perspective, Sally's response regarding an ideal habit was wholly oriented toward conception. It is as though she interpreted the question to refer to an ideal habit when conception is the objective. "Once a month . . . during the menstrual period," she said, "unless best to avoid conception." But Mrs. Warren was also completely well-adjusted to marital sex, including a higher frequency of marital sex, when pleasure rather than reproduction was the object in view. She found it to be "Usually very delightful." It is a pity that she did not also respond to the issue of an ideal habit when pleasure rather than procreation was the object, but she did not.

Still, in her celebratory approach to conception combined with her avowal of desire and delight, she clearly serves as evidence against rather than in favor of the stereotype of repression. She was not repressed. We will see in Chapter V that scholars have sought reinforcement for the repression stereotype in the supposed fact (I will dispute it) that the Mosher women tended in general to prefer a frequency (their "ideal habit") that was less than their own actual frequency. They would have picked up a negative attitude toward sex, in other words, that made them dissatisfied with the need to submit to a lot of it. Sally Warren would seem technically, at first glance, to support the contention of these scholars, given that her stated ideal was once a month, while the actual frequency was about once per week. A close look at her as an individual rather than a statistic, however, reveals that such an inference would be oversimplified and, in fact, misguided. In her response of once a month, she was probably thinking

108 Cowan 1874, p. 170.

more of the purpose of conception than of pleasure. In any case, it is clear that her response should not be used statistically to support the repression theory – in essence, that sex was a nuisance to Victorian women and even repugnant. Feeling sexual desire once a week and finding intercourse to be very delightful suggests exactly the opposite. If all women had been like Sally Warren, the repression model would be a non-starter.

III

The remarkable Coalition for Repression

The previous chapter documented a prescription for behavior: how middle-class Victorian women ought to think and act. It is far-fetched, however, to suppose that they might have conformed to those instructions without tremendous pressure from around them. Evangelical and medical advice are highly unlikely to have been enough. As it happens, that pressure did exist. It was essentially unanimous, coming at Victorian women from all quarters so that there was virtually no place to hide. Surprisingly enough, it was even internal, that is, one of the members of the Coalition for Repression was middle-class Victorian women themselves. There is considerable overlap among the categories forming the coalition, so that individual persons belonged to several of them at the same time, but each category represents a distinct social role with its own motivations. The other five coalition members besides women were men, husbands, parents, the church, and the middle class.

Why would the members of this coalition want to push women so strongly in the direction of chastity? It was not just whim or passing fancy. Each group had a great deal to gain for itself, both vitally and urgently. I hope to provide an increased understanding in this chapter of the primary forces behind the intended sexual repression of women in the nineteenth century – so singular a movement in British and American history.

We already know what they wanted to accomplish. They wanted women to be what we will call "pure," that is, modest, chaste, virtuous, simple, godly, and domestic. This combination of six qualities would yield a number of benefits to the members of the coalition, but prominent among them, certainly, was the deterrence of pre-marital and extra-marital sex.

We will be chiefly concerned with societal changes in both values and behavior among three groups of actors, considering in particular the changes that took place around the transition from the eighteenth century to the nineteenth. The first group comprises the members of this coalition. A linchpin of the value changes characterizing the group was middle-class respectability.[1] On the behavior side, our particular interest will be in the pressure applied by them to middle-class women toward purity, and especially toward the component of chastity. The second group comprises Victorian women themselves and their possible compliant change toward chastity, domesticity, and the other dimensions of purity. The third group comprises those individuals taking an active interest in the morals of art, chiefly writers and critics but also including publishers, purveyors of books, and, at times, the general public. Our primary concern regarding values and behavior in this third group will be changes in the kinds of things that could and could not be published. The first two groups will together constitute the subject of the present chapter; the third becomes the subject of Chapter IV.

Innocence

Scholars claim on excellent evidence that the Victorian cultures in Britain and America were closely similar, with adopted influences going in both directions.[2] There is one way in which they differed, however, and that is in the respective strategies they used to achieve the goal of purity in young, unmarried women. In Britain, particularly before 1880, the strategy has been described as *Innocence*, with a pinch of *Passionlessness* and a dash of *Dependence* thrown in. In America and in late nineteenth-century Britain, it was the combination of *Autonomy* and *Self-Control*. There is no basis for claiming that the two cultures were identical rather than just closely similar. For that reason, and especially in view of the difference

1 Cominos 1963.

2 Howe 1975.

in socialization strategies just noted, inferences about sexual behavior in either society must be based on evidence clearly pertinent to that society.

In a 1973 chapter, the historian Peter Cominos indicated that innocence, in this sense, denoted blissful ignorance. It was "an exalted state of feminine consciousness, a state of unique deficiency or mindlessness in their daughters of that most elementary but forbidden knowledge of their own sexuality, instincts and desires." Many prominent authorities believed strongly that once innocence was lost, the daughter's chastity became vulnerable. In the words of the educator Miss E. M. Sewell, "If a girl's mind is not pure – if her own instincts are so blunted that she cannot *feel* evil before she can explain it –if she cannot shrink from it without knowing why she does so – may God help her! For the wisest safeguards which the best friends may provide for her will never be sufficient to secure her from danger."[3]

We will see from American data that Miss Sewell was wrong; innocence was not necessary to secure young women from danger. Nevertheless, her views represent the dominant ideology in Britain for most of the Victorian period.

Through his research, Cominos goes on to inform us that the state of innocence was achieved through a severe regimen of early and continued training and constant guarding and watching. The idea was to prevent young women from having any knowledge whatever of the existence of the concept of sexual relations and thus from having any thoughts at all relating to sex. "To preserve innocence, the struggle had to begin early. . . Children ought to be punished for doing or saying anything not refined or modest just as they were for lying. . . . Infractions deserved sharp and instant punishment. It was useless to warn, reprove or advise. What was aimed at was not comprehension, but obedience."[4]

The stuffy concept of propriety, so striking in the novels of the period, became a dominant feature of normal middle-class Victorian life, and propriety meant, in part, zero words or actions that might undermine adherence to the qualities mentioned above: chastity, modesty, and so forth. Anybody who skirted too close to the line in conversation, for example – any visitor, any

3 Both quotes are from Cominos 1973, p. 157.

4 Cominos 1973, p. 158.

servant, any friend – produced a clear reaction of disapproval. Girls must have no knowledge whatever of what was on the other side of that line nor even any suspicion that there was a line at all.

Training daughters for innocence was consequently difficult because of its comprehensive strictness. Moreover, it was challenging because of the constant threat of the rearing up of sexual interest. Almost any young woman would frequently feel the pull of desire. Even if such feelings were not understood by her at all, they would still be disturbing and might lead her to reach out in dangerous ways. Religion was one important strategy for dealing with this aspect of the task. Men were urged to conquer their sexual instincts by complete sublimation through exercise and work. Middle-class women, on the other hand, barred from meaningful work, were taught to sublimate desire, of whose sexual nature they should be completely unaware, through religion – the love of God.[5]

Professor Welter comments on this strategy: Religion functioned "as a kind of tranquilizer for the many undefined longings which swept even the most pious young girl, and about which it was better to pray than to think."[6]

Still, hormones were an ever-present danger, as was random information that might arouse curiosity. The other device for ensuring innocence, therefore – a device that was both far more troublesome to execute and far more harmful in its side effects – was to dictate and supervise every aspect of life. If girls and young women had zero reliance on their own thoughts, then dangerous or risky thoughts could be kept out of their minds. If all the information coming to them was controlled, then none of it could be threatening to the dimensions of purity. In this way, with their every activity prescribed, supervised, and guarded, middle-class British daughters would become dependent, deficient in ego strength. Not only would they not be able to decide their behavior for themselves, but it would never even occur to them to try. The decisions would be made by others.

Daughters were to fulfill a role, the script being written in advance. This is radical training, but the fact that the model was broadly followed in real life is evidenced by the comments of astute observers of the day. The philosopher

5 Cominos 1973, p. 163.

6 Welter 1966, p. 153

John Stuart Mill wrote: "Their ideal of character is the very opposite of that of men; not self-will, and government by self-control, but submission, and yielding to the control of others."[7] And the outspoken nurse Florence Nightingale commented on the same syndrome: "Women don't consider themselves as human beings at all."[8] An interesting example is D. H. Lawrence's Lady Chatterley in his novel, *Lady Chatterley's Lover,* who, in difficult circumstances, fulfilled her prescribed role without the hint of a critical thought until she was inspired to discover that she had an independent identity as a person through the awakening of her sexuality.[9]

It is well known that at the same time as strict propriety ruled the middle-class Victorian home, there was also a thriving commerce in "immoral" and downright pornographic literature and art. So-called immoral fiction was not sexually explicit in the mode of the modern novel, although it did frequently contain narrations of female desire and hints of illicit sexuality.[10] In the main, it portrayed strong women who made monkeys out of men, often while displaying defiant attitudes and verbally rebelling against the traditional, prescribed roles. Its appeal was to married women and prospective brides who felt some measure of dissatisfaction with conventional gender roles and the related rules and practices. It was a late nineteenth-century phenomenon and may have captured the stirrings of impending change.

Pornography thrived throughout the century,[11] as did prostitution. In addition, police and trial accounts in daily newspapers were surprisingly explicit about seduction, rape, adultery, and other crimes, particularly in England.[12] It appears, therefore, that there were ample sources from which daughters could learn about sex. It was part of the training for innocence, however, to shield young women completely from such springs of pollution. Pornography could be obtained only from clandestine sources and was consumed almost exclusively

7 Cominos 1973, p. 161.

8 Cominos 1973, p. 160.

9 Lawrence 1928.

10 This brief characterization of immoral fiction follows Garrison, 1976.

11 Marcus 1966.

12 Boyle 1984.

by men. The milder immoral fiction was aimed at and read by married women and renegades.

Newspapers were commonly to be found in the Victorian home, to be sure, but young women would not have been able to read them and in fact would not have dreamed of being interested. One would be extremely hard-pressed to find instances in the novels by major Victorian writers of any young woman reading a newspaper, although men were at them all the time. One of the key characteristics of the age was the doctrine of Separate Spheres, very commonly appealed to in Victorian books and articles and apparently accepted and internalized completely by all except public rebels. Separate Spheres meant that the outside worlds of business, finance, politics, public policy, and international affairs were exclusively the concerns of men. The province of women was demarcated in terms of the management of children, the household, charities and good works, the social calendar, and closely related concerns. Newspapers were, therefore, institutions within the sphere of men. Women would rarely, if ever, consider looking into them. It is not that women might often be tempted to look into a newspaper but would refrain. Rather, seeing the paper, it would not occur to them to pick it up. It might as well be a cricket bat. It was outside of their sphere. It was a thing that men did, and they were women.

It is important to remember that this kind of training and its goal, the standard of purity, were characteristic of the middle class. Many in the leadership of that class considered the laboring classes to be debauched and depraved, and therefore not only different but morally dangerous. We saw in the last chapter that there was some truth to this characterization in the late eighteenth century and the early years of the nineteenth. Scholarship has shown, however, that as the Victorian era progressed into its late stages, the prevailing moral code as concerned sexuality in the working class was not radically different from that of the middle class. Instead of working-class morals spreading upward, as many in the middle class feared, it worked quite the other way around: the moral Victorianism of the powerful middle class seeped quite substantially into the outlook and behavior of the lower orders. One significant disparity, however, did persist. When a working-class couple became formally engaged or reached a mutual decision to marry, sexual intercourse was permitted and was common both in cities and in agricultural areas. This was the source of a certain amount of illegitimacy and heartbreak, but by and large, the marriages did occur and the practice led only to a substantial number of prebridal pregnancies.[13] We will keep this important factor in mind as we explore sexuality in the novels of the period and examine statistical records for evidence bearing on our principal concern.

On the wedding day, the need for innocence evaporated. On the wedding night, innocence itself came crashing down. The training and guarding were over for good. The standard of purity, however, still remained. Assuming that premarital sex had been effectively prevented, extra-marital sex was still a concern of the coalition. The strictures of chastity (in this context, marital fidelity), modesty, virtue, simplicity, godliness, and domesticity remained in full sway. The model for the middle-class Victorian wife became the Angel in the House. This was the title of a long poem by Coventry Patmore that sold a quarter of a million copies and was popular in Britain and America during almost the entire last half of the nineteenth century. According to one contemporary, it "pleased all women and many men."[14] To the modern ear, the poetry is likely to seem overly sentimental, adulatory, and long. A sample (from Canto IV):

> And still with favour singled out,
>   Marr'd less than man by mortal fall,
> Her disposition is devout,
>   Her countenance angelical;
> The best things that the best believe
>   Are in her face so kindly writ
> The faithless, seeing her, conceive
>   Not only heaven, but hope of it;
> . . . Her modesty, her chiefest grace,
>   The cestus clasping Venus' side,
> How potent to deject the face
>   Of him who would affront its pride!

13 Barret-Ducrocq 1993. D'Emilio and Freedman 1988, p. 74. Thomas 1959, p. 206.

14 Gay 1999, pp. 291-294.

Wrong dares not in her presence speak,
    Nor spotted thought its taint disclose
Under the protest of a cheek
    Outbragging Nature's boast the rose.

The qualities of character that are exhaustively described and lauded by the poet in this perfect woman are chiefly modesty, attractive conservatism of dress, gentleness, chastity, goodness, the desire to please, selfless devotion to her children, angelic fellowship, submission to her husband, and dedication to his cares. The all-too-probable traits of such a woman that are not brought out, of course, are mindlessness and boring, as we saw in the previous chapter. The question is how closely the model of the Angel in the House was followed. We will get some feel for the answer both in the individual portraits and in our group-level analysis of the Mosher survey.

Autonomy and Self-Control

The scene in America was quite different, especially considering that these were two cultures so similar in almost every other respect. Purity was still very much the standard for the deportment of middle-class women, but all of its dimensions except godliness were somewhat more relaxed in America. Beginning with domesticity, we will see that in this aspect of purity and in the related doctrine of Separate Spheres, for example, America was historically more precocious than Britain. Higher education for women and women in the professions started earlier in America than on the other side of the Atlantic, as was the case as well with women's suffrage. In related fashion, modesty was still a valued trait, very much so, but friends and neighbors in America were not aghast at a woman's speaking her mind, as they might well have been in Britain. This was at least partly because the strategy of behavioral autonomy rather than dependence meant that women had more of a mind to speak.

Virtue in the sense of moral rectitude was seen in both Britain and America as more integral to the character of women than men, who had the vicissitudes of business and politics to contend with. Sexually, however, virtue did not preclude a lot of hugging and kissing among unmarried and especially courting young couples in America – a freer standard than in Britain. Chastity still meant a complete ban on premarital and extramarital sexual intercourse, but many unmarried American women independently arrived at the determination that, if they were spiritually elevated by being in love, they could still consider themselves as remaining chaste while taking and allowing liberties beyond hugging and kissing but short of the boundary of sexual intercourse.

The dimension of simplicity means that the other dimensions of purity – modesty, chastity, and so forth – come to the woman naturally, that is, without affectation. There was the sense in both cultures that women possessed the traits composing purity more instinctively than do men. We will see momentarily that simplicity is the trickiest of all the dimensions of purity because it could be taken to imply a biological base, that is, that women were somehow more virtuous and chaste than men as a consequence of their *physiology*. Terms such as "natural" and "instinctive" were very often used in this connection and almost always used ambiguously, that is, the writer never says that all women are more virtuous than all men because of their physical make-up, but the writer does not say it is because of their early training and socialization, either. The impression or feeling is left that there is something vaguely necessary about the generalization that virtue comes more readily to women, and this feeling served the purpose of repression quite well.

The American historian Ellen Rothman has devoted considerable study to patterns of courtship in the United States from the Puritan period to the late twentieth century.[15] In a 1982 article extracted from the research, she tells us that young men and women:

> Encountered each other in meeting, schoolroom, and shop; they met on the lanes and commons of the village and in the houses of neighbors and kin. Young men and women born in the years after Independence enjoyed a high level of self-determination. This meant not only that they were free to choose their own mates but that they socialized with little parental supervision.

15 Rothman 1987.

> In groups they went berrying, riding, picnicking; they sang and danced together at parties, balls, and at the singing and dancing schools that were popular in small towns and villages. Although these events were often group affairs, twosomes were not discouraged. A young man and woman who were interested in each other could spend time alone as well as in the company of friends and relations. They were allowed to go off walking or riding together, to sit alone in the parlor late at night, and to make unchaperoned visits to family and friends.
>
> In some cases, parents made little or no effort to oversee their children's courting behavior; in others, the family took active steps to give a young couple privacy. Sometimes this meant that family members went out for a walk or early to bed when a suitor came to call. Since in most houses the parlor was the only space considered appropriate for courting activities, this was often the only way a couple could visit alone without going out themselves.[16]

Although this wide latitude of freedom, autonomy, and independence was granted, there was at the same time a rigid expectation of self-control. "Romantic love was defined to include sexual attraction and gratification but to exclude coitus between unmarried couples. This meant the posting of intercourse as not only 'off limits' but as an altogether separate terrain, accessible only to married people. There were, of course, couples who failed to observe those limits; for them, crossing the boundary line was a risk, albeit one they were willing to take."[17] According to Professor Rothman as well as the implications of the Mosher survey, not very many took that risk. Every young woman knew – and some readers will remember this terminology from their own youth – that whatever else you did, you did not "go all the way." Of course, there is also ample evidence that most women had little or no idea what "all the way" really meant. In Chapters V and VI, we will see that only a minority of women had a good notion of what was in store for them on the wedding night even in America. For most, hugging and kissing was the extent of sexual indulgence

16 Rothman 1982, pp. 410-411.

17 Rothman 1982, p. 415.

during courtship. For the few who experienced heavy petting, there seems to have been an instinctive sense that a line must be drawn at a certain level and further liberties resisted. It was apparently not necessary to be sophisticated about the details of sexual intercourse to feel the presence of that line.

Thus, although purity was an institutional standard in both cultures, it was a less exacting standard in America, and, most particularly, the strategy for achieving it there was substantially different. Why this difference should have existed, at least until late in the century, is not much pursued by the relevant scholars, and such analysis would be a digression from our purpose here. Suffice it to speculate that in Britain the major historical precursor was the wild license of the Restoration and its aftermath, understandably producing a felt need to counter extreme with extreme. In America, on the other hand, the important prior background was the independence and informality of the frontier spirit, starting in the settlements on the coast and moving gradually westward.

Scholars agree that in the late nineteenth century there was a convergence. Innocence as a strategy became less capable of being implemented and enforced in Britain as changes in modern life began to give women more freedom. Railway travel and the bustle of the cities increased the frequency of associations outside the family. Opportunities for genuine secondary and higher education for women began to open up. The voices of outspoken women pressing for the vote and other measures of equality were more and more widely heard. Parents felt the need to grant more independence and to rely more on their daughters' "strength of character to say no," as the historian Peter Cominos put it in 1973.[18] In America at the same time, the same forces of modernization were taking unmarried women farther and farther from the observation and guidance of church, neighbors, and community. There was a sense that temptations had become stronger. Chaperonage began to be introduced in the upper-middle and upper classes, and both young men and young women realized that stricter rules needed to be adopted and respected to offset the abandonment of almost all other constraints.[19] The standard of purity unquestionably prevailed in both cultures until the First World War. The strategies for achieving it were initially

18 Cominos 1973, p. 165.

19 Rothman 1987, pp. 207-208.

quite different but moved with the times on both sides of the Atlantic toward a more moderate middle.

To what extent was the standard of purity actually adhered to by middle-class women both at the beginning of Victoria's reign and toward the end? That question remains. For the moment, we continue to develop an appreciation of the forces that urged and supported it.

Passionlessness

Women do not care about sex. They would rather not be bothered except that they know it is occasionally necessary in order to have children. We have already seen that many physicians asserted this notion as fact in the latter half of the century. What a boon to the coalition if only they could get women to believe in it and act accordingly!

The characteristic referred to came to be known in more recent scholarship by the somewhat awkward term "passionlessness." It has been defined as a concept conveying "the view that women lacked sexual aggressiveness, that their sexual appetites contributed a very minor part (if any at all) to their motivations, that lustfulness was simply uncharacteristic."[20] It is an idea that was advanced by many elites because they felt that its acceptance would help them in their cause: the cause of chastity. The coalition powerfully wanted women to be chaste. In the strength of that desire, many convinced themselves that women were indeed chaste by nature, and that if this fact were brought forcefully to women themselves in their training and socialization, so that they believed in it and internalized it, it would help them to act out the character, that is, to remain chaste. It would help largely by enabling women to resist easily the advances of men – even their husbands, given that frequent intercourse was widely considered to be both physically and spiritually unhealthy. A belief in passionlessness might also help by deterring men. They would then have to see themselves, presumably distastefully, as forcing women to do something repugnant to their nature as opposed to yielding to a natural impulse.

20 Cott 1978, p. 220.

One would not want to propose seriously that it was biology that made women sexually passionless. That would imply that all women were essentially the same in this regard. On the contrary, it was too plain that there were many women whose sex drive was apparently as strong as that of men – in the upper and lower classes certainly and not only in the Britain and America of the day but historically – for example, in the culture of the late seventeenth and eighteenth centuries. Also, biological passionlessness would not fit well with other elements in the drive for purity. It would bring out an embarrassing inconsistency. Biological passionlessness is readily seen to clash with insistence on training for innocence and self-control. If young women were naturally passionless, why struggle so hard to keep them from understanding their passions? Why fear that their passions might lead them into indiscreet behavior?

No, what the moralists undoubtedly meant was that passionlessness is a psychological property. They were not explicit about this, probably because that would too easily have involved them in complex issues with uncertain implications, such as why some women became psychologically passionless while others did not. Their simple implication, and it was a moralizing one, was that women brought up in the "right" way, the generally respectable way, did not care for sex. The authorities were bold enough to write about passionlessness even with this vagueness hanging over the exact meaning of the term because they fervently desired to influence behavior in the direction of what would be expected from women with no sex drive.

On the face of it, they would have a hard time. There is no evidence that parents, educators, or even moralizers tried to influence behavior by inculcating in girls and unmarried young women the idea that they were sexually passionless. In England, such an attempt, with its necessary introduction to the forbidden concept of sex, would have meant the undoing of all training for innocence at a stroke. In America, there is excellent evidence from the Mosher survey that whatever small knowledge of the wedding night a few young women may have had, it hardly ever came from parents. Parents usually did not talk to their children about sex and so could not have explained to them the meaning of passionlessness. Also, books on the subject were available only to very few.

How might parents hope to lead their daughters to believe that they had no sex drive without talking about sex?

It turns out, intriguingly, that it is not necessary to be explicit about the concept of passionlessness in order to use it to influence behavior. Professor Nancy Cott has pointed out that passionlessness is logically implied by the combination of certain of the dimensions of purity.[21] If a woman is virtuous and chaste without guile or affectation (the latter two traits referring to the simplicity component), that is, if she so thoroughly, sincerely, and honestly sees herself and feels herself to be chaste and virtuous – without forcing it or faking it – then she is to all intents and purposes passionless. To hope to influence behavior by inculcating psychological passionlessness in young women, then, it was only necessary to train them positively for modesty, virtue, and chastity (don't get close to men), and negatively at the same time against guile, affectation, lying, dissembling, and subterfuge. You are virtuous and you are without guile or pretense, therefore you are *really* virtuous, that is, psychologically passionless.

For married women, the story is different. There would have been even greater utility in the doctrine of passionlessness. One could be explicit about the concept because one did not have to worry about bringing up a forbidden subject. Married women could read the relevant medical scribblings and learn that they were supposed to be without sexual inclination. For those who experienced little or no desire or pleasure in sex it would be reinforcing. They would feel normal. It could, for example, help to prevent them from drifting into a relation of adultery and also help them to resist the inclinations of their husbands toward too frequent marital sex. For many of those who did feel desire and pleasure, the doctrine would lead them to feel *not* normal and bring on feelings of shame or guilt, as noted earlier, providing the same sort of incentive to avoid adultery and a high frequency of intercourse desired by their husbands and even themselves. The doctrine could, therefore, be useful for the coalition in the cases both of the married women and the unmarried – at least in theory. The question would be whether it influenced behavior in these ways in practice. There is some bit of evidence from the Mosher survey that it did, at least

21 Cott 1978, p.225.

attitudinally: a few of the women (three out of the forty-five) believed that sex was "necessary" for men but not for women.[22]

Lastly, there is another side to the subject that we have not yet touched upon. Acting as though passionlessness were valid, desire or no desire, could be useful to women of the Victorian period. In theory, anyway, there was often something to be gained by making a husband feel that his sexual advances were an imposition. More on this under Women, below.

The Church

Turning to the members of the coalition, the idea is to explore the motives of the various parties for putting extreme pressure on women in the direction of purity, highlighting in most cases the component goal of chastity. The majority of these motives prevailed and still do prevail in other historical periods than the Victorian, but in a milder form. It is important to recognize that in the circumstances of the Victorian age these interests were especially keen, and therefore the zeal with which they were pursued was especially intense. The pressure exerted on women was great – and indeed so great that there is good reason to believe that the pressure accomplished its purpose.

Churches in any age tend to preach morality. They also stand to gain in wealth and status if they successfully increase their influence over some or all segments of the population. In the early nineteenth century, as it happens, there were two circumstances that particularly intensified these motives. First, the churches (as well as many other social and political institutions) were genuinely terrified by the French revolution of the late eighteenth century and the threat of contagion that it posed. A certain amount of discontent in the laboring classes existed in most advanced societies as the Industrial Revolution gathered steam, often based in a wretched set of circumstances powerfully recorded in several Victorian novels, such as *Mary Barton* and *North and South* by Elizabeth Gaskell and *A Hazard of New Fortunes* by William Dean Howells. The fear was that the French example would inspire a similar uprising domestically, leading to the ruin of families, wholesale executions, the anarchic overturning of stability, and

22 I count Blanks number 1, 18, and 23.

a drastic loss of social role and influence for the church. Second, at the same time, churches feared that the continuing blasphemies and profligacy of segments of the aristocracy, rooted in "Fashion," as described in the last chapter, would filter downward to pollute the morals of the newly expanding middle class. This class, at the time, represented a unique opportunity for the church to increase its status, power, and influence dramatically as compared to its role in connection with the aristocracy (in Britain) and the working classes. Both of these currents had to be blocked.[23]

Churches were therefore strongly motivated at this time to take action to save both themselves and a social system in which they might reasonably be expected to prosper. They needed to spread adherence to religion and, through it, the acceptance of high moral standards and attachment to social stability. The role and status of women, generally more pious than men to begin with, presented a golden opportunity. Because the lot of women was so much less important than that of men in the social system, they were likely to be susceptible to devices that would raise their status and self-esteem. If they were married, they were also likely to be able to influence their children and their husbands toward churchgoing and religious observance. The strategy suggested would be to emphasize purity, thereby making exalted moral beings out of women and raising both their sense of self-worth and their influence. The strategy was adopted, as we have seen, and the results were first the onslaught of sermons, books, and pamphlets issued by Evangelicals in the late eighteenth and early nineteenth centuries, carrying over to the angel-in-the-house syndrome that lasted for most of the rest of the Victorian period. The church was also of critical importance for the coalition by reason of efficiency: it applied the desired pressure not only individual by individual, as within families, but broadly to the mass female public through its influential sermons and writings.[24] Christianity was salient to the women of the day. The extreme pressure toward purity, when applied by the church, would have had great meaning for them. It was a good bet that they would, in general, adopt the role marked out and use it much as the church desired and anticipated.

23 Cott 1978, pp. 223, 225.

24 Smith and Hindus 1975, p. 551.

The Middle Class

In the nineteenth century, the new and growing middle class opted for respectability.[25] Little, if anything, in the current chapter is as important as the previous sentence for understanding the Victorian repression of female sexuality. Respectability meant, in particular, saving, investing, and thereby increasing wealth rather than using it for high living as in much of the British aristocracy – lavish entertaining, fox hunting, multiple palatial residences, and so on. But it also meant acquiring some more modest status symbols in terms of housing, dress, and transportation (carriages), plus attending church, adopting the manners of ladies and gentlemen, and subscribing to a moral code with conservative regulations in such areas of conduct as sexuality, gambling, and public drinking. Since the middle class was distinguished by acquiring more money than the laboring class (and even than much of the aristocracy), individuals could have used this wealth for conspicuous luxury and debauch. That they did not indicates that they were more interested in durable social status than in short-term material pleasures, many of which would have decreased rather than increased their social standing. The category of persons with highest status at this time was, of course, the British aristocracy, but noble birth as a means to social position was not open to the middle class on either side of the Atlantic. Moral respectability (with a dose of hypocrisy in a few areas, such as male sexual behavior) and the accumulation of wealth were the only practical paths to elevated status available. Historically, the middle class was urged in this direction by the highly influential output of eighteenth-century writers such as Joseph Addison, Richard Steele, and Samuel Richardson and also, strongly, by the Christian churches.[26]

The area of sex was troublesome, however, and here hormones (still using the term in the sense of natural, biological sexual inclinations and urges) won a public policy victory. It was a victory that directly benefited only men, not women. A great many men indulged in premarital and extra-marital sex in violation of the clear moral commands accepted by the system. These sexual relations were almost exclusively with lower-class women and above all with

25 Cominos 1963.

26 Cott 1978, p. 223.

prostitutes. The prevalence of this general behavior could not possibly have been hidden, but it was not paraded. It was an open secret. If this lax sexual behavior had extended to middle-class women, making the middle class a thoroughly promiscuous one, all pretense to respectability would have been lost. It was necessary for the status position of the middle class that wives and daughters embody the standards of respectability by remaining pure, no matter what the men were doing.

Thus arose a pernicious double standard: men's sexual activity was condoned, while for women, even so much as the thought of sexual indulgence was strictly out of bounds. At the same time and necessarily, there was a universally recognized division of all women into two distinct categories: the respectable and the depraved, the Madonnas and the Magdalens,[27] with no grey area in between. Unmarried, middle-class Madonnas were not to be sought as sexual partners. Thus, with females of their class (except for one's wife) entirely closed off to middle-class men, the demand for prostitutes became enormous, and prostitution flourished. In an article of 1959, Professor Keith Thomas tells us that, "In 1841 the Chief Commissioner of Police estimated that there were 3,325 brothels in the Metropolitan district of London alone and this calculation takes no account of part-time prostitution produced by inadequate female wages."[28]

Yes, there were physicians, feminists, and other reformers who argued strenuously against the double standard. The physician T. L. Nichols wrote persuasively in 1872, for example, "There can be no right of men to destroy a certain number of women, making them the victims of their lusts, in order that those they marry may be virtuous."[29] Persuasive, but it did little good. The reformists did eventually prevail, but not until very late in the century and, arguably, not fully until the 1960s. Gradually, in other words, both the double standard and the discriminatory division of women into two categories were overcome – not by increasing the continence of men, but, as the requirement of respectability declined over time, by the relaxation of the norms governing

27 Trudgill 1976.

28 Thomas 1959, p. 198.

29 Quoted in Cominos 1963, p. 45.

the sexual behavior of women. For the time being, however, during almost all of Victoria's reign and beyond, desperate pressure on its women toward purity was applied by the respectable middle class.

Morality was enshrined by the middle class in laws. The British parliament passed the Obscene Publications Act in 1857, amended but not repealed as late as 1959 and 1964. This outlawed (but did not succeed in eliminating) pornography and other items that might corrupt the morals and behavior of susceptible individuals.

In the latter part of the century, contraception became a major issue. It was widely considered that if contraception were written about and accepted, it would encourage unmarried middle-class people to have sex with each other and married ones to have sex outside of marriage, as well as having sex too often for health and moral rectitude even within the marriage. Most authorities, therefore, strenuously opposed contraception on moral grounds, thus cutting the married woman off – even the pure married woman – from a potential means of rescuing the quality of her life and even her life itself.[30] In England in 1877, Richard Bradlaugh and Annie Besant (rhymes with pleasant) published a book – written, as it happens, by an American – that contained information on contraceptive methods. They were brought to trial under the Obscene Publications Act and were found guilty, but, on appeal, they were acquitted on a technicality. In the meantime, the public became not only intensely interested but clearly aroused in favor of the defendants, which rendered contraception essentially acceptable thereafter in the court of public opinion.

In America, a fanatical and indefatigable zealot by the name of Anthony Comstock got the U.S. Congress to pass a similar law in 1873. He proceeded to travel extensively and tirelessly around the country digging up pornography and materials relating to contraception and arranging for prosecutions under the Comstock Laws. The practical results were not entirely as Comstock wished. It is true that there were many arrests and convictions and that hundreds of pounds of supposedly obscene literature and goods were seized and destroyed.[31] The public in this period, however, was not in sympathy with the Comstock

30 Cominos 1963, p.22. D'Emilio and Freedman 1988, p. 154.

31 D'Emilio and Freedman 1988, pp. 159-160.

Laws, especially as affecting access to birth control. There was a thriving black market in birth-control devices. Even prosecutors and the courts sympathized with family privacy, making it extremely difficult to achieve successful prosecutions under these laws.[32]

The Comstock Laws were not finally repealed until 1983.

What the obscenity laws in both countries did accomplish was to reinforce the making of sex into something that must be hidden, particularly from pure women who might otherwise be contaminated.

Back in England, the parliament in 1864 also passed the Contagious Diseases Act, strengthened and extended geographically later in the decade. The trigger was the fact that members of the armed forces in disturbing numbers were contracting venereal diseases from prostitutes who congregated in certain cities with a large military presence. The act originally had effect in only a few ports and army towns but was eventually extended to eighteen subjected areas. It provided that women who appeared to an enforcement officer to be prostitutes could be detained for a medical examination. If found to be infected, they were confined to a medical facility – a "lock hospital" – for as much as a year.[33] Women (who of course did not have a vote) were incensed. For one, any designated officer on a whim could stop any woman and subject her to the insult and indignity of a medical examination – by male doctors, of course. In 2010, the State of Arizona passed a law providing that policemen could detain any person they thought might be an illegal immigrant and require proof of citizenship or legal status. Hispanics in Arizona were insulted and infuriated at the indignity just as women were by the Contagious Diseases Act in nineteenth-century England.

In addition, the Contagious Diseases Acts were the most flagrant imaginable admission of the double standard of sexual behavior. It takes two to have sexual intercourse. Only women, however, received any censure or punishment for the spread of diseases in this manner – diseases that they obviously caught from men. In addition, a substantial proportion of these women became prostitutes only because they had been seduced by men – very often middle-class men – and lived in a social

32 Tone 2000. I am grateful to Karen Lystra for recommending Tone's article.

33 See for example, *Wikipedia:* Contagious Diseases Acts.

system that gave them almost no other option. An unmarried middle-class woman who was known to have committed the unspeakable act could be a middle-class woman no longer. Thus, the ranks of middle-class Victorian women remained pure by expulsion.

Ironically, the Contagious Diseases Acts had a notable, positive side effect. They animated feminist leaders to a greater intensity of action, and because of this, the acts can be credited with contributing in a major way to the eventual passage of women's suffrage and better consideration of women and their property in the laws of marriage and divorce. The Contagious Diseases Acts were repealed in 1889, but the categorization of women as either respectable or depraved was not so easy to undo.

The requirement of respectability permeated middle-class Victorian life, both in day-to-day, private interaction and in public policy. The salience of the requirement of respectability cannot be exaggerated. Its paramount importance for the interests of the middle class served to put extreme pressure on women to be pure.

Parents and Husbands

This section is short, but the brevity should not be misleading. Among members of the coalition, the interest of parents and husbands in chastity and the pressure they brought to bear were the most intense and direct of all.

A woman was a form of property to her parents before her marriage and was literally and legally the property of her husband afterwards. As such, her seduction was an instance of property damage or even theft. It is true that this was also the case before the Victorian period and in a certain light afterwards as well. The great English literary figure and moralist Samuel Johnson wrote in the eighteenth century, "Consider of what importance to society the chastity of woman is. Upon that all property in the world depends. They who forfeit it should not have any possibility of being restored to good character; nor should the children of an illicit connection attain the full right of lawful children."[34]

34 Quoted in Trudgill 1976, p. 16.

But the interest of parents and husbands in chastity was more intense during the Victorian period than it was either before or afterwards. For a woman to be known not to be a virgin or to have committed adultery was not quite such a calamity in the eighteenth and twentieth centuries as it was in the nineteenth because there was no supreme value of middle-class respectability to intensify the transgression. In the Victorian age, the importance of respectability meant that such lapses destroyed the value of this particular form of property and were in fact life-shattering for either parents or husband or both. In the case of parents, there was an added urgency. After the Victorian period, a woman who never married could have a career or at least a job that paid enough to sustain her in modest comfort. In the age of Victoria, a known, fallen woman would be highly unlikely ever to marry. She either became a prostitute or, if her father did not cast her out, became a drain on his resources and that of his heirs for the rest of her life.

As property, a woman was in the same category as a carriage or a necklace or a house. She was not generally tradable in the marketplace like these other commodities (with rare exceptions in life,[35] mirrored in such fiction as Thomas Hardy's *The Mayor of Casterbridge*), but she was similar to them in that she conferred status. A chaste daughter or wife was an asset in this regard. The purity of women was critical for social standing. It may not be readily apparent that the possession of a pure daughter or wife raised the status of a parent or husband as a carriage did, for example, but it is easily seen in the negative; that is, a woman known to be unchaste would certainly lower the status of husband or parent – unavoidably, radically, and irrevocably. Moreover, whereas an insurance policy could protect a family from losses due to the theft of a carriage or damage to a house, only chastity and modesty could protect it from the costs of damage to the virtue of a daughter or wife. Within families, the purity and especially the chastity of women became a paramount value and a dominant concern.

35 Thomas 1959, p. 213.

Men

Historically, it appears that men in general, that is to say all middle-class adult males, were motivated on two grounds to exert strong pressure on women in the direction of purity: one was primarily for the sake of chastity and the other for domesticity.

Take chastity first. Why would men want women to be chaste? One would think that just the opposite would be true, making it easier for men to succeed when sexual possibilities arose. Of course, men would be motivated by such concerns as property and respectability, but these would be in their roles as husbands, fathers, or members of the middle class and not just simply as men.

I have, in fact, concluded that men did not have a strong concern for chastity exclusively in their role as adult males. However, the reasons for thinking that they did insist on chastity simply as men contribute to one's understanding of Victorianism as it bears on the sexuality of women, and it will be well to review them.

Recall that Victorian morality made much of the distinction between body and soul, or appetite and reason. This common teaching, apparently quite widely internalized, emphasized the great moral importance of ruling one's life by soul or reason rather than allowing oneself to be governed by appetite. One does not know to what extent this moral principle affected behavior in real life but let us grant for the sake of argument that the effects were considerable.

Clearly, Victorian men were attracted to women, as most men are in any age. The body-soul duality quickly arises in this regard. It was possible to have a carnal, lustful attraction to a woman, and it was also possible to have a purely spiritual affection, as in the love of God or of deep friends. Giving in to the former would be allowing body – the base, animal nature – to gain ascendance. Harboring the latter would be a creditable expression of soul. Interestingly enough, the common, widespread definition of romantic love accepted by nineteenth-century and earlier writers was as a feeling toward another person, say as a man toward a woman, that was constituted jointly by both of these components – carnality and affection. For example, quoting Mrs. E. B. Duffey in 1873, "Love in its truest, purest, highest form is that of strong, unselfish affection blended with desire."[36] It is an appealing definition and one to which we will refer repeatedly.

However, if one's morality were heavily influenced by the body-soul duality, these two possible lanes of attraction – the spiritual and the carnal – would present a major problem. One woman could hardly be the object of both kinds of feelings at the same time, or the feelings would become mixed up together, and the spiritual would be dirtied and indeed spoiled by the carnal. It could be very difficult for a man to maintain in his conscience that his regard for a woman was spiritual, controlled by soul rather than appetite, when at the same time he lusted after her energetically. Therefore, if this male mindset were both widespread and powerful, there was an emphatic need to have a class or category of pure, virtuous women in the world whom one could love only ethereally, and non-pure women who would be the objects of lust. It is in this sense that men, as men, would want respectable middle-class women to be chaste. It enabled them to see themselves as being ruled substantially by soul and reason rather than completely by body and appetite.

Unmarried men nourished on these teachings would look respectfully for sweethearts among the modest and virtuous women of their class while frequenting prostitutes to relieve desire. Husbands would require their wives to "lie still and think of the empire" once or twice a year while consorting with servants and prostitutes in the interim for responsive sexuality. In sum, we have the reasoning that men – as men – wanted middle-class women to be chaste because they were ruled by the body-soul distinction.

This seems fairly reasonable at first glance, on a theoretical level, but there is little if any hard evidence for it. True, it is consistent with the fact that the trade of prostitution increased in America and flourished in Victorian England as it perhaps never has done before or since,[37] but the incidence of prostitution might well have had little to do with the body-soul distinction. It might be mostly explained by the notion that as members of the middle class and as husbands, future husbands, and parents, men had a high stake in the chastity of

36 Lystra 1992, p. 60, quoting Mrs. E. B. Duffey, 1873. See also Gay 1999, p. 45 ff.

37 Smith 1973a, p. 51. Thomas 1959, p. 198.

middle-class women because of their concerns for respectability and property, as reviewed earlier, while at the same time feeling a need for a sexual outlet.

Not only is the evidence lacking, but it can hardly be believed that this psychological orientation actually prevailed in the practical world of nineteenth-century love and sex, even though Sigmund Freud was convinced that it did prevail and considered love on the part of Victorian men to be immature on that account, that is, immature because it could not combine the two necessary components of romantic love into feelings for one woman.[38] Certainly, it is possible for a man to love a woman only spiritually, but the Victorian novels are full to overflowing with suitors who clearly loved their young, unmarried heroines with physical attraction as well as with deep affection. In the novels, anyway, what Freud would have considered mature – combining the two forms of attraction – was the rule rather than the exception. Consider it this way: In almost every single case, the reader will find that the young man who was in love with a young woman of his class considered her to be very beautiful. If the sole basis of his attraction were spiritual, why should he care how beautiful she was? After all, the heterosexual man does not generally care if his close male friends are beautiful – the ones that he appreciates and loves very deeply as a friend. This beauty that the novelist tells us about as being perceived by the man is a way of communicating to us that he is physically – that is, sexually – attracted to her, although there is generally a spiritual component involved as well – the "affection" component of the definition. In short, these heroes of the novels loved their young goddesses in both ways, nicely fulfilling the definition of romantic love but directly contradicting the implications of the body-soul duality, which would require that the pure woman be loved only spiritually.

There is also abundant anecdotal evidence of such true, double-sided romantic love in the history books.[39] For example (anticipating material from the letters and diaries of Chapter VI), here is an excerpt from a letter by Charles Kingsley to his beloved Fanny Grenfell, written in 1843. Kingsley was a widely-read English novelist but also an Anglican minister. See how faithfully he adheres *not* to the requirements of the body-soul duality but to

38 Thomas 1959, p. 207. Cominos 1963, p. 229.

39 E.g., Gay 1999, Rothman 1987, Lystra 1992.

the definition of romantic love, explicitly affirming the blending of affection with desire, soul with body. In his letter, he tells Fanny of his morning daydream (it seems quite intimate, but in fact they did wait to consummate their love until after the wedding).

> This morning I awoke at 5, & as I lay, white limbs gleamed before me, & soft touches pressed me, & a wanton tongue – yet chaste & holy!, stole between my lips! . . . What is sensuality! Not the *enjoyment* of *holy glorious matter,* but blindness to its spiritual meaning! . . . How much more delicious when in each others' arms, the flesh and the spirit shall tend the same way, increasing each other's delight! Bless God Bless God![40]

Crossing the Atlantic, here are excerpts from two letters of Nathaniel Hawthorne, American author of *The Scarlet Letter*, to his betrothed, Sophia Peabody. In the first, written in 1841, he expresses the spiritual side of his love. He refers to Sophia as "wife" but in truth they were not yet married, and, like Charles and Fanny, they also waited for the wedding to consummate their love. In the second excerpt, from a letter of 1842, he voices the carnal side of his feelings, anticipating the joys of the flesh when they would be husband and wife.

> Now good bye, dearest, sweetest, loveliest, holiest, truest, suitablest little wife. I worship thee. Thou art my type of womanly perfection . . . Thou enablest me to interpret the riddle of life, and fillest me with faith in the unseen and better land, because thou leadest me thither continually.[41]
>
> Even the spoken word has long been inadequate. Looks – pressures of the lips and hands – the touch of bosom to bosom – these are a better language. But bye-and-bye, our spirits will demand some more adequate expression even than these.[42]

---

40 Charles Kingsley to Fanny Grenfell 1843. Quoted in Gay 1999, pp. 308-309.

41 Nathaniel Hawthorne to Sophia Peabody, 1841. Quoted in Lystra 1992, p. 41.

42 Nathaniel Hawthorne to Sophia Peabody 1842. Quoted in Gay 1984, p. 457.

As a final example, I have broken up an excerpt from a letter of 1867 by Lyman Hodge, a Yale graduate and merchant, to his future wife, Mary Granger. The first passages indicate the spiritual side of his love, the second show the desire he feels at the same time:

> And now love, you with the warm heart and loving eyes . . . whose feet I kiss and whose knees I embrace as a devotee kisses and embraces those of his idol, . . . my life, with your generous womanly soul, my heart's keeper – Good night:
> And now love, . . . whose picture I kissed last night and whose lips I so often kissed in my dreams, . . . whose caresses are so dear and so longed for awake and in slumber, making my heart beat faster, my flesh tremble and my brain giddy with delight, . . . my darling whose home is in my arms and whose resting place my bosom, . . . good night: a good night and a fair one to thy sleeping eyes and wearied limbs, the precurser of many bright, beautiful mornings when my kisses shall waken thee and my love shall greet thee.[43]

These plentiful young men in love challenge the validity of the theory of Freud and a great many Victorian writers who believed that the two components could only rarely be fused by Victorian men.[44] It is almost certainly true that these smitten young men wanted their brides to be virgins, but surely not just in order that they might worship them in the future with zero carnality. In short, Victorian men do not seem to have been ruled by the body-soul distinction in this particular. That being the case, they had no stake from this source in the chastity of young, middle-class women.

Once married, if the young bride made it clear that sex was repulsive to her, this might certainly drive the frustrated husband into the arms of prostitutes. But if she were receptive (we have already seen that some Mosher women were indeed receptive), and given that she not only was lovely but right there in the bed and not downtown in some whorehouse, it is hard to

43 Lyman Hodge to Mary Granger, 1867. Quoted in Lystra 1992, p. 68.

44 Thomas 1959, pp. 207-208. Cominos 1963, pp. 23-24.

see that normal men would not allow the carnal to follow the ethereal, thus again fusing the two components.

In sum, men wanted middle-class women to be chaste, but the motive was not rooted in the dual nature of love. It is doubtful that they developed desire-free romantic attachments in great numbers. They certainly had an interest in female chastity but for other reasons.

Perhaps there was a reason other than the body-soul duality why men, as men, wanted middle-class women to be chaste. It is frequently suggested that they had a stake in chastity because of the danger of pregnancy.[45] A first objection to this alternative explanation is that if a man were not a husband or father or brother, why should he care about pregnancies? The fact is, however, that men did care even if they were confirmed bachelors and therefore had no status to lose by an illicit pregnancy – among acquaintances, for example. That is, they did not necessarily care about the pregnancy itself. They had no property-motivated stake. They cared because the sex act that produced the pregnancy was a transgression of the moral code in which they did indeed have a stake. Even if not husbands or fathers, the spread of non-marital sex would threaten the respectability that was critical for the status of their class, the middle class.

In the nineteenth century, the vehement moral opposition to contraception contributes to this conclusion regarding pregnancy as a motive.[46] The basis of the opposition was that contraception would lead to illicit sex and thus to the wholesale violation of chastity.[47] But if the only reason for upholding chastity was the danger of pregnancy, good contraceptive methods and devices should have been welcomed! The more effective they were, the less need there would be to worry about pregnancies. Yet, contraceptives were not welcomed. It appears that authorities opposed to contraception were not so much concerned about preventing pregnancies as about preventing the illicit sex act itself; contraception, they feared, would exacerbate the problem. Thus, the widespread and strenuous opposition to contraception shows that the danger of pregnancy cannot have been much of an explanation for the general obsession with chastity.

45 Thomas 1959, pp. 209-216.

46 Thomas 1959, p. 216.

47 Cominos 1963, pp. 21-23.

I would conclude that in putting pressure on women to be chaste, men were not acting as men but rather as parents, husbands, and members of the middle class. Their reasons for applying that pressure were not ultimately the two-component theory of love or the danger of conception, but rather the motives of property and respectability, both of which acted to maintain or increase status in the Victorian social system. What we derive, then, from this review of the motives of men for demanding chastity in middle-class women is increased support for the importance of these inter-related motives – property, respectability, and status.

We do not, on these grounds, however, remove the category "Men" from the coalition. It emerges that men did act as men not for the sake of chastity but in their zeal to enforce another dimension of purity: domesticity. One must agree with others that the underlying motive was simple: to protect themselves from competition. There was no problem for middle-class men in women's undertaking laboring-class roles, such as domestic service or dressmaking or factory work or taking in laundry, but a threat was apparently felt when, in the 1870s in England and a little earlier in America, women began to press for admission into higher education in general, into the professions in particular, and into the medical profession even more specifically. A valuable article from 1973 by Professor Joan Burstyn speaks directly to the topic.[48] These efforts on the part of women to be admitted into general institutions of higher education (and not just to teacher training programs) had been kept under control by arguments, convincing to public opinion, that women were intellectually inferior to men. However, women began to demonstrate – by succeeding in college courses in small numbers, by actually becoming doctors in even smaller numbers, and by competing successfully with boys and young men in certain examinations – that the intellectual inferiority argument was faulty.

At the same time, it became clear that women had served the public and their country extremely well by performance as nurses, especially through the well-publicized efforts of Florence Nightingale and Mary Seacole, who pioneered modern nursing practices in the Crimean War of 1853-1856. If women could withstand the rigors and daunting technical challenges of wartime

48 See Burstyn, 1973.

nursing, the public began to feel that they could also excel as physicians. Added to this, there was demand by women patients for women doctors in the fields of gynecology and obstetrics. Threatened medical men had to come up with a better argument.

The first ploy was to claim that women were plainly physiologically different from men and that, therefore, they were meant for different types of work in life and different kinds of education. Especially, it was argued by physicians both in America and Britain that the stress and strain of professional education would harm the reproductive systems of women. They would be able to compete intellectually and succeed in examinations but only at the expense of damage to the critical organs. "They intended to show conclusively," Burstyn tells us, "that the Victorian ideal of modest womanhood was based on sound physiological principles that could be ignored only by endangering the human race."[49] Excessive strain and mental competition during puberty and the later teenage years would be disastrous. The human body had only a fixed amount of energy at any given time. Young women needed all they could muster during the maturing years for the formation and growth of their reproductive systems. It was folly to drain this energy by the stress of arduous mental labor. Examples of the dangers were claimed but, as usual, without identifying individuals or referencing published case studies so that the claims could be verified. As one incidence of such assertions, Burstyn quotes the American physician Edward A. Clarke: "They graduated from school or college excellent scholars, but with undeveloped ovaries. Later they married, and were sterile."[50]

In particular, the development and healthy maintenance of their reproductive systems demanded that women rest during menstruation, necessitating a different pattern of education from that of men. But more than that, it necessitated different types of mature work. "Who would want a doctor who was available only three weeks out of four? Or a barrister who might have to miss a case because she was 'indisposed'?"[51] Women must not only be modest, virtuous,

49 Burstyn 1973, p. 80.

50 Burstyn 1973, p. 85.

51 Burstyn 1973, p. 86.

and chaste, but domestic. A woman of intellect needed to apply her gifts to the raising of children who would be major contributors to their society.

On these various grounds, male physicians and like-minded citizens blocked access by women to higher education by voting against it on boards whenever they could – and that was often. Men added to the pressure on women to conform to the model of purity not only as husbands, fathers, and members of the middle class, but as men – the group that held a monopoly on access to higher education and the professions at the time and wanted to keep it.

In making the argument based in menstruation, of course, the doctors were forgetting about or omitting mention of those women who had been working reliably in factories for years – four weeks out of four. It was not this counter-example, however, that defeated their attempts. Rather, it was the example of middle-class women themselves. Many women and some men kept the pressure up, and women did succeed, showing that they could not only lead full student and professional lives in spite of menstruation but could be successful wives and mothers at the same time. As the century progressed, there slowly began to be broader demand for middle-class women to work in middle-class occupations. By the 1890s, objections to women in higher education and the professions had begun to unravel even for married women, and the trend was never reversed. However, the unraveling was not rapid. Men kept a surprising proportion of women, and especially married women, in apron strings for a surprising number of years after Queen Victoria's death in 1901.

Women

The members of the coalition for repression urged women to be pure and, as a consequence, to be psychologically passionless. Surprisingly enough, there could be an attraction in this position to some women, as individuals who had little or no power. It was a potential source of self-respect, strength, and influence. Being pure could be seen not so much as a relegation to the sidelines of active life but as an exalted state in which one could serve as a positive example.[52] In America, moreover, there was an egalitarianism that meant that any woman

52 Cott 1978, p.228.

could hope to marry her lover regardless of class, making her chastity and thus her continued eligibility precious to her.[53]

Married women could use the tool of purity to rectify their unjust image as beings designed primarily for sex and procreation. This release could give them the space needed to increase their self-esteem and develop their faculties.[54] Instead of seeing women as the victims of Victorian sexual standards, it is therefore possible that women helped to maintain those standards themselves as a means of rising out of the abject role to which history had consigned them.[55] To escape inferiority, one choice would be to strive for complete political, economic, and social equality, but that road would be extremely long and difficult given the mindset of the times. On the other hand, one could become an angel in the house overnight.

As it happens, women used both of these routes simultaneously. They began the struggle for equality by seeking the same intellectual education that was available to their brothers. Paradoxically, they strengthened the education strategy by appealing to the traditional gender ideology. In the previous section, we looked at women's education in the Victorian age as something that men tried to prevent. We now examine the other side of the same struggle: education as an opportunity that women tried to create. A second valuable journal article in connection with these events was written by Professor Ellen Jordan in 1991. The following discussion owes much to her analysis.[56]

The central political problem in seeking access to solid preparatory and higher education for women was the moral stance that women must be pure, which in this context especially emphasized the "domestic" component of purity. It was widely believed that intellectual education for women would only turn their heads away from their proper sphere. The hook used by early feminist leaders, educators, and students to get around this roadblock was the following: "A woman should, according to the current gender ideology, be a companion to her husband, a teacher of her children, and a pervasive moral influence within the home. But only an educated woman could perform these functions adequately; therefore, academic education was in fact the

53 Smith and Hindus 1975, p. 552.

54 Cott 1978, p. 233.

55 Cott 1978, p. 235.

56 See Jordan, 1991.

best preparation for marriage and maternity."[57] The claim seems strong in its details – education making for more companionable wives and more competent mentors of children – with the possible exception of the link between education and "pervasive moral influence." Advocates argued cogently, however, that people could only exercise good moral judgment if they had been trained to think logically and rationally.

In fact, the argument quoted above can be a formal logical demonstration in its own right. It has been labeled "the bluestocking syllogism," bluestocking being a term applied at the time to intellectual women. The model syllogism from Logic 101 goes something like this:

> All men are mortal.
> Socrates is a man.
> Therefore, Socrates is mortal.

Following this pattern, the bluestocking syllogism would be:

> All women who are a good moral influence make good wives and mothers.
> A woman with an intellectual education is a good moral influence.
> Therefore, a woman with an intellectual education makes a good wife and mother.

That link between "intellectual education" and "good moral influence" is not airtight, but it is essentially quite reasonable and was persuasive at the time – not universally, but significantly.

The bluestocking syllogism, presented not as an academic exercise but as an elaborate and flowing argument in speeches and pamphlets, was a brilliant bit of political strategy. Once accepted as valid, see what other astounding feat it can perform:

> All good wives and mothers are truly feminine women.
> A woman with an intellectual education makes a good wife and mother (the conclusion of the bluestocking syllogism).

57 Jordan 1991, p. 442.

Therefore, a woman with an intellectual education is a truly feminine woman!

This was critically important because the parents of middle-class girls and young women did not care much about the content of their education, but they did care supremely about preserving and enhancing femininity. Feminist leaders and liberal educators, on the other hand, were concerned to train young women in the classical languages, science, ancient and modern literature, and, above all, in reasoning ability and habits of independent thought. It might take many generations to achieve these goals by pushing hard for the general equality of women against formidable societal resistance. The gamble was that the goals could be achieved much sooner, almost immediately, by asserting that "your goals are our goals" – we all want to develop good wives, mothers, and truly feminine women.

It worked. There was a lot of opposition – for example, the following appeared in the prestigious scientific journal *The Lancet* in 1868: "We believe that to apply the same systems of education and training to both sexes alike, and to open the same paths to both, would be to act in defiance of natural laws and to diminish the usefulness and lessen the moral and spiritual influence which women unquestionably exert."[58]

The opposition was not quite strong enough, however, to quell the impetus for change, based as it was on accepted standards of gender ideology. Schoolmistresses, collegiate educators, and even parents found themselves able to support the teaching of broad culture and rational argument without feeling that they were endangering the femininity of their charges. The times were apparently ready on both sides of the Atlantic for a gradual abandonment of the more extreme aspects of the Victorian ethos. As an example, leaders in the women's movement publicly urged the opening of middle-class occupations to women. How could they do that without exposing the bluestocking syllogism as an egregious hypocrisy? How could education make good wives and mothers if the educated women were out working in middle-class occupations? The answer is that such careers were advocated for *single* women. There was no danger of making bad wives and mothers out of them if they were not wives and mothers at all. The comparable campaign on behalf of married women did not reach significant intensity until the early twentieth century.

58 Quoted in Jordan 1991, p. 458.

Notice, however, that the wedge established on the basis of the bluestocking syllogism and its derivatives meant that women seeking an education must allow themselves to continue to be ruled by the ideology of purity. Indeed, they must continue to believe in it. All evidence suggests that it was not hypocritical at all. In spite of being allowed an intellectual education in ever-increasing numbers, women were still expected – and expected themselves – to be chaste, modest, virtuous, simple, godly, and domestic. Nearly one hundred percent of single, middle-class women who worked, for example, quit work the minute they got married, and, as noted above, this lasted until well into the twentieth century both in Britain and America. For reasons both of self-esteem and opportunity, therefore, women put pressure on themselves to conform to the traditional standards of purity. For the time being, they became members of the Coalition for Repression.

Outcomes

How shall we define the prevalence of repression? Shall we concede that middle-class Victorian women were sexually repressed if at least half of them can be shown to have been essentially asexual – or perhaps sixty percent or seventy? Suppose we adopt a loose dividing line in order to have something concrete in mind as we attack our central mystery for a solution. We would not want to say that the hypothesis of repression fails if there were one single instance of a middle-class woman having a premarital or extramarital affair or having two or three pleasant one-night stands. There will always be exceptions. Few public policies or social regimes can be one hundred percent effective. Thus, let us take a ninety/ten view, that is, if we can conclude with confidence that fewer than ten percent of Victorian women had such affairs or one-night stands, we can safely accept the traditional view – the stereotype of repression. Looking at the other side of the coin, it means that over ninety percent of the women in question remained chaste, as desired by the coalition. If the evidence leads us to conclude that ten percent or more did not remain chaste, then we relinquish the repression theory and accept that Victorian women were more modern in their sexual attitudes and behavior than traditionally thought.

In light of the Victorian social scene as outlined above, it is hardly credible that such sexual affairs or pleasant one-night stands were common. Ten percent of Victorian women having affairs would be doubtful, and fifteen or twenty percent would be truly astonishing in the atmosphere created by such intense pressure and vigilance. It would mean that women commonly just thumbed their noses at all of these valued people and social forces that indoctrinated them, pressed them, and depended upon them to be pure.

The remainder of this book is devoted to gathering evidence on whether this extreme socialization actually did succeed in repressing almost all middle-class female sexuality. The evidence is not one-sided. Some of it supports repression based on the ninety/ten benchmark, and some of it supports the opposite theory that claims much more modern attitudes and behavior. In the end, I hope to make sense of it all. The evidence will be drawn from love letters, novels, vital records, and the Mosher survey. At this point, one would have to expect the evidence to be convincing in favor of the repression hypothesis, but there are more sources to consider. Before launching into the following three chapters, in which novels, the Mosher survey, and love letters are respectively considered, let us take a moment to consider important data from vital records and apparently representative personal experience.

If we consider the Puritan period of the seventeenth century to be a period of strict sexual morals, the post-Restoration period of the eighteenth century to be one of quite loose moral standards, and the Victorian period to be strict again, we would expect the historical prebridal pregnancy rates to be a good reflection of these characterizations. They should be low in the Puritan period, high in the eighteenth century, and low among the Victorians. They are. The numbers indicate – not perfectly, but reasonably well – the amount of sexual intercourse taking place among unmarried couples who then proceeded to get married and have a child. In the Puritan period in America (around 1680), approximately 10% of first births to married couples came within eight and a half months of the wedding. By the late eighteenth century (1800), this rate had risen to the extremely high level of 27%, so that more than one out of every four first babies was conceived before the wedding. In the early nineteenth century, 1801-1840, the rate declined to 18%, and at the height of the Victorian era (1889), it was back down below 10% again.[59] On the face of it, this is strong evidence that Victorian women, at least American Victorian women, were not sexually loose, and the data can be seen as supporting the hypothesis that the rigorous socialization for repression had its effects.

Men will make advances, even in gentlemanly, Victorian fashion. To keep the statistics so low, women must have resisted most of the time, showing the effects of growing up as a female in a Victorian home – that is, revealing a moral code that had thoroughly penetrated her being and that made her sharply different from the women of today. Again anticipating material from the letters and diaries of Chapter VI, here is an excerpt from the diary of Maud Rittenhouse, written in 1882 after an incident on her front porch: "He says, if I loved him as he loved me I wouldn't care for the whole world to know that he held me in his arms and kissed me good-night. But I told him it was highly improper." And the following is a brief excerpt from a letter of Emma Lou Story to George Bellows in 1906: "I didn't think that you thought me that sort but now you know that I'm not. . . . I haven't any doubt that girls have the same feelings at times but being girls can't give way to it the way a fellow can."

If the man pushes harder, the virtuous Victorian woman's resistance is more firmly expressed. Here is Kate Nickleby responding to the unwanted advances of Sir Mulberry Hawk in Charles Dickens' novel, *Nicholas Nickleby:*

> "Do me the favour to be silent now, sir," replied Kate.
>
> "No, don't," said Sir Mulberry, folding his crushed hat to lay his elbow on, and bringing himself still closer to the young lady; "upon my life, you oughtn't to. Such a devoted slave of yours, Miss Nickleby—it's an infernal thing to treat him so harshly, upon my soul it is."
>
> "I wish you to understand, sir," said Kate, trembling in spite of herself, but speaking with great indignation, "that your behaviour offends and disgusts me. If you have a spark of gentlemanly feeling remaining, you will leave me."[60]

59 Smith and Hindus 1975, p. 561.

60 Dickens 2006, Chapter 19.

The data from vital records showing so sharp a decline in prebridal pregnancies from the post-Restoration period to the Victorian are extremely important to us. On the surface, anyway, they demonstrate beyond a doubt that repression was successful and that theories to the contrary must be viewed with suspicion. Unfortunately, these are not national statistics collected universally as a matter of course by medical personnel and recorded by bureaucrats. Rather, they come primarily from parish records in a set of scattered localities that may or may not be representative of the country as a whole. More importantly, although they constitute an excellent indicator of the quantity of illicit sexual relations in the system, they do not in themselves tell us exactly what we want to know. To gauge repression, we would like to have data on the number of unmarried middle-class Victorian women who had sex – whether or not they got pregnant and whether or not they later got married. Such data do not exist.

However, two factors show us that the figure of ten percent extracted from the vital records is, if anything, too high. For one, these data overwhelmingly record the experience of working-class women, not middle class. The British historian Tim Lambert concluded that in the nineteenth century at least eighty percent of the English population was working class.[61] Estimates for America indicate about the same.[62] Furthermore, we know that intercourse for engaged or committed couples was largely acceptable in the working class, especially in the early part of the Victorian period, whereas it was not acceptable in the middle class at all. This means that if we could examine middle-class women alone, the proportion of first births under eight and a half months would most probably be lower than ten percent. A second factor is that, although data representing all sexual intercourse before marriage for Victorians do not exist, such data do exist for women in the immediate post-Victorian decades, enabling a trend to be established. The data indicate that the portion of middle-class Victorian women who lost their virginity before marriage is undoubtedly under ten percent. It would be a digression to report these other data here, but they become germane and will be described in the following chapter.

61 Lambert, Tim undated.

62 *Wikipedia*: American Middle Class.

Turning to personal experience, a few scholars have made a deep study of love letters of the period, unfortunately pertaining mainly to America and hardly at all to Britain. Several of the accounts in these letters not only provide data on individuals but have the feeling, by the way they are worded, of being representative – of telling us something about the orientation of the general population toward sexuality in their era. We will look at just one such American account here. The written record applying to Britain is tiny, but there does exist at least one account, and that one is consistent with the data from America. Together, these anecdotal glimpses into personal experience indicate the influence achieved over the minds of women by the coalition for repression and thereby strengthen the statistical record as a valid indicator of Victorian sexuality.

Annie Cox, twenty-one, and Winan Allen, twenty-six, were in love in the 1860s. Annie seems,, by her writing, to be quite an ordinary, average, middle-class young woman. They became formally engaged in the summer of 1863, and during part of that time, Winan lived with Annie and her parents in Madison, Wisconsin. They were waiting to marry until Winan could finish his law degree and set up a practice. They were intimate, which was not at all unusual, but in this case they apparently allowed themselves once to go all the way. We will see that this was indeed unusual, but what is of interest here is not so much the lapse as Annie's reaction to it – not so much her individual behavior as what her words imply about the success of the coalition in influencing the minds of young women.

In a letter to Winan, she wrote:

> When temptation to wrong suggested itself from natural passions and opportunity, 'twas my mission to have been *fine*, giving you a kind refusal and leading your mind away and beyond. In the first instance, I failed in the full possession of my reason & judgments thus giving strength to your desire and weakening my better nature. We made firm resolves and the next opportunity showed how they were kept [in other words, no repeat]. . . . God only knows how I detested myself. . . . I own I think you to blame in some degree. That is, in not accepting

> my first denial. . . . We have both done wrong. I having done much the greater because I should have acted the part of a true, noble, Christian woman. . . . I know this experience will be for my good, though it would have been better if it could never happen.[63]

Earlier, I mentioned another Annie, Annie Besant. A contemporary of Annie Cox but living in England, she was a vigorous and highly influential campaigner for contraception and the legality of contraceptive advice. She came to this role in rebellion, however, as a result of adult experiences, for as a child and young woman she had been pointed in a totally different direction. From the age of eight, her education deepened the emotional and religious side of her character and turned her into a pious Evangelical. Tales of the early Christian martyrs inspired fantasies wherein she vicariously experienced martyrdom, being "flung to lions, tortured on the rack, burned at the stake." She passionately lamented that these heroic religious deeds could not be realized again in her own lifetime. Just as her education precluded the reading of romantic novels, so reveries of romantic love were absent from her daydreams. "No knowledge of evil had been allowed to penetrate" her dreamy life. She was "kept innocent of all questions of sex." In her childhood and youth, "the budding tendrils of passion" were entwined about two ideals, Christ and her mother.[64]

We have reviewed the motivations and some of the actions of the coalition for repression and have glanced briefly at the probable results in several personal accounts and in data on prebridal pregnancies. At this point, it seems impossible to conclude other than that the traditional view of the sexuality of middle-class Victorian women – the view that they were severely repressed – is essentially correct. Evidence from the Victorian novels analyzed in the next chapter will not alter this conclusion but will qualify it in some respects. Evidence from the Mosher survey and the love letters of Chapter VI tell a different story.

63 Rothman 1987, p. 130.

64 Cominos 1973, p. 163, quoting and paraphrasing from Besant's autobiography.

Third Interlude: Portraits 7 – 10

Portrait 7: Molly Attenborough[65]

This is another case in which, rather than taking the questionnaire home to complete, the patient was interviewed by Dr. Mosher, who noted down her responses. Almost all of the answers are tersely rendered. Moreover, no exceptional circumstances are noted that might have led me to produce a narrative account of considerable length, as occurred with several of the other respondents. But Molly Attenborough was forceful in expressing several interesting views. Without frills, she appears to have provided Dr. Mosher with a straightforward example of the kind of woman's-life information the good doctor sought to analyze.

Molly was born in 1871, and she was interviewed by Dr. Mosher in 1913 at age forty-two. The date of her marriage to Attenborough was not supplied, but we know that she gave birth to her first child in 1903 at age thirty-two. She had attended college at Iowa State University for one year. We do not know Attenborough's occupation. It must have been interesting, however, because Molly indicated that the first child, a healthy boy, was born "in the tropics." He was delicate at first, which Molly attributed to the location, but he soon grew stronger.

About a year later, Molly suffered an episode of amoebic dysentery, but she did not say whether or not this occurred while still in the tropics. Shortly after recovering, she conceived for the second time, and the baby, a healthy girl, was born in 1906. Subsequently, in 1909 and 1912, Molly had two miscarriages. The couple did not practice any specifically mentioned form of birth control except after the first miscarriage. At that time, Molly indicated that her husband advised taking precautions because he did not want her to conceive again until she was strong. The method used was "douches of bichloride."

As to knowledge of the sexual relation before marriage, Dr. Mosher wrote, "No knowledge. Did not know what marriage meant." The initiation took place, however, two or three days after the wedding. In the early years, they had intercourse about twice a week. Around the time of the interview, they were having intercourse only once in two to three weeks, depending on whether they had

65 Mosher 1980, Blank No. 44, pp. 430-435.

leisure. The couple did not have intercourse during Molly's pregnancies except for a few rare occasions during the first one. When asked if she had any sexual desire during her pregnancies, Molly responded that she did not feel any desire during the first pregnancy but that she did during the second. "At other times have you any desire for intercourse?" The response was a simple "Yes," amplified in the follow-up to specify that it generally occurred just before or just after her period. To the question whether intercourse was agreeable, the answer again was a simple "Yes."

The answer was "No" to the query whether she always had an orgasm. Dr. Mosher indicated that her time reaction was slower than her husband's. However, the negative response did not mean "never." She did attain orgasm at least sometimes because she responded that she rested better when she did and experienced a "temperamental uplift." When orgasm was not attained, Molly indicated that it did not bother her a great deal. Dr. Mosher's notation on the form was that it made "very little difference."

Molly endorsed the view that the primary purpose of intercourse is reproduction, but she considered pleasure to be a "very strong" second. She conveyed to Dr. Mosher an almost paradoxical bit of philosophy on this latter subject. Here is Dr. Mosher's sketchy rendering: "If women enjoyed intercourse, the demands on them would be much less. Males desire less when more perfectly satisfied." It seems that the old bit of wisdom regarding intercourse from that eighteenth-century gem, *Aristotle's Compleat Master Piece*, applied, in Molly's opinion, to men as well as to women: "Women in general are better pleased in having a thing once well done than often ill done."[66] Her sense was that by experiencing and revealing deep satisfaction, women made men feel more satisfied in turn, resulting, she predicted, in a pattern that emphasized quality over quantity. The paradox arises in her apparently thinking to maximize the pleasure from this source – for both men and women – by limiting it. This notion occurs several times in the Mosher survey, including from Dr. Mosher herself. One wonders whether it might not be as broadly applicable today as it apparently was in both the eighteenth and nineteenth centuries?

66 Anonymous 1752, Chapter I, Section III.

Molly went on to express her opinion – quite attractively, I think, even in Dr. Mosher's shorthand – about reasons other than reproduction that are sufficient to warrant intercourse: "Oneness – uplifting like music. Very little that is animal about it. The comradeship of it." She agreed, then, with many of the Mosher colleagues unknown to her that this aspect of married life carried special value for preserving and enhancing the relationship.

Thus, Molly Attenborough started out not knowing what to expect but soon discovered that she felt desire as a regular part of life and enjoyed the sexual relation with her husband both in terms of physical pleasure and for the welcome psychological qualities it contributed to their union. She was one who did not experience orgasm regularly or even very frequently, but it apparently was enough. For her, the reliability of orgasm seems to have made "very little difference."

Portrait 8: Lillian (Lily) Anderson[67]

Mrs. Anderson was born in 1853 and married her husband, Hector, in 1875. She had been married for 38 years when she filled out the questionnaire for Dr. Mosher in 1913 at age sixty. Most of her life was enviably good, but there were a few rocky periods, the last of which, judging by the tone of her responses, left her downcast.

As a youngster, her health was excellent, and it continued to be so after her marriage – with a few exceptions to be noted. She attended Vassar College, but it is uncertain for how many years – not long enough, in any case, to earn a degree.

The Andersons' first child came within a year of the marriage. Seven more children followed, the last being born when Lillian was thirty-eight. Thus, she was blessed with eight healthy children, five boys and three girls, all of whom survived to maturity. Lucky Lily! That record was not common in the nineteenth century.

After the first child, the Andersons took a stab at birth control, using what she referred to as a "Good-year rubber ring." This vague description sounds most like a cervical cap or other precursor of the diaphragm. In any case, Lillian developed what she referred to as "congestion of the uterus" during the following three-year period, and she suspected that the condition was caused or aggravated by this device, at least in part. She allowed that there may have been other causes, as well, including "the lack of an orgasm." This latter terminology is ambiguous. She probably did not mean she failed completely to reach orgasm for three years, because orgasm was a pretty regular event for Lily, and she felt that its occurrence was largely under her own control. "A matter of will, mostly," she said. "Seldom beyond absolute control." We can suppose that orgasm failed with more than usual frequency during this period, and we are left to speculate whether this might not have been an effect rather than the cause of the congestion of which she spoke. Whether the condition was actually uterine congestion or the more common pelvic congestion (both being essentially an issue of varicose veins in the region) is uncertain, but pain is common to both conditions, and that may well have interfered with her sexual gratification.

67 Mosher 1980, Blank No. 47, pp. 449-455.

After two years, they abandoned the "Good-year rubber ring," and their second child was conceived shortly afterwards. Subsequently, conception was "left to chance," and "from that time on," she wrote, "my health was excellent until the menopause began."

While not explicit, her responses make it quite definite that whatever this congestive condition was, the symptoms evaporated at that point. The twelve years from age twenty-six to age thirty-eight, during which she had her last six children, were wonderful ones, characterized by "good health and good spirits." Thereafter, there were no more children, but Lillian's life continued to be satisfying until the age of forty-five, fifteen years before her session with Dr. Mosher. One thing we do not know, unfortunately, is how Mr. Anderson felt about this continually growing family. We do not even know whether Lillian knew how he felt. What we do know is that repeated births did not cause her husband to rein in his sexual activism, at least until after the eighth child came into the world.

Intercourse took place within two days after the wedding and about twice a week thereafter except during menstruation. This practice continued as usual even during the pregnancies, which was relatively uncommon among the Mosher women. When asked if she felt sexual desire during her pregnancies, Lillian said that she could not remember for sure, "but think I probably had more than when not pregnant, as there was not the fear of conception present." Her responses tell us that, in her case, arousal was "always a response to affection." At such times, intercourse was an agreeable event for her, but at other times, that is, when affection was not prominent, it was "an offense, simply endured."

In the cases of several of the Mosher women, some of whose portraits we have already sketched, orgasm was not the sort of critical factor one might have expected it to be. They were either content without it or would not have minded very much if there had happened to be less of it, nor did reliable orgasms necessarily insure a satisfying married life. In Mrs. Anderson's case, it was different. Orgasm was important. When asked how she felt immediately after having attained orgasm, she wrote, "Under ideal conditions relaxed and sleepy." How about the next day? "And the next day filled with the joy of life – mentally and physically alert." What if there was no orgasm? "If I remain indifferent, there is no effect on me. But if not and I remain unsatisfied the result is bad, even disastrous, nerve racking, unbalancing."

Asked next whether intercourse were a necessity to man, Lillian answered, "Apparently," by which she undoubtedly meant, "Apparently, judging by my husband." And to woman? "Probably." She went on to explain that intercourse was "apparently a necessity for the *average* person." [Emphasis hers.] "It seems to me that only superior individuals can be independent of sex relation with no evident ill results." Her judgment that those who are independent of sex are "superior" indicates an influential exposure to the conservative view. Judging from this remark alone, one would have expected Mrs. Anderson to subscribe to most if not all of the advice and opinions of Dr. Acton, Dr. Cowan, and their like-minded colleagues. Not so, as we have already seen. In contradiction, or at least showing ambivalence on her part, her feeling that sex was necessary for the average woman indicates a glaring rejection of the conservative position and the stereotype of repression. This is another in a series of instances showing many of the Mosher women as having been of two minds, convinced of the conservative beliefs because those beliefs had been drilled into them and embracing a more liberal stance at the same time because of their own personal experience.

Her answer to the question about ideal habit has much in common with that of a great many of the other Mosher women. They had a tendency toward what seemed to them the sensible judgment that the ideal is not a matter of numbers but of individualized comfort and adjustment. What counts is that intercourse occur when it is desired, and desired by both partners, and not simply by the passage of a certain number of days. In Mrs. Anderson's case, she emphasized "peace of mind," "repose," "response to affection." She guessed that this would amount to "once or twice a month in the hey-day of life." Thus, her numerical ideal was less than her actual frequency of intercourse (twice a week, except during menstrual periods), but she as well as many other Mosher women would feel that one's actual frequency should be irrelevant to the ideal, which would instead be governed by the guidelines of peace of mind, repose, and response to affection – whether this happened to mean more sexual intercourse or less. Also, we can add Lillian Anderson to Sally Warren as warnings that unexamined statistics can be misleading. The fact that the "ideal habit" for many of the women was less than their actual frequency – wanting less than they got, in short – does not make them instances of support for the stereotype of repression. Mrs. Anderson, like Mrs. Warren, liked sex and valued it. That is primary. These women were not repressed.

About the time she reached her forty-fifth year, Mrs. Anderson began to have serious difficulties. There were "two or three years excessive menstrual flow, with attendant soreness." At that point, she became conscious of what turned out to be the growth of a fibroid uterine tumor (generally benign). Orgasm was seriously inhibited and she attributed the growth of the tumor to that lack of satisfaction, a lack, as we have seen, that she would frequently have intensely abhorred. Undoubtedly, however, the force of causation goes the other way, with the orgasm being prevented by pain during intercourse occasioned by the presence of the tumor. Here is how she described this period of time: "Began about 45th year to flow excessively for 5 & 6 days at menstrual period. Sometimes spend several days in bed; last day or two sometimes in much pain; always the same pain & soreness in lower front of abdomen. . . . At this time began to suffer from intercourse; unresponsive, would not recover from one experience till time for another. Congestion, pain in the back, unnerved, wretchedly unhappy and morbid . . ."

As the tumor became larger, starting about age forty-eight, the flow lessened, but an aversion to intercourse was still sustained because of the pain it caused. We remark in all of this the clear circumstance that regular intercourse was still taking place. However, Mrs. Anderson told Dr. Mosher that she kept her troubles to herself. She embarked on a mind-over-matter campaign to block the sensations of intercourse, thus avoiding the pain. But this physical trouble was not all that was going on at the time. She wrote of "much sorrow and misfortune in family history during these years – loss of money, first death of oldest son. Husband's health broken. He never really recovered." Meanwhile, she began medical treatment for the tumor and probably – coincidentally – went into full-fledged menopause at the same time. She reported that she took a certain pill three or four times a day for two years, after which the tumor was essentially gone. She returned to the doctor at the end of the third year, which would have been about age fifty-one, and there was still no sign of it. Of course, she credited the medicine with absorption of the tumor, but that is unlikely. There is no known chemical cure even now. Such fibroid tumors depend on estrogen, and with the curtailment of estrogen secretion in menopause, they often disappear by themselves. Nine years passed between the disappearance of the tumor and the session with Dr. Mosher, but the protocol gives us no information at all about the quality of life for Lillian Anderson during that last period.

In writing of her husband's difficulties during the worst years, Lillian credited him with being the "kindest and most chivalrous of men." She concluded in the following self-deprecating vein: "I often wonder whether I am responsible – whether I have been below normal and been a drain instead of a stimulant – whether nature made me for a good mother but did not fit me for a good wife."

NO! No, Lily, do not take the blame for this on yourself. You have definitely upheld your end of the bargain for all these years. During those critical six years, you were suffering, you were ill, you were in pain. Hector Anderson might be, as you said, the "kindest and most chivalrous of men," but he was not there for you in your hour of need. He continued to make unremitting sexual demands, as though nothing had changed, after you became uncharacteristically unresponsive and it was almost killing you. Perhaps you should have made more of an effort to discuss it with him, although that was not the kind of forward behavior expected of women in your day, but he also, without question, should have broached the subject with you so that you might have sought a solution together. He unfortunately was treating you not as a wife, as he might well have done, but as a Victorian wife.

Portrait 9: Deirdre Mueller[68]

Mrs. Mueller was probably forty-two when she filled out Dr. Mosher's questionnaire. The exact date is not given, but other information makes it highly probable that it was in 1892, making her one of the respondents from the early, Wisconsin phase of the study. Several of the responses, which were written by herself rather than second-hand by Dr. Mosher, give the impression of a basically cheerful outlook. For example, she spoke of her father as being "at 68, hale and hearty," and her mother as being "66, and very well indeed." However, fate dealt her one severe blow which, although papered over by her naturally upbeat orientation, remained an enduring sorrow.

In her answers to many of the dry, factual questions, she showed what might be a thoroughness, or fastidiousness, or perhaps a tongue-in-cheek lightness in responding to uninteresting questions with overly precise answers. For example, she gave her paternal grandmother's age at death as "96 years less 19 days." Perhaps there was a family bible available to her that was used for careful record keeping. Her father's age when married was "25 yrs. 7 months," whereas her paternal grandfather's was "26 yrs, 11 months," and so on. Besides the family bible or other record, she also took the trouble to get answers to questions about her mother from her mother herself. One interesting bit of information supplied by her mother was in answer to Dr. Mosher's question about "prenatal influences before your [Deirdre's] birth." All concerned believed that such influences on the physical health or character of the child were usual. She quoted her mother as follows:

> Life moved on in a quiet and systematic way, but brought me into contact with delightfully agreeable and congenial people outside my home-circle, and you do not need to be told that my home life has been from the first bright and cheery as a dear husband's unswerving and tenderest love could make it.

The last part is quintessentially Victorian; it could be a sentence out of Dickens.

68 Mosher 1980, Blank No. 12, pp. 128-139.

Picking out a few details of Mrs. Mueller's life before her marriage, we find here one of several cases among the Mosher women in which the consistent occurrence of severe menstrual pain totally disappeared after marriage. It is hard to think why this would be so except to conjecture that the effects may well have been psychological. Dr. Mosher had a long-term interest in menstrual pain and eventually published the illuminating results of an extensive study of patients.

Deirdre herself, born in 1850, was of Scotch-Irish and English parentage. Her husband, of Dutch and German descent, was ten years younger than she. They both went to Oswego Normal School so that, even considering the age difference, they may have met through community ties. She had further schooling in Ann Arbor and Cambridge, England and received a Bachelor's degree; he went to Cornell and Indiana and received a Master's. Deirdre said that her health before marriage was "generally delicate – Malaria, weak heart, tendency to hysteria." As to the latter condition, she was "on the whole, much quieter and better since marriage." This is our first hint that her young husband – only twenty-four when they married – was good for her.

We also learn that she had "a very complete knowledge" of sexual physiology before her marriage, which she "obtained from lady physicians who were my friends." Unlike the majority of the Mosher women, Deirdre married late – at age thirty-four – and therefore was more likely to have professional women as friends before her marriage and to be exposed to information about sexuality. It is very possible that acquiring a good deal of knowledge in this particular way was of benefit to her in contributing to a positive attitude toward sex, although we will see that such knowledge did not relate to the quality of sexual experience in the group of forty-five women as a whole.

Dr. Mosher asked if she habitually slept in the same bed with her husband and her reasons either for doing so or not. Her answer was:

> Yes . . . I sleep much better and feel altogether more comfortable. The first year . . . I had a separate bed, believing that was the right thing; but I abandoned it entirely before the end of the year.

We see two things here. First, the standard Victorian training apparently influenced her to the extent that she believed that separate beds would be the right thing. Second, the marital relation itself influenced her enough in the opposite direction to induce her to throw over that notion and please herself by joining her husband regularly in bed, which would not ordinarily be an easy change for a Victorian woman to make.

The Muellers had had one child by the time of the study, born at an unspecified time during the eight years they had been married. This was a boy. There were no other pregnancies. Mrs. Mueller said he was perfectly formed but very large – twelve pounds. The baby died during the birth process. She wrote that the doctor attributed the death to the length and severity of the labor. Her illness afterwards, no doubt affected in large measure by her grief, was also both long and severe. "I think I have never had quite the *strength* since." [Emphasis hers] She did not mention why there may have been only that one conception, but it is questionable now whether there were others, even after her participation in the study. How might the marriage itself and this tragic event have affected her experience of sexual relations? In particular, did the death of her child and the unlikelihood of further conceptions embitter her attitude?

She gave their frequency of intercourse as once or twice per month, with no indication that it had changed over the years. Asked whether she experienced desire, she entered simply, "Yes." How often? She answered somewhat vaguely that she thought it was more before and after menstruation. Mrs. Mueller did not volunteer any information in the questionnaire on whether or not she was trying to have more children. She did say, however, when asked if she ever used any means to prevent conception, that there was or had been – she does not say which – some "selection of time for intercourse."

To the question whether intercourse was agreeable to her or not, she again simply answered, "Yes." Did she always have what Dr. Mosher called a "venereal orgasm"? Her response was, "Almost invariably." One may well wonder whether Dr. Mosher's respondents fully understood what she meant by this terminology. Even the word "orgasm," let alone "venereal," might have been strange to these women, given their presumed lack of prior experience and even of second-hand knowledge. Deirdre did have knowledge, however, and although we cannot be sure that it included the concept of orgasm, or if she understood the meaning from her own marital experience, the follow-up questions leave no doubt that she was answering the question as Dr. Mosher meant it. Asked how she felt on the occasions when she did achieve orgasm, she replied, "Absolute physical harmony." And the next day? "Hard to say; often a greater feeling of strength and composure; sometimes, physical weariness." How about the occasions when she did not achieve orgasm? "Depressing and revolting." No mincing of words on that one, and therefore no doubt about the feelings. However, Mrs. Mueller apparently took these occasions in stride, and the adjustment was all the easier in that they did not occur very often. Deirdre stands as one example, in any case, in which a Victorian woman came to incorporate her sexuality as an integral part of her life and had expectations of it that rose to the psychological level of demands.

At the same time, Mrs. Mueller's desire and her positive experience of orgasm clearly did not lead her and her husband to have sex with great frequency – just a moderate once or twice per month. When asked what would be the ideal frequency, or "habit," she responded:

> No *habit* at all, but the most sensitive regard of each member of the couple for the personal feeling and desires and health of the other. In fact, pure and tender *love*, wide awake to the whole of life, should dictate marriage relations. [Emphasis hers.]

We have no way of being sure whether Mueller, her husband, went along with these wishes whole-heartedly, but it is important that he apparently did go along with them.

We also see here the apparent effect of the ethos of the romantic age in placing love in a position of supremacy. Love should motivate all marital behavior. Deirdre did not think that intercourse was necessary either to man or to woman. She did feel, however, that pleasure was a true purpose of intercourse – "Not sensual pleasure, but the pleasure of love." Love holds sway over biology: "True and passionate love . . . is the prime condition for a happy conception, I fancy." When asked what other reasons besides reproduction are sufficient to warrant intercourse, she answered, "I do not think this reason alone warrants it at all; I think it is only warranted as an expression of true and passionate love."

Deirdre Mueller experienced one very severe blow in her life but it apparently did not affect her love for her husband nor her ability or inclination to express that love in sexual communion.

Portrait 10: Irene Morrison[69]

Irene was born in 1855, received the normal schooling for the daughter of a farm family, went on to get a B. S. degree from Cornell University, taught school for a few years afterwards, and then got married. At the time of filling out Dr. Mosher's questionnaire, most probably in 1894, she had been married for fifteen years. Her husband was seven years older and also earned a B. S. degree from Cornell. He was a college professor at the time of the study.

We have noted in several of the portraits that aspects of the health or character of a child were often attributed by Victorians to events in the mother's life during pregnancy. Irene, in this case, noted that she had an aversion that was "absolutely uncontrollable" to a certain insect, millipedes. In answer to the question on prenatal influences, she explained that "the millipedes were thick that summer before my birth, and my mother disliked them very much." Her mother, unfortunately, had been a nervous invalid for twenty-two years, ever since her menopause. The family attributed her condition to the change of life itself. As moderns, we would expect that there must probably have been some other cause.

Like Deirdre Mueller, Irene had considerable knowledge of sexuality before she got married – in her case at age twenty-four. She had read some medical books but, more importantly, she gathered "a good deal of particular knowledge from my experience with the life on the farm, in seeing the farm animals during all processes of breeding." In addition to that, Irene was one of very few Mosher respondents who most probably was told about copulation by her mother.

By his choice, Irene and her husband did not regularly sleep in the same bed. Nevertheless, she gave their frequency of intercourse as twice per week "in the earlier years of married life" and about once per week during the last six years. Asked if she had ever used any means to prevent conception, she responded that she had not. Many of the women mentioned timing, at least, but she did not. She used douches for personal hygiene but had not taken contraceptive measures. In spite of this, the Morrisons had no children. Indeed, there were no conceptions at all. Unfortunately, Mrs. Morrison did not note this fact or remark upon it in any way, nor did she say whether they had been trying or would like to have

69 Mosher 1980, Blank No. 18, pp. 199-210.

children and, if not, why not. There is, moreover, nothing in her responses that we might use as a basis of speculation.

Sexual desire was not a part of her life. In response to the question on this topic, she wrote, "No especial desire for intercourse ever." Choosing to respond to the further question about when desire is experienced in relation to her period, she appended mildly, "But it seems more natural within ten days after menstruation." Thus, she does not appear to have been averse to having sex, or to have been bothered by it, or to consider it a nuisance; it simply did not seem to have been a major event – either positive or negative. There is then Dr. Mosher's other question about whether intercourse was agreeable to her or not. She wrote, "Sometimes agreeable, sometimes not, depending on physical condition." It seems, especially in light of her other responses, that Mrs. Morrison was interpreting this question a little differently from most of the other respondents. The others were reflecting on intercourse in general as they had experienced it and relating whether it had on the whole been pleasing or displeasing. Mrs. Morrison seems rather to have been relating the question to each occasion as it began to arise and telling Dr. Mosher how receptive she was on that occasion, so that the answer, "Sometimes agreeable, sometimes not," meant that receptivity depended on how she was feeling at the moment – on her physical condition.

One would expect that the frequency of her receptivity might well have depended on whether or not she commonly experienced orgasm. If she did not, it is understandable that sex would not have had great appeal. Therefore, given the lack of desire and a receptivity that was only occasional, a guess would be that orgasm must have been infrequent in her case or even absent altogether. The relevant questionnaire item was, "Do you always have a venereal orgasm?" Her answer was, "Usually." Did she truly understand what the question was getting at? She probably did. Her answer to the follow-up question on how she felt afterwards is:

> Sometimes a feeling of exhaustion but often followed by wakefulness and nervousness. But the nervousness is more pronounced when there is no venereal orgasm.

Later, she volunteered again that sexual intercourse made her nervous or irritable.

It seems, as it already has in other cases, that the frequent experience of orgasm does not necessarily imply either subsequent desire for intercourse or even reliably positive feelings about the prospect. At this point, Mrs. Morrison seemed to be cool toward marital sex – not an enthusiast. From the fact that she had no desire whatever and only sometimes found the prospect of sexual relations agreeable, one would be tempted to categorize her as a typical Victorian wife according to the traditional view and chalk up one point for the hypothesis of repression.

That, however, would be a mistake, and the key to understanding it lies in the fact that Irene Morrison did not interpret marital sex as essentially a physical experience. That aspect did not really register strongly on her consciousness. The entire subject matter for her was spiritual instead. She allowed that intercourse may be a physical necessity to man, but she viewed it as a spiritual necessity to woman – not just a spiritual experience, but a necessity.

> The marriage relation should be nearer than any other. Sexual intercourse is the means which brings this about. Loving relations have a right to exist between married people and these cannot exist in perfection without sexual intercourse to a moderate degree. This is the result of my experience. . . . To me, personally, [having sex] once a month . . . would keep alive in me the sense of nearness which I regard indispensable to a happy marriage.

She mentioned once a month as a basis, but on the subject of ideal frequency she added, as did so many of the others in the Mosher survey, "But *the* ideal must be a compromise between two and must be the best for *both*." [Emphasis hers.]

Whether by indoctrination or otherwise, and in spite of the frequent experience of orgasm, Mrs. Morrison was rather unmoved by the physical experience of sex. As she indicated, however, the result of her experience of marriage was that she placed a high value upon the sexual relation nevertheless. This was not just because her husband needed it or demanded it, but because she herself felt that it expressed her love, kept their nearness alive in her, and bound them together. Thus, contrary to first impressions, sexual relations occupied a much more important place in Mrs. Morrison's life and outlook than the conservative doctors of Chapter II would have preferred.

IV

The Victorian novels provide evidence

And so we turn to the novels. Here certainly is the source of most of our impressions about the lives of Victorian women. Perhaps these great works are not as widely read now as they were during the first half of the twentieth century, but still they rise to the surface in high school English classes and many are interpreted for millions of viewers in the modern cinema. The previous two chapters dealt with the strong advice given to middle-class Victorian women regarding how they should behave and the equally strong motivation of almost everyone around them to make sure that they conformed to that advice. The question is whether they did conform. Ordinarily, a large assortment of written documents of the period, taken together, would give us that information – newspapers, magazines, letters, contemporary histories, court records, scholarly books and articles, surveys, celebrity statements, and so on – but in this case they are inadequate. They are mainly silent on the subject of middle-class sex. The silence itself should be taken as evidence on the side of conformity – no smoke should mean no fire – but it is not decisive evidence because of the rigid taboos that existed against the public airing of sexual topics.

In this event, it is natural to make use of the art of the period, and especially the novels, as a source of information. Novels written during a certain period about life during that same period should present an accurate picture. Collectively, they should give subsequent readers a good idea of how ordinary people behaved, what were the corresponding norms, the salient preoccupations, and the differences in values across the generations that co-existed during the time portrayed. Some novels, of course, will be about special subgroups, such as the criminal underworld or the very rich, but many will be about a broad segment of the ordinary population that spans the social-class spectrum. If the novels tend to agree in their portrayal, there is every reason for substantial confidence in the picture they collectively paint. The Victorian novels should have a special advantage and a special disadvantage for this purpose. The advantage is that they tend to be (delightfully) long and to have huge casts of characters of different types, backgrounds, and outlooks, so that each novel packages a wealth of historical information. The disadvantage is that the taboos against the public airing of sexual topics might well be considered to make all the novels similar in an absence of the information we seek in the present case.

We will find that the norms against sexual content in fiction were not as thoroughly restrictive as one might guess from a superficial consideration. The novels do provide evidence pertinent to our quest.

The Compromise

We know that the prevailing morality not only condemned illicit sexual behavior but also prohibited talking about it, especially in the company of middle-class women. The virtue squad would consider sex in a novel to be scandalous and would raise such an outcry that sales of the novel would be seriously endangered. The standards governing just what was and was not acceptable were never explicitly codified, but, although always on the prudish side, they tended in general to be a little stricter during the middle Victorian period, roughly the 1850s through the mid-1890s, and a little looser both beforehand and afterwards.[1]

If the prevailing moral norms are to affect the content of fiction, they would ordinarily do so in one or both of two ways. The first and most common way is for the norms to be internalized by the authors themselves, so that the taboos are observed without drawing especial attention to themselves – a form of self-censorship. The second is enforcement through a medium. If authors are not inclined to conform, certain persons or institutions attempt to press them into

1 Tillotson 1954; Stang 1959; Trudgill 1976.

the mold. In the nineteenth century, both of these mechanisms were in evidence. From the turn of the century through the 1840s, Jane Austen, Walter Scott, Charles Dickens, and William Thackeray, for example, felt little or no desire to be any more daring in print than their general audience felt comfortable in reading. At the same time, the standards were not quite as strict then as they soon became, so that the degree of latitude they felt available to them was not distressingly confining. This does not mean that they wrote about sex with the abandon of a modern novelist but that they adhered to the moderately strict standards of the day without feeling much external pressure.[2]

Beginning in the late 1840s, with the tightening of the rules, even Dickens and Thackeray were criticized, and others such as Wilkie Collins, George Meredith, and Thomas Hardy came under extreme pressure. Still, if the medium through which the pressure was exerted had been the publishers and literary critics alone, as would ordinarily be the case, the writing of these and other authors would almost certainly have been at least somewhat different – for example in capturing the passion of intimate scenes. This is especially true in that the various publishers and critics were not equally eager to apply prudish standards. Some were inclined to be more liberal than others. As it happens, however, there was another medium of pressure, one that imposed severe constraints and that had more homogeneous influence. This was the Mudie Library.

During the 1840s, Charles Edward Mudie developed a commercial lending library for scientific books and novels, our particular concern being with the latter.[3] He bought up thousands of copies of the first printing of a great many novels, thus becoming extremely important to publishers, and rented them out to the general public. His business model was the precursor of the original Netflix model; that is, he charged a guinea (one pound plus one shilling) for a year's subscription, allowing customers to read one volume at a time, return it, borrow another, and get through as many volumes in a year as they could manage under this system. To maximize his profits, he forced publishers to publish novels in three volumes, so that different parts of the same copy of the same novel could be read by three paying customers at the same time. A

2 Tillotson 1954.

3 The discussion is based primarily on Landow 1972.

portion of the public read some of the novels in serialized form in the numerous literary magazines of the day, but most depended on books. The retail price of a novel in three volumes was about five times the cost of the same novel in one volume. Mudie bought them at a very substantial discount, but the cost to ordinary middle-class families put frequent book buying beyond their means. Thus, they depended on Mudie and his few competitors. Some citizens could even get through a large quantity of novels quite cheaply if they were fast readers and had the time to devote to it.

Although the Mudie Library operated mainly in England, it had a profound effect on America as well, in a way that particularly concerns our present subject. Mudie became a censor. Given his commercial respect for the prevailing norms, he refused to carry any novel that would in any passage bring a blush to the maiden cheek. Beginning in the 1850s, this concern was accentuated because of the rapidly growing practice of reading novels aloud in families. Critics could and did differ on the extent to which the maiden cheek should be an important critical criterion. For example, Mudie bought three hundred copies of George Meredith's *The Ordeal of Richard Feverel,* but after seeing the reviews and reading the novel himself, he refused to carry it. The section to which he and presumably his subscribers objected was one in which a woman, for various stuffy and selfish reasons, was persuaded by others to seduce a young man. In his 1959 book on the nineteenth-century English novel, Professor Richard Stang quoted from an article in the influential *Saturday Review* that was, in its own terms, quite favorable to Meredith's novel, although it would clearly be negative to Mudie:

> "He [Meredith] does not allow any conventional notions of impropriety to stand between him and the description of scenes he thinks necessary to carry out his main purpose. . . . There is much that is repulsive" in this section of the novel, but "it is the repulsiveness of a horrible truth. There is nothing shadowy, vague, or mock-moral about this portraiture of immorality. . . . We do not object to this. It is quite right that there

> should be men's novels, if only it is understood at the outset they are only meant for men."[4]

Here, the *Saturday Review* critic not only rejects the cheek of the Young Person[5] as the ultimate criterion but asserts the guideline, often echoed, that truth, or facts, are permissible as long as they are not made more repulsive than necessary. This benchmark of "fact" was important but by no means universal. Some critics were more squeamish in determining which factual events or descriptive details were "necessary," that is, some critics would prohibit the mention of most immoral behaviors even if the existence of that type of behavior were conceded to be a fact.

Professor Stang went on to cite another pertinent review:

> *Blackwood's*, for instance, found that the plot of *Yeast* [by Charles Kingsley], in which the daughter of a landowner falls in love with her father's gamekeeper [although he leaves the country and she dies before anything can come of it], was "really a little too much; for, if we consider it rightly, it implies an entire departure from the modesty of woman, not to say a depraved instinct. . . . Such things doubtless have taken place, but they are not to be mentioned with honour, or judged with leniency; and we cannot help thinking that the writer who unnecessarily brings forward such aberrations, and who treats them as if society were at fault in not recognizing unions of that kind, ought to be treated with severest censure."[6]

Thus, the critics differed among themselves on what was permissible in fiction. Mudie, however, was a homogeneous arbiter on the conservative side with vastly more power than any critic. His refusal to carry a novel could and did easily threaten the author with the difference between financial success and failure. Nevertheless, his influence, though great, was not complete. Novels

4 Stang 1959, p. 208, citing the *Saturday Review*.

5 This, rather than "maiden" is the original terminology of John Podsnap in Dickens' *Our Mutual Friend*, Chapter 11.

6 Stang 1959, pp. 217-218.

could still be published, as Meredith's was, and enjoy at least modest success outside of the Mudie orbit. We will see the results of this complexity of forces in the pages ahead.

Every important novelist of the period was attacked at some point – very often by potential publishers when the work was in manuscript – for lowering the standards of purity of the novel, sometimes for depicting crime, decadence, or similar immoral or disgusting topics and sometimes for drawing attention to sexual transgressions.[7] This in itself shows that the authors were not inclined to give in readily to the radically squeamish segment of the public. Moreover, they almost always fought back vigorously, often on the grounds that it was better to deal openly with factual immorality and unpleasantness than to sweep them under the rug. Somehow, in the end, the works in question did get published, even when including at least some of the content that was objectionable to conservatives. We must therefore expect, upon examining the novels, that the objections of the more squeamish moral policemen were not quite enough to prevent novelists totally from representing the sexual side of the world around them in print.

In fact, the record indicates that a compromise seems tacitly to have been struck, one that is important for our attack on the conflict between two theories of the sexuality of Victorian women. The writers could include immoral or unpleasant behavior that existed and contributed to a realistic picture of contemporary life but on three tough conditions. I mention the first two here and delay the third, *necessity*, until a bit later. First, *delicacy*: such subjects must be handled delicately, considerately, even obliquely. The public was easily shocked. Second, *expiation*: immoral behavior must not be supported. Those who sin should not evoke our sympathy and, even if they do, they must pay the penalty. There were conservative and liberal critics, but even the liberal ones imposed standards of delicacy and expiation that were constraining, especially in limiting the detail and vividness with which the writers were permitted to exercise their art on these subjects. [8] Nevertheless, the compromise makes it possible for us to guess that the collective picture painted by the major novelists must

7 Stang 1959, p. 217.

8 Tillotson 1954; Stang 1959.

faithfully capture the role of middle-class sexual activity in the system, even if detail and color are omitted. In other words, the silence imposed by the norms was severe but not absolute.

One consequence is that although fornication might, on this reasoning, be represented in a novel, it could never be appealing, and this also has substantial importance for our investigation. It suggests – even demonstrates – that the frequency of middle-class premarital sex must have been quite low. How does it do that? By what means?

The beauty of sex marks a distinct difference between the modern novel and the Victorian. In many modern novels, as we will see in a moment, the sexual relations become a component of the content of beauty. The sexual experiences are frequently uplifting, or at least meant to be. In the nineteenth century, however, fornication was distinctly immoral and consigned to ugliness. In large measure, the doctors, the clergymen, and the social opinion leaders considered fornication to be the manifestation of a base instinct. Religion was uplifting; animal behavior was degrading. For a nineteenth-century novelist not only to mention premarital sex but to dwell on it as a beautiful experience would have been such a gross violation of beliefs, norms, and respectable sensibilities as to make the manuscript not only unpublishable but burnable. If the book were somehow published, both the author and publisher would have been subject to prosecution.

Does this mean that there was very little beautiful premarital sex in middle-class Victorian reality? It probably does mean just that.

But before showing the logical connection, take a moment to consider the practical side of things. On the practical side, most of the premarital sex that existed in that severe normative regime and chaperoned environment would have resulted from one-shot seductions or capitulations to desire in which the woman was highly likely to feel scared, guilty, and confused. Beauty would hardly have had a chance. In practical terms, as well, prolonged illicit love affairs, where beauty might have prevailed, would have been extremely difficult to carry out in secret. Pragmatically speaking, it is doubtful whether widespread premarital sexual relations in the category of "beautiful" could have existed in Victorian times.

Turning from the practical to the logical, we can observe that whenever premarital sex truly is broadly accepted in a social system, and is quite common rather than exceptional, a good deal of it is highly likely to be appealing. That is in the nature of things. If this situation of acceptance had indeed been the case in the nineteenth century, it would have been problematic, to say the least, for the authorities to sustain a set of highly prudish norms governing social relations and, in particular, to enforce publishing taboos that ruled out beautiful sex. Beautiful sexual affairs, even if officially immoral, would have been pressed by the authors and some critics as fact, reality, commonly practiced, broadly accepted, and justifiable in a novel on those grounds. We cannot be certain at this point that appealing affairs would have been alluded to as such in nineteenth-century novels if they had occurred with some frequency in real life, but it is an eminently reasonable supposition. Let us assume for the moment that appealing rather than only shameful sex would indeed, under those accepting circumstances, have figured appreciably in the novels – and indulge me for trying your patience by returning to Logic 101:

> If a fair quantity of appealing affairs had existed, they would have been alluded to in the novels (the assumption we just made).
> They were not alluded to in the novels (this is jumping ahead of ourselves, but for a good purpose).
> Therefore, a fair quantity of appealing affairs did not exist.

> If premarital sex had been common, there would, in reality, have been a fair quantity of appealing affairs.
> A fair quantity of appealing affairs did not exist (just shown).
> Therefore, premarital sex was uncommon.

And thereby, as well, the model of repression is supported. Regarding the validity of the reasoning just offered, much hinges on whether we can justify the very first premise: the assumption that an appealing quality of sexual relations would have figured significantly in the novels if it had formed a non-negligible part of middle-class life. Support for this assumption is provided a bit later in the chapter. That support is of substantial importance because the above logic is tight, and the end result, as stated, is rigorous confirmation of the traditional view of repressed Victorian sexuality.

With a few minor changes, the same as has been elaborated above with respect to premarital sex may be said as well of adulterous sex.

Intimate relations within a marriage, however, might seem to be a different story. Such relations were not immoral. One might therefore expect to see at least a modest amount of married sexuality in the novels – or allusions to such activity at the very least. Taking a broader look, however, one must actually predict quite the opposite. Descriptions of appealing marital sex would have been unthinkable. The Victorians cared deeply about privacy. A firm distinction between the public and the private spheres is a major theme of Professor Karen Lystra's important book on relations between the sexes in Victorian times.[9] Professor Laura McCall concluded, based on a very extensive analysis of nineteenth-century novels and stories, that Victorians firmly believed that "expressions of [physical] love belong in the personal realm of imagination and in private spaces . . ."[10] Certainly, detailed or vivid descriptions of interaction in the marriage bed would have been considered grossly indelicate, which we have seen to be a major criterion of suitability. The maiden cheek would have burned intensely. Moreover, there would not have been a need and therefore a license to allude to it, even delicately. There would be no *necessity* for such references in the plot and, truly, no place for them.

The novels that are important for our subject are novels of romance. The plot or subplot generally has a young man and young woman endure a series of events that create suspense, and in the end, they acknowledge their deep love for one another and get married (or sometimes not, as in Trollope's *The Small House at Allington*). The end. We are formally satisfied. There generally is no interest whatever in what happens between them afterwards. Recall from the quoted passages above that the critics frequently used the term "necessary," meaning necessary to bring to the notice of the reader a true social condition that should have awareness and moral attention. Necessity was thus an important element of the compromise along with delicacy and expiation. In proper proportion and

9 Lystra 1992

10 McCall 1994, p. 80.

with delicacy, the author would inform or remind the reader of the factual composition of the relevant world. Marital sex, however, was not sinful or immoral and was very well known to be commonly practiced; the audience has no need to be informed, and there would be no point in describing or even alluding to it. From what we have seen, essentially all publishers and critics would flatly reject such allusions as being highly offensive and at the same time totally unnecessary. We are about to look closely at the novels to see just what they do and do not contain, but whereas it would not be surprising to find allusions to crime, for example, or abject poverty, decadence, premarital sex, adultery, or marital cruelty, there is no reason at all to anticipate allusions to marital sex.

Proceeding by sample survey

If a writer wanted to characterize the treatment of sexuality in Victorian novels – exactly the position I am in at this point – the obvious method would be to provide some sort of analytical structure and fill it with illustrations and quotes from the novels themselves. There are two fatal problems with this procedure. The first is a matter of objectivity. If I were to provide examples from this novel and that novel to make a case or prove a point, how would you know that I have not been biased, even unintentionally? If I am picking and choosing, how does the reader know that I have included, in just proportion, instances that might militate against my eventual conclusion as well as in favor of it? The second problem is a matter of negativity. Everyone knows that even if there is a little sex in Victorian novels, there is not much. But to demonstrate this, how does one show what is *not* there? It is extremely awkward and maybe not at all possible to use examples of text to show the extent to which sexual behavior was not present. The text never says, "At this point, they did not make mad, passionate, animal love."

The sample survey solves both of these difficulties.[11] Step one would be to define a population of novels that would satisfy what we want to mean by "the novels," that is, the group from which our impressions of middle-class Victorian

11 It is uncommon to address a survey to works of literature. Content analyses are plentiful, as for example that reported in McCall 1994. A survey is broader in scope. The present analysis in fact included several content analyses with their coding results given in Appendix III-B. The bulk of the information, however, comes from the wide range of precoded, forced-answer questionnaire items.

sexuality are primarily derived. Step two would be to take a random sample of those novels. Step three would be to administer a questionnaire or survey to those novels and/or to characters within them as respondents. An admirable way of getting information about the sexual behavior of Victorian women would be by survey – drawing a sample of real, live women and asking them to answer the questions in a questionnaire. The latter is exactly what was done for forty-five American women in the Mosher survey.

We are, of course, much too late to extend Dr. Mosher's work to a larger sample. What we do instead is to address the same kind of questionnaire to the characters in the Victorian novels, dealing afterwards with the question of whether their responses are equivalent to those that real people would have given. In this way, we solve the problem of objectivity by getting the same information from all of the relevant characters in all of the sampled novels. No picking and choosing. At the same time, we solve the problem of negativity by asking a question and permitting the character to say "No," meaning, "No, I did not do that." This is possible because various passages of text make it abundantly clear that nothing disreputable happened even though the absence of the behavior is not explicit and therefore cannot be demonstrated by a quote. Although not explicit, in other words, in almost all cases it is clear beyond a shadow of a doubt. As long as the sample was correctly selected and is, therefore, representative, this method enables universal statements – as for example, "There is very little voluntary premarital sex on the part of middle-class women in Victorian novels." Not only does the sample-survey method work to permit such statements, but it would in fact be very difficult to justify such statements rigorously by any other method.

The population I eventually decided on contains one hundred and ninety-five novels. Since I also decided to address the survey separately to "love couples" within the novels and there is an average of about four love couples per novel, that makes a total of 780 respondents.[12] The questionnaire is long – forty-six

12 See Appendix III-A. A love couple is defined as a pair of individuals who get married, or, who remain unmarried while at least one of the two is romantically attracted to the other, for love, lust, or convenience, including those who are seen to form a potentially adulterous pair.

questions in most cases and sixty in some.[13] To address the questionnaire to all respondents in the population would delay the publication of this book by about two years' worth of research hours. For reasons of this nature, we generally sample – in the knowledge that a random sample of decent size is very close to being as good as the whole population.

The population of novels from which the sample was drawn is given in Appendix I.[14] It contains all the novels I could find to read by the authors of the great nineteenth- and early twentieth-century texts – novels such as *Pride and Prejudice*, *Ivanhoe*, *David Copperfield*, *Vanity Fair*, *Middlemarch*, *Jane Eyre*, *Barchester Towers*, and *Tess of the d'Urbervilles.* There are thirteen novelists in all, including several known by the biographies to have been considered great by the other greats and who continued to be widely read long after their deaths. Several major novelists are omitted because they wrote of adventure or other themes rather than romance, including Stevenson, Conrad, Mark Twain, Melville, and Lewis Carroll. Also, because of the sampling method employed, several major authors were omitted because they wrote only one major novel – for example, Emily Brontë, the author of *Wuthering Heights.*

The sampling method itself presented a large and unfortunate difficulty. Since the novelists did not each write the same number of books, strict random sampling (for example, giving each of the one hundred and ninety-five novels a number and picking numbers out of a hat) would be likely to oversample some relative to others, yielding a lopsided rather than a true and useful representation. Anthony Trollope, for example, wrote forty-three novels, while Charlotte Brontë wrote only four and Austen, Thackeray, Gaskell, and Eliot six apiece. A strictly random sample would be likely to be heavy on Trollope, giving undue weight both to his particular approach and to the chronological stage of Victorianism that he represents. At the same time, many of these other writers might well be omitted altogether. In practical terms, there was no valid solution to this problem.

13 The questionnaire for the first love couple in a novel is included in Appendix III. It contains all sixty items. For the second and further love couples only the first forty-six items were used, the rest having to do with the novel in general rather than a particular love couple.

14 An inadvertent and unfortunate omission was Nathaniel Hawthorne.

The method I finally chose was to pick a strictly random sample of two novels from each of the thirteen authors. Instead of one good random sample of twenty-six novels, therefore, what we have is a pooling of thirteen small random samples of two novels each. Still, the method does have some of the important advantages conferred by probability theory.[15] The final sample of twenty-six novels on which the analysis is based is given in Appendix II. Appendix III-A gives the complete questionnaire.[16]

Sex in the novels

To put the treatment of nineteenth-century novels in perspective, I will provide several illustrations of the treatment of sex in modern novels. I do not offer the most graphic examples. It is more to the point to include, where relevant to the discussion, one or two fairly tame but nevertheless revealing texts.

Beginning with the phenomenon of desire, consider the following brief passage from Alison Lurie's 1965 novel of sexual awakening, *The Nowhere City*:

> They kissed long and deeply. "Is it always like this with you?"
> Ceci had shut her eyes; now she opened them again: wide, golden. "No," she said. "Sometimes." She raised her head slowly, sleepily, supporting it on one hand, yawned, smiled. "But I knew it was going to be like this for us."
> "How could you know that?"
> "Easy. Because I wanted you the first time I looked at you."[17]

15 While it does not result in a random sample of anything, the method has a strong feeling of being properly representative for our purpose and is not entirely divorced from probability theory. For example, if a given sexual behavior has a 10% probability of occurring in the novels of each author, the probability of missing it entirely by this sampling method is about .06; that is, we have a 94% chance of finding at least one instance. Moreover, the random selection of novels for each author means that estimation errors on the high side for one author are likely to be counterbalanced by estimates on the low side for another so that they would tend to "average out;" that is, the aggregate is unlikely to be affected by consistent distortion.

16 Also included in Appendix III-B is the "codebook" for the open-ended questions. In addition, I offer the complete data set as an Excel spreadsheet to all who are interested. Please write to lmohr@umich.edu.

17 Lurie 1965, p. 82.

We have seen that some nineteenth-century physicians taught that proper women had no desire at all. On the other hand, we have seen in portraits from the Mosher survey that many did feel desire and were quite aware of it. Lastly, we can appreciate that descriptions of female or even male desire would no doubt be considered indelicate by most nineteenth-century critics and readers. If it were deemed objectionable but not necessarily immoral, even allusions to desire, let alone descriptions, would be judged as "unnecessary" and therefore unwelcome. We should, therefore, expect to find very little sexual desire in the sample of novels.

In the survey, we ask the woman who forms part of the "love couple"[18] whether in her thoughts and feelings for the man there has been any sexual content. The twenty-six novels in the sample yield ninety-seven love couples. Of these, the answer is "No" for ninety-six of the women. The one exception occurs in *The Golden Bowl*, by Henry James. In this novel, Maggie Verver is married to the prince. Her physical desire towards him is mentioned explicitly several times. Once, it is stated that his approaching her in a physical way would melt her.[19] Although nothing like this ever occurs in the novels of James's contemporary and good friend William Dean Howells, who is also represented in our sample, we see that by 1904, when *The Golden Bowl* was published, such allusions were no longer considered prohibitively indelicate. Mudie had died in 1890 and his lending library was defeated by the growth of free, public libraries. It ceased operating in 1894.

Aside from this question about thoughts and feelings, we also asked whether either the man or the woman verbally expressed physical attraction or desire. The answer is yes in just five of the ninety-seven cases. Tellingly, all of these occurred either early in the period or very late, that is, during transition times when standards were strict, to be sure, in comparison with modern or eighteenth-century norms, but not as strict as in the middle Victorian decades. In three of the five cases, the man tries openly to seduce the woman, declaiming frequently about her attractions and charms. The woman in these three cases wants no part of it at all and strongly resists. Two of these are in Sir Walter

18 See Note 12 or Appendix III-A for the definition of "love couple."

19 James 2009, p. 254.

Scott's novel, *Woodstock*. Scott stood out as a notably decent, principled, and very proper human being and author. He was not writing to push against a current that he considered overly prudish, as we will find in the case of many of the mid-period novelists. Rather, he was chronicling the kinds of events that were accepted as existing at the time and were written about without particular notice.

The third case of desire expressed in the course of attempted seduction in our sample occurred in Dickens' early novel, *Nicholas Nickleby*, published in 1839. There, the arrogant, lewd, and villainous Sir Mulberry Hawk persistently and forcefully tries to overcome the resistance of Nicholas' sister, Kate, declaiming her attractions and charms without any apparent constraint or moral scruple. Kate is an early example of the "pure" Victorian woman, presaging the angel in the house and demonstrating that the change to a prudish moral code was in the process of evolving.[20] She successfully struggles against and escapes Sir Mulberry's presumptuous coercion, although not without suffering indignities. Such indelicate scenes do not occur in Dickens' later novels. Also in *Nicholas Nickleby*, the repulsive Miss Squeers admires the turn of Nicholas' leg, giving us the fourth instance of expression of attraction or desire – a comic and very mild one, as it happens, but still, a kind of indelicate allusion that is totally absent from the mid-period novels in the sample.

The last of the five examples occurs in *The Golden Bowl*. The prince, as we have seen, is married to Maggie Verver, but he is also loved by Maggie's close friend, Charlotte, who tells him at one crucial point, "I've wanted everything."[21] Again, all five of these instances are from the transition times. There are zero verbal expressions of physical attraction or desire in the sampled novels of the mid-Victorian period.

---

20 This is not to say that there were no earlier examples. Almost a hundred years earlier, in fact, all of the heroines in the novels of Fanny Burney and Samuel Richardson and even most of those in Smollett and Fielding were similarly chaste and virtuous. However, these characters existed side by side with others whose sexuality was considerably more relaxed. Virtuous fictional women were not invented in the early nineteenth century; it was then, however, that they became the rule rather than the exception and served as the models that exemplified the pretentions of the emerging moral code.

21 James 2009, p. 218.

One might expect desire to be expressed between engaged couples, looking forward to the wedding night and afterwards. This never occurs. Not one man or woman among the forty-one love couples who do get engaged expresses such a feeling or is reported to have a thought about the momentous wedding night or the physical intimacy anticipated in the marriage. This is a departure from the relative freedom of the previous century that illustrates well the change in norms governing publishing that was ushered in along with Queen Victoria.

Consider the following excerpt from Smollett's *Roderick Random*, published in 1748, in which Roderick has just married his beloved Narcissa and displays candidly the desire he felt beforehand and his anticipation of the wedding night:

> When she left the room, her face overspread with a blush that set all my blood in a state of fermentation, and made every pulse beat with tenfold vigour! She was so cruel as to let me remain in this condition a full half-hour: when, no longer able to restrain my impatience, I broke from the company, burst into her chamber, pushed out her confidante, and locked the door, and found her — O heaven and earth! — a feast a thousand times more delicious than my most sanguine hopes presaged! But, let me not profane the chaste mysteries of Hymen. I was the happiest of men![22]

Finally, even if the characters do not themselves express attraction or desire, the author might allude to it. That does happen in three cases besides the melting of Maggie that we touched upon earlier. Two occur in the sampled novels of Wilkie Collins. One is so innocent that no critic would have objected to it. It literally involves bringing a blush to the maiden cheek. The beautiful, deaf and dumb young heroine Madonna blushes deeply at the mention of Zack's attractiveness, Zack being the young man she secretly loves and who, unfortunately for her, turns out in the end to be her half-brother. There is a minor character named Francine de Sor in Collins' *I Say No* who is foreign born and clearly a person of vulgar instincts and predictably low character. She is unabashedly attracted to the clergyman Miles Mirabel and continually plots to win him for her

22 Smollett 1748, location 8553.

own. Collins indicates that she experiences "sensual passions" and "measureless desires."[23] The final case, like Madonna's blushing, is a borderline example of desire. In George Eliot's *Daniel Deronda*, the villain, Grandcourt, has a long-running affair with Lydia Glasher, persisting even after he marries Gwendolyn Harleth, a heroine of the novel. Lydia is said to have been Grandcourt's one great passion.

What we see with regard to desire, then, is that expressions of or allusions to it could be made early and late in the century, when the morality hawks were less exacting. During the middle decades, intimations of desire were very few and so tame as hardly to be noticeable. The exception is the sensual passions and measureless desires attributed to Francine de Sor. Somehow, Collins got away with that one.

We must conclude either that desire was very rarely felt by women (note that in five of the nine total instances just reviewed the desire or attraction was in fact experienced by men) or that sexual desire was frequently experienced by both men and women, but the constraints of delicacy and necessity served to limit its reporting. Which is it? Probably the latter. We may take for granted that there would be more desire in the system than actual sex. We will soon find, however, that the incidence of illicit sex in the novels is about equal to the incidence of desire, implying that the recording of desire is suppressed. Here, we most likely are witnessing an excellent example of the compromise in action, so that delicacy, along with the requirement for necessity, constrains the artistic portrayal of desire. The public would essentially be saying, "You may include – but with delicacy, of course – the sin itself (illicit intercourse) rather than allow us to avoid all knowledge of its existence in our midst, but you don't have to include the objectionable sidelights (such as desire)." We will see in Chapter VI that enough desire was expressed in love letters to convince us that there was a good deal of it around. That so little appears in the novels is an indication that the writers were constrained in this regard, probably uncomfortably constrained, by the requirements of delicacy and necessity. Still, the absence of desire contributes to the impression of "no sex" that the novels convey.

23 Collins 19??, p. 257. (Chapter XLII)

Raising our sights to bolder behavior, we may wonder whether there is any sexually charged touching among these couples. If allusion to desire in a novel would be considered indelicate and unnecessary, petting or just touching would be even more so.[24] If they do not commit the actual sin that most concerns the respectable public, the cheek of the young person demands that the mention of subordinate activity, though scandalous, is not to be condoned. It is, however, mentioned frequently in modern fiction. Consider for example this passage from Penelope Lively's novel, *The Photograph*:

> They climb: the steep grassy slope, the winding trail. "Does this thing have a name?" she asks. "They all have names. This is Cat Bells." There is soft, caressing wind, and sunlight that flees across the hillside. She comes close and wraps her arms around him. They kiss. Pressed up against him, she runs her hand down and finds his erection: "I think we'd better get off this mountain," she says.[25]

At least as often, the touching would be done by the man. This is from Sue Grafton's "alphabet" series of mysteries:

> At 10:00, when the phone rang, I knew it was him. . . . I reached over and picked up, saying, "Hey. . . . Where are you?"
> "Rosie's. Come join me."
> "You trust me to walk half a block by myself? It's pitchy dark outside."
> "I was going to meet you halfway."
> "Why don't you go the whole distance and meet me here."
> "We can do that later. For now, I think we should sit and stare into each other's eyes while I put a hand up your skirt."
> "Give me five minutes. I'll step out of my underwear."
> "Make it three. I've missed you."
> "I've missed you, too."

---

24 This does not include sensual touching of the hand, which occurs with great frequency in Victorian novels. For some reason, this slight violation of feminine modesty in a fictional portrayal was universally condoned.

25 Lively 2003, p. 192.

> By the time I locked the door behind me and reached the front gate, he was waiting on the other side of Henry's wrought-iron fence. . . . I slid my arms around his neck. He tilted his head and ran his mouth down along my throat and across my collarbone. The fence pales were cold, blunt-tipped spears that pressed against my ribs. He rubbed his hands up and down my arms. "You're cold. You should have a jacket on."
> "Don't need one. I have you."
> "That you do," he said smiling. He eased a hand between the fence pales, ran his fingers under my skirt and up between my legs. I heard him catch his breath and then he made a low sound in his throat.
> "Told you."
> "I thought it was a metaphor."
> "What do either of us know about metaphors?"[26]

As it happens, this particular instance is of interest because the man in early Victorian times would not have caught his breath in surprise. In his book, *The Other Victorians*, Steven Marcus brought to our attention the lengthy manuscript called *My Secret Life*, written by a wealthy, sexually obsessed, anonymous Victorian and existing in very few copies. Warning: the sexual terminology in this work is explicit. At one point in his extensive and informative analysis of *My Secret Life*, Marcus reports:

> We learn as well that during the early part of the period women, "even ladies," wore no drawers. Some time after the turn of the middle of the century, women began to wear undergarments, and this change in fashion is not welcomed by our author. "More and more this fashion of wearing drawers seems to be spreading," he complains in Volume IX. "Formerly no woman wore them, but now whether lady, servant, or whore, they all wear them. I find they hinder those comfortable chance feels of bum and cunt, of which I have had so many."[27]

26 Grafton 2004. pp. 244-245.

27 Marcus 1966, p. 98.

Quite aside from *My Secret Life*, we see what is likely to occur in fiction when its social setting accepts sexuality in its various forms and feels little compulsion to suppress it. The nineteenth century was different. In the entire sample of novels and love couples, there is only one instance of touching – a very mild instance to be sure. It is our old friend Francine de Sor. "Without waiting for it to be offered, she took Mirabel's arm, and pressed it to her breast as they slowly walked on."[28] If delicacy constrained the chronicling of desire, it would certainly most severely constrain descriptions of petting. The question, though, is whether the compromise is functioning to cover up a fairly common behavior or is simply reflecting the true state of a world in which sexual touching was vanishingly rare. Love letters that we will treat in Chapter VI suggest that there was a moderate amount of petting in America among committed or engaged couples but little among others, so that its scarcity in the novels may well be due to actual absence rather than imposed constraints on writers. There is, unfortunately, no comparable record for Britain, where most of our novels take place. At any rate, the quantity of sexual touching in the novels rounds to zero.

There are forty-four marriages among the love couples in the sampled novels. In none of these cases is there a reference to the events of the wedding night, nor is there ever a description of the morning after in terms of the feelings that linger in the wake of such events. In thirteen of the forty-four cases, children are produced. In none of those thirteen cases is there a reference to the physical experiences or love passages that brought the children into being. They simply appear. Children, it seems, are one of the phenomena that somehow tend to materialize after a marriage. We will soon see that there are, in addition, a number of instances of unmarried sex, and they also sometimes result in children. Not only is there no reference whatever to the love act that produced those children, but in several of the cases, the only way in which the reader can tell that sexual intercourse has taken place is by the revelation of a pregnancy or the appearance of a child.

Lastly, in none of the marriages or cases of illicit sex in the sample is there a reference to the quality of the intimacy, whether good, bad, or indifferent. The reader often comes to appreciate, with regard to many of these love couples,

28 Collins 19??, p. 257. (Chapter XLII)

that their long-awaited physical union must have been an intense and lovely experience. To record it, there would be no need to be vulgar or even graphic. The description could be gentle.

In his early work, *Goodbye, Columbus*, for example, Philip Roth was more gentle than he became in the later novels:

> Later that night, Brenda and I made love, our first time. We were sitting on the sofa in the television room and for some ten minutes had not spoken a word to each other. . . . When I began to unbutton her dress she resisted me, and I like to think it was because she knew how lovely she looked in it. But she looked lovely, my Brenda, anyway, and we folded it carefully and held each other close and soon there we were, Brenda falling, slowly but with a smile, and me rising.
>
> How can I describe loving Brenda? It was so sweet, as though I'd finally scored that twenty-first point.[29]

This twentieth-century excerpt alludes to the quality of the experience, which was appealing. In contrast, the text of our nineteenth-century novels never provides even the faintest suggestion that there might have been beauty in a coming together of the love couple – even the recently married, passionately attracted love couple.

The scarcity of intimations of desire, the absence of touching, the complete absence of anticipation of marital sex, the complete absence of reference to the consummation of a marriage or love affair or the conceiving of children, the complete absence of any reference to the quality of a sexual encounter – all of these absences combine to give to the reader the striking impression that there is simply no sex in Victorian novels. You read and read and eventually develop the consciousness that these people, amazing as it may seem, were almost unbelievably proper and lived their lives with no attention to and almost no experience of sex. The suggestion must occur that there may well have been a corresponding lack of sex in Victorian society itself. That would be making a leap from fiction to reality – from the novels to the real world. The leap may

29 Roth 1963, pp. 32-33.

indeed be a valid one, or close to it. It is wrong, however, to make the jump. That is because all of these absences were governed by the strictures of delicacy and necessity. There was no necessity of bringing sexual touching and so forth to the attention of the reading public, thereby severely threatening a blush on the cheek of the young person, and therefore no license to do so. The taboos imposed a silence on these matters regardless of the rate at which they might have transpired in the real world. In other words, while the fictional silence on these particular subjects creates an exceptionally strong impression of prudery, it tells us little or nothing for sure about actual behavior.

How would Victorians themselves have reacted to the absences I have just pointed out? We can only guess at this point, but there is a reasonable inference to be made, and it speaks more persuasively to the question of Victorian behavior than do the absences themselves. These novels were immensely popular. The reading public could hardly wait for the next book from one of our authors or the next installment of one of their novels in a monthly magazine. Mudie got rich. If this public had been well aware that the missing sexuality was actually prominent in their real world, the books would have seemed like fake propriety – a prudish, unrealistic avoidance. It is hard to imagine that the audience would have been so avid and the books so popular. "Where and when are they talking about? What world are they in? This stuff is out of touch with reality!" The inference based on these conjectures is that what Victorians were reading was a just reflection of behavior in their everyday world, that is, that there was as little illicit sex in reality as there was in the fiction. In that case, reading the novels would have been quite comfortable and also deeply satisfying, given the monumental talent of the writers.

Sexual intercourse itself is a different matter. Unless it occurred between people who were married to each other, it was a crime, and it was sinful. On that basis, there were good grounds for bringing it to light – revealing it with delicacy, of course, under the onerous constraint of the maiden cheek, as well as under the imperative of expiation. These apparently were the terms of the compromise worked out over time. Unlike desire, touching, and the other subordinate sexual behaviors, however, the disqualifier of necessity does not apply. The sinful and criminal nature of fornication allowed that it was necessary to bring it to light. On this basis, then, we should expect many more allusions to illicit sexual intercourse in the novels than to the subordinate behaviors reviewed. That is exactly what we do find.

There are five cases within the sample in which a man tries to get an unwilling woman to have sex with him. This treatment would seem to pierce the boundary of delicacy. However, three of the five are early examples. We have noted them before in connection with desire. Two are in Scott's *Woodstock* (1826), and one, Sir Mulberry Hawk and Kate Nickleby, is in Dickens' novel of 1839. During that transitional period from post-Restoration culture to deep Victorian, the constraints on novelists were looser than they soon became.

The fourth of the five cases occurs in Dickens' much later novel, *Hard Times* (1854). In that novel, Louisa Bounderby is in a very unsuitable and unhappy marriage. James Harthouse falls in love with her and tries to get her to elope with him, finally expecting her to join him in a hotel room on the appointed night. She does not, however, arrive. Unlike the earlier cases, there is nothing explicitly about sex here, only love and elopement, yet, given the hotel room and the whole idea of eloping, it is clear to both the characters and the reader that adultery is what is being urged. Harthouse does not then die for the sin of attempted seduction into adultery. He is crushed and defeated and leaves for the Middle East. Had he been successful in his aim, it would certainly have been different for these lovers. Paying dearly for the sin would then have been required for both Louisa and James.

The fifth case is the famous rape in Thomas Hardy's *Tess of the d'Urbervilles* (1891). Alec d'Urberville leads the innocent Tess into a foggy wood and goes off for a while, leaving her to sleep on the ground under his coat. He returns and lies down with her. Later, she has a child. The scene is handled with such delicacy that it is ultimately uncertain what actually happened, in particular whether he really did rape her or just aroused and seduced her. In the end, Tess kills Alec and is hanged. That Alec the villain must die is readily understood, but the sexual sins of Tess have been forced upon her by circumstances that left her no real alternative. She is a highly sympathetic character. Yet, she must die, both for the sin of illicit sex and the crime of murder.

We recognize here that although desire, touching, anticipation, and the quality of sexual encounters were forbidden, assaults on women by men could be conveyed in fiction, even in the middle Victorian period. They had to be presented in such a way as to avoid precipitating a blush on the maiden cheek, which would be no easy task, but reputable publishers and even Mudie would in the end accept such accounts.

In the knowledge that justifying the inclusion of such incidents depended on their factual correspondence with reality, I suggest that writers would have exercised this limited freedom in rough proportion to the frequency and importance of such events in the real world around them. If they were present but rare in reality, for example, they would be present but rare in the novels, with each author being influenced by the guideline. Surely, one cannot infer from the novels to the society in exact percentages, but one can see that we would derive a different feel for the practices of the times if such events occurred, for example, two or three times in almost every novel in the sample. The strong impression would then be that they must have been quite a common feature of Victorian life. What we actually find, however, is only five and, more to the point, only two such incidents in the sampled novels published after 1840. If the novels do indeed reflect reality – and I am in the process of making the case that they do – one infers that there was very little of such behavior in Victorian times.

The incidents just reviewed have been attempts at seduction or coercion. More often, no doubt, the hearts and minds of both man and woman would have tended in the same direction.

Here is a modern example from A. S. Byatt's 1991 novel, *Possession: A Romance*:

> "No, that's why I---"
> "Feel safe with me---"
> "Oh no. Oh no. I love you. I think I'd rather I didn't."
> "I love you," said Roland. "It isn't convenient. Not now I've acquired a future. But that's how it is. In the worst way. All the things we – we

> grew up not believing in. Total obsession, night and day. When I see you, you look *alive* and everything else – fades. All that." . . .
> Cold hand met cold hand.
> "Let's get into bed," said Roland. "We can work it out."
> "I'm afraid of that too."
> "What a coward you are after all. I'll take care of you, Maud."
> So they took off their unaccustomed clothes, Cropper's multicoloured lendings, and climbed naked inside the curtains and into the depths of the feather bed and blew out the candle. And very slowly and with infinite gentle delays and delicate diversions and variations of indirect assault Roland finally, to use an outdated phrase, entered and took possession of all her white coolness that grew warm against him, so that there seemed to be no boundaries, and he heard, towards dawn, from a long way off, her clear voice crying out, uninhibited, unashamed, in pleasure and triumph.[30]

There are nine instances of unmarried sex in the sample in which the woman enters into the relation voluntarily.[31] I want to give the flavor of these encounters because they are so different from what we experience in the novels of today. One instance occurs in a very early novel, Jane Austen's *Pride and Prejudice*, and two in very late ones, Henry James' *The Ambassadors* and *The Golden Bowl*, leaving six in the middle period.

One might tend to think of Jane Austen as the most proper of all nineteenth-century novelists, but, in fact, in *Pride and Prejudice* Lydia and Wickham do elope, not to get married but to live together in sin. Furthermore, they do not die. Arrangements are presently made to enable them to get married, and the delayed marriage sets matters to right. Lydia is not ruined for life, as would have been the case in a novel after 1840. This may be seen as a reflection of the standards of behavior – the moral code in force – around 1813, when *Pride and Prejudice* was published.

30 Byatt 1991, pp. 550-551.

31 There is in fact a tenth case, the bigamous marriage of Nancy and Laban in Howells' *The Leatherwood God*, but I omit it from consideration because everybody believed that Nancy's first husband was dead.

The situation is similar in the examples from James. In *The Ambassadors*, Chad and Madame De Vionnet not only are not married to each other, but Madame De Vionnet is still officially married to someone else. In both of these cases – Austen and James – the sexual encounter is only alluded to and not described, so that substantial delicacy is implemented. Atonement for the sin, however, is not demanded in these transitional periods. As with Lydia and Wickham, nothing particularly bad happens to Chad and Madame De Vionnet. Finally, in *The Golden Bowl*, Charlotte and the prince have apparently had a previous affair when both were unmarried, and now they apparently have another sexual encounter when each is married to someone else. I say "apparently" twice because delicacy leads James to convey these events in language that enables a very high probability that they occurred, but not absolute certainty. Planning to spend the afternoon at an inn – an inn to which they have been together in the earlier days – Charlotte says, "These days, yesterday, last night, this morning, I've wanted everything." And the prince replies, "You shall HAVE everything."[32] Again, in this case, there is no real atonement. Astutely managed by Maggie, Charlotte and her husband, Mr. Verver, abandon England for America, leaving Maggie and the prince alone together and on track to enjoy a satisfying marital relationship.

For the six cases of voluntary illicit sex in the middle period, however, there is punishment in addition to the comparably oblique treatment of the actual sex. Mary in Collins' *Hide and Seek*, Feemy in Trollope's *The Macdermots of Ballycloran*, and Fannie in Hardy's *Far from the Madding Crowd* all become pregnant. In spite of the reader's sympathy with these women, and especially with Fannie, they all die an early death. The three others suffer a fate worse than death in the eyes of the respectable Victorian middle class, worse in part because it is inflicted and enforced by the social system itself. These dire consequences are more certain than death, so that the warning to others by their example is more immediate and more threatening. The offending women are banished from polite society forever. Sara Jethro in Collins' *I Say No* is a self-imposed outcast. She can barely get herself to talk to any respectable person because she knows that they would not touch her if they knew of her sin. Moreover, in her particular case, she is haunted by guilt and oppressed by the knowledge that she was responsible in

32 James book 3 end of chapter 9.

large measure for the suicide of the man she truly loved. In Meredith's *Lord Ormont and His Aminta,* the pair in the title are married, but Aminta, who is treated shabbily by her Lord, falls in love, over time, with young Matthew Weyburn. In these circumstances, the young couple cannot possibly unite and manage a decent life. The solution is to flee not only polite society but all British society by taking up life in Switzerland.

The most interesting case is that of Lydia Glasher in *Daniel Deronda* by George Eliot. She has left her husband to become the mistress of the villain Henleigh Grandcourt, bearing him four children and expecting them to inherit his wealth. These expectations are threatened when Grandcourt marries the heroine, Gwendolyn Harleth. However, Grandcourt badly mistreats Gwendolyn, and she grows to hate him. They have no children together. Grandcourt then dies in a boating accident, and it emerges that he leaves his name and the bulk of his estate to his and Lydia's illegitimate son. Lydia is a minor character. If she had entered into an illicit relationship as a major character, she undoubtedly would have died for her sin and there never would have been four children – perhaps just one – but her role in the novel is dominated by her status as a mistress. As such, she became part of the double standard. It was known that some men kept mistresses. The dire punishment for the woman was not death but ostracism. In the division of women into the respectable and the depraved, the Madonnas and the Magdalens, mistresses were automatically placed in the latter category – no matter who they were or where they started out. Grandcourt himself is not ostracized; that is part of the double standard. He just dies.

The impression one gets from pleasure reading is that there is no sex in Victorian novels, but we have seen that this is not accurate. It is misleading. The impression results mainly from the requirement for delicacy. Within that hallmarking and very severe constraint, rape and seduction could nevertheless be exposed, as well as voluntary, illicit sexual union.[33] What we

33 In the nine instances of illicit sexual union, all of the women except two were middle class. Mme. De Vionnet in *The Ambassadors* can be considered upper class, and Fannie, in *Far from the Madding Crowd*, was working class. That matters very little in the novels, however, because the characters tend strongly to be treated as subject to middle-class morality no matter who they are. Martha and Jem in Gaskell's *Cranford*, for example, are both working class, and as a plighted pair, one would not be surprised if they had sex before the wedding. In fact, in the movie version they do (Curtis and Hudson 2008), but not in the novel. They are held to the standards of the author and her audience, not their own.

find, in sum – by no means a novel finding in literary scholarship – is that there is definite sexual content in Victorian novels, even voluntary sex on the part of middle-class women and even when sex is defined as coitus and not loosely defined to include kissing and blushing. Therefore, any lack of sex in the novels is not due completely to constraints forced upon the authors by Mudie and the critics. The examples above show that Victorian novelists could and did write about sex, even if the modes of expression they were compelled to use were far from explicit.

At the same time as we see that there is permissible illicit sex in Victorian novels, however, we also become aware that there is very little of it. In the findings recorded above, fewer than ten percent of sampled love couples, as defined, are involved in rape, attempted seduction, or voluntary intercourse during the middle period – the 1850s through the mid-1890s. Considering voluntary intercourse alone, fewer than ten percent of the sampled women participate in voluntary sex over the full historical range of the novels, including the early and late transitional periods. One might object that there is probably a lot more sex in Victorian novels than the instances cited but that they occur outside of the observed sample. That is true,[34] but our inference would be that for every love couple outside of the sample that is what we might call sexually active, there are at least nine love couples that could be but are not.

While the novels in the universe from which we sampled were widely read both in Britain and America, it is true that eleven of the authors were British and only two were American. The scholar Laura McCall helps to fill in our picture by having conducted an analysis of 304 female characters extracted from 104 American novels and stories published between 1820 and 1860. In her 1994 article, McCall categorized fifteen percent of the women as "impure." This number appears to be somewhat greater than our own finding. However, McCall's definition of impure was broad. It included not only sexual relations outside of marriage, but contemplating such a relation even if it were not consummated, and a woman trying to break up a relationship

34 For the interested reader, several of the novels of the period come quickly to mind: Gaskell's *Ruth* and *Mary Barton*, Hawthorne's *The Scarlet Letter*, Trollope's *The Vicar of Bullhampton* and *Dr. Wortle's School*, Eliot's *Adam Bede*, Kate Chopin's *The Awakening*, Hardy's *Jude the Obscure*, Olive Schreiner's *The Story of an African Farm*, and James' *The Wings of the Dove*. There are more.

between couples who were engaged or married in the hope of winning the man for herself.[35] Although there are differences in the time period covered and in exactly what is counted, we see both that there is rough conformity between the two studies in finding only a small quantity of actual, illicit sex and rough conformity, as well, between British and American writers. Thus, if we can accept the fiction as painting a faithful picture of reality, we would conclude that the reality consisted of both a very small amount of serious illicit sex and a quantity that was approximately the same in both geographic venues.

Returning to our inspection of the sample of novels, a rather bold but still tentative conclusion at this point is that the small amount of intercourse and seduction in the novels reflects a correspondingly small amount of sexual activity in Victorian life. Repression prevailed. We are led to this tentative conclusion in a three-step process. First, the novelists were permitted to write (with delicacy) about such behavior if it was faithful to reality and not just, for example, an attempt to be revolutionary. Second, with this permission, they included only a very small amount of sexual activity. And third, that was their picture of life. They might have written about a lot more of it, but they would have been slammed by the critics if such amounts had been unrealistic. Further, the conclusion is robustly reinforced by two subsidiary arguments: the logical demonstration offered earlier regarding the absence of appealing sexual encounters and by the great popularity of these essentially sexless novels among contemporary Victorians.

A question of information might arise. The question would be whether the novelists, although they would not intentionally either exaggerate or minimize, could know enough to have a realistic picture of how much illicit sex there actually was in the system. After all, it is the kind of thing that people try hard to keep secret. It is well to keep in mind, however, that the level of such behavior in Victorian times would be at least roughly observable. That is because coitus without good contraceptive devices tends to result in pregnancies, and pregnancies are observable. They are observable in women's bodies, in sudden lengthy trips out of town, in hastily arranged marriages, in births too soon after

35 McCall 1994, p. 83.

weddings, and in illegitimate babies. Unlike the present day, there were virtually no effective contraceptive devices readily available to Victorian lovers. The only real possibility was withdrawal, and that is much less likely to be employed by scared youngsters overcome by desire than by established married couples. The prevalence of these pregnancies would indicate the approximate level of premarital sex in the system.

My conclusion above was that finding some but only a very small amount of illicit sex in the sampled Victorian novels means that there was some but only a very small amount of illicit sex in the real Victorian world. This is, of course, an important conclusion for us because it gives strong support to the repression model, thus going far toward clearing up the mystery. But this is using fiction to demonstrate reality, and for that reason the conclusion needs to be bolstered.

We have seen that if there had been a much larger amount of illicit sex in the real Victorian world, it is highly unlikely that these novels would have been so popular. That is a reasonable bolster. But besides the audience, there were also the authors. If there had been a lot more sex in the system, it is inconceivable that these particular novelists would have distorted that reality by writing about so little of it. The fact is that they strained at the ropes. Collins, Meredith, Hardy, Gaskell, Eliot – they all pushed outward against the prudish boundaries. The historical record as it stands shows their rebellion against the squeamishness that did exist. Their principles led them to try their best to write about the reality they knew and to resist the pressures to distort it by toning it down. If what actually existed was a large amount of illicit sex all around them and if the moral policemen had allowed them to paint the picture as long as it were faithful to reality, then the social and artistic principles of these authors would have yielded a large amount of illicit sex in the novels. It is not what we do see in the novels, and therefore it is not what existed in the social reality.

But it is not only these particular authors. There is a general principle here. All evidence points to the fact that a loosening of sexual *behavior* in the system is followed by a loosening of the norms governing publication. Consider the following examples in which rules governing social and literary behavior adjusted themselves to actual moral practice in the community. The scholars Daniel Scott Smith and Michael Hindus present good data to show that as the general Puritan influence waned in America in the late seventeenth century, illicit sexual activity increased and the punishments of the church for those offenses became gradually less severe, showing the movement of social norms in response to actual practice.[36] With the Restoration of the monarchy and crowning of Charles II in England in 1660-1661, morality sank and the resulting change in norms permitted the bawdy literature of Restoration comedy to flourish.

Recognizing the persistence of these looser morals throughout the eighteenth century, we saw in Chapter II that toward the end of the century, when the rate of premarital sexual relations was still high, the novel *Pamela* (1740), with its intense and salient sexual preoccupation, could be recommended from the pulpit. True, the novel was supposed to be morally uplifting (recall the subtitle, *Virtue Rewarded)*, but it also dwelled endlessly on seduction. In our own examples, we found that in the early 1800s, when sexual behavior still had some of its eighteenth-century permissiveness, Jane Austen could write about illicit sexual activity with protagonists going unpunished. In the early 1900s, a transition time marked by middle-class women joining the work force and going to college, pleasure seeking among the urban working-class, and married sex taking place increasingly for pleasure rather than procreation,[37] Henry James could do the same. With the significant expansion of premarital sex after the First World War, the publisher of D. H. Lawrence's *Lady Chatterly's Lover* could be tried by jury for obscenity, found not guilty, and could immediately sell thousands of copies to the general public. The next dramatic expansion of nonmarital sexual activity, in the 1960s, was followed by the breathtaking exercise of freedom to represent sex in fiction, cable television, and the cinema that we witness today.

These have all been examples in which the rules relating to sexually related publishing either remained lax or, especially, loosened substantially, depending on what people were actually doing sexually in the social system. This is not to claim that

36 Smith and Hindus 1975, pp. 553-555.

37 D'Emilio and Freedman 1988, pp.171-201.

recognized moral norms of any sort always follow in time rather than precede the corresponding behavioral practice, but to make a narrower point. It appears that the norms governing publication in particular – just what it is permissible to represent in print, film, conversation, and otherwise – tend to follow behavioral practice rather than evolving independently and influencing, in turn, how people behave. I will pick up that thread in just a moment, but first a very brief digression to pick up another thread that was intentionally dropped a few pages back.

In the last two examples above, we saw that sharp changes in actual sexual behavior patterns after the First World War and during the 1960s permitted equally sharp changes in what could be published. In particular, I want to draw attention to the fact that one of the kinds of things that could be published, or shown in film, was sex as a beautiful experience. That was pretty new. Premarital sex was no longer consigned to ugliness. Projecting that – as well as the general idea in all of these examples – onto the nineteenth century, we would infer that if in that Victorian century there had been a similar broad acceptance and common practice of premarital sexual affairs among couples in love, we would similarly witness sexual relations as an element of beauty in Victorian literature. This is important because it provides support for the key first premise in the logical demonstration that I offered earlier. I repeat it here for convenience.

> If a fair quantity of appealing affairs had existed [as in the 1920s and 1960s], they would have been alluded to in the novels. (Just supported.)
> They were not alluded to in the novels.
> Therefore, a fair quantity of appealing affairs did not exist.
>
> If premarital sex had been common, there would in reality have been a fair quantity of appealing affairs.
> A fair quantity of appealing affairs did not exist. (Just shown.)
> Therefore, premarital sex was uncommon. (Repression prevailed.)

The unanimity of the range of historical examples offered above does not necessarily prove that if a substantial amount of premarital and extramarital sexual intercourse had been socially accepted in the mid-nineteenth century, the social rules regulating sex in literature would have been more relaxed. Clearly, however, it does argue strongly for that conclusion.

And now, back to the fiction-to-reality claim we arrived at earlier, namely, that finding some but only a very small amount of illicit sex in the sampled Victorian novels means that there was only a very small amount of illicit sex in the real Victorian world. We can now support that claim by supposing that the opposite were true (that is, a substantial amount of illicit sex did exist in the Victorian reality) and rejecting that supposition. The model is the following: If you had flipped the switch, the light would certainly have gone on (we accept this to be true). But the light did not go on. Therefore, you could not have flipped the switch. In our case: If there had indeed been a substantial amount of illicit sex in the Victorian reality, the rules would have been different, the authors would have taken advantage of the relaxed rules, and the novels would have been quite rich in sexual content. But they are not. Therefore – necessarily – there could not have been a substantial amount of illicit sex in the Victorian reality. Again, repression is seen to have prevailed.

I have been using the content of the novels and what we know about the Victorian novelists and critics to show that the traditional stereotype of Victorian sexual repression is valid. Several strands have led to the same conclusion – the popularity of the novels, the absence in them of sex as an appealing experience, the principle that moral norms in published work tend to follow in time the behavior they supposedly portray, and the artistic motivations of the writers. None of these strands in itself constitutes an airtight proof. It should count heavily, however, that each is persuasive on the surface and that there are so many of them, all tending in the same direction.

As it happens, there is also indirect statistical validation beyond the direct evidence from the prebridal pregnancy rates. The large and impressive Kinsey report on women, published in 1953, covered a small segment of individuals born before 1900. Since the interviews were carried out in the mid-1940s, this subset of women would, for the most part, have been born in the decades of the 1890s and 1880s; their coming of age would have been very late in the Victorian period when the moral code was relaxing. The authors of the report found that among women in this early subset who were unmarried by the age of twenty-five, fourteen percent had had premarital coitus, which I would consider to be a "small" amount, showing the effects of repression. (The figure for those born between 1900 and 1910, coming of age after the First World War, was thirty-six percent, which I would consider "substantial.")[38] The Kinsey finding shows that our number of roughly ten percent based on a sample survey of the novels is about right, considering not only that the Kinsey women were born later than the characters in the Victorian novels but that they included women from the working-class as well as the middle class. The Kinsey Report, in other words, gives us confidence that the sample survey of the novels yields data we can count on. And there is more. An extensive survey of one thousand married women was carried out by Dr. Katharine Davis in 1920, the women being mostly middle class and having been born, on average, in 1882. This study found that just over seven percent of the women had had intercourse between age fourteen and marriage.[39]

The conclusion once more, based on this analysis, is that there was only a small amount of illicit sex in the middle-class Victorian reality, much smaller than the quantity that existed both beforehand, in the eighteenth century, and afterwards, in the twentieth. It is tempting to conclude that the amount was so small precisely because of the Victorian socialization for repression detailed in Chapters II and III, and I believe that this is indeed the case. It has not yet been demonstrated, but that will come in the final chapter with an examination of love letters. As surprising as it might seem to my cocktail-party respondents from Chapter I, the fruits of repression prevailed in the age of Victoria. It would seem that the mystery has therefore been solved beyond a shadow of a doubt and that the palm goes to the traditional stereotype of repression – but that is *not* the case. The mystery is not that simple – not open and shut. We need to look at the Mosher survey and the love letters.

---

38 Kinsey, et. al. 1953, p. 298.

39 Davis 1929, p. 59. Relative to the Kinsey report, this percentage is almost certainly depressed by the inclusion of women who married young, say under the age of twenty-five.

Fourth Interlude: Portraits 11 – 14

Portrait 11: Mary Pennington[40]

The responses in this case were written by Dr. Mosher as she interviewed Mrs. Pennington. That means that many of the answers were abbreviated and perhaps even paraphrased.

Mrs. Pennington was relatively young at the time of the interview – twenty-eight – but she already had two children and would probably go on to have more. I say that not because of her declared intentions but because she depended for contraception, at least up to the time of the interview, on the timing of intercourse and harbored the common belief that the safe time was halfway between menstrual periods. Her response to the question about frequency of intercourse was "3 – 4 times during the safe period," and her view of the ideal frequency was "Several times during midmonth." On the subject of the children, Dr. Mosher appended notes showing that, as a researcher, she had a particular interest in the fact that Mrs. Pennington bore these children after having an ovary removed. That occurred shortly before her graduation from college, about six months before her marriage. The case helped to demonstrate to Dr. Mosher that removal of one ovary did not necessarily imply sterility and might not even diminish fertility.

Mary was born in 1892 and got married in 1914, five and a half years before she was interviewed by Dr. Mosher for the project. She received an A.B. degree from Stanford in 1914 shortly before the marriage. Unlike almost all the other Mosher women, however, and indeed the great majority of the women of her day, marriage for her did not mean taking on the roles of wife and mother exclusively. She did not give any details about her job, but she mentioned that within a matter of just a few weeks after giving birth to her second son she went back to the university and took charge of, or at least had a major responsibility in, getting an issue of a magazine out and through the press. Her husband also went to Stanford, but she did not indicate that he received a degree. Asked his occupation, Dr. Mosher recorded Mary's answer unhelpfully as "Office."

40 Mosher 1980, Blank No. 29, pp. 318-329.

Mary claimed to have what Dr. Mosher called "full knowledge" of the sexual relation before her marriage, gained from talking to two physicians. In several other cases, Dr. Mosher indicated the same status by saying that the patient knew "what marriage meant." It is evident that what is signified by these terms is understanding that sexual intercourse is a normal part of married life and understanding as well what is basically involved in sexual intercourse. Several of the women whose cases we have presented in these portraits so far have also had "full knowledge," but in this respect the subgroup of women in the portraits is not typical of the whole. We will see that only forty percent of the Mosher women either definitely or probably had attained this level of sexual sophistication. The majority were clueless.

One of our important interests regarding the women of this early study, in judging the extent to which they tend to support or refute the hypothesis of repression, is in whether sexual desire was a significant part of their lives. Asked the question whether, at times, she had a desire for intercourse, Mrs. Pennington's recorded answer is "Occasionally." This marks a change in feeling or at least in awareness. It is in contrast to a note at the end of the file indicating that Mary was "never conscious of any physical sex need before marriage." There are, in addition, a few indications of a somewhat more compelling role for desire in her case. She said that at the time when her second child was conceived her desire had been "much stronger," indicating by the emphatic recall a definite consciousness of the feeling, and she also reported that sexual intercourse served to decrease nervous tension, especially when she "has felt the need."

She found that sexual intercourse was agreeable to her. On orgasm, her recorded response is "Not always." This is less precise than one would like, but her further comments indicate that it was not a rare event. Asked about the effects immediately afterwards when she did achieve orgasm, her response was "Always relaxation and satisfied," and on the effects the next day, "Relaxed the next day. Calmer. Gets more tired by night if she is overworked."

Mary's birth date, sometime in April of 1892, is the latest of all the Mosher women. Only two others were born as late as the 1880s, all the rest coming earlier. There is the interesting question, therefore, whether Mary Pennington was a Victorian woman or post-Victorian. The issue is not so much the date of 1901, when Queen Victoria died, but rather the knowledge that the strictness and pervasiveness of Victorian morality began to wane in the 1890s and tottered fairly radically during and after the First World War, 1914-1918. At the same time, significant vestiges of Victorian morality did persist even into the 1940s and beyond. It was not a black and white process.

There are a few indicators to help us judge in this case. Asked whether she habitually slept with her husband the recorded response is, "Yes. Like it, enjoy it – only time for being together." This might seem post-Victorian except that her response is similar to that of many of the other women we have considered so far. One of Mrs. Pennington's responses concerning the true purpose of intercourse was, "Simply – sweeps you out of everything that is . . . every day." This can be considered typically Victorian in that it shows how totally unprepared she was for the combined physical and emotional effects of the sexual relation. She had the experience of feeling transported, carried completely out of herself. On the other hand, the experience of sex is hard to convey to another by any medium or means and ultimately difficult to appreciate except first-hand. Even some modern young women might have a reaction similar to Mary's in intensity and the sense of novelty and uniqueness.

Her other responses on the subject of the true purpose of intercourse were very close in tone to those of the other women we have considered. She said:

> A higher purpose than physical enjoyment. . . . A strength to go on. Union, which brings something to both. . . . If people are to live together as married people your bond must be strengthened. It makes a more close bond and reproduction is the highest tie.

"Victorian" as a cultural category is vague around the edges, and Mary Pennington's particular questionnaire does not constitute a concrete demonstration of the respondent's status one way or the other – Victorian in culture or post-Victorian. On the whole, however, the impressions of culture evoked by her responses correspond reasonably well with those of the other members of the group. Certainly, they do not clash. Although she became a teenager after the turn of the century, it seems that Mrs. Pennington was still essentially a Victorian woman.

Portrait 12: Yvonne McNair[41]

There is a good deal that is not clear about the lives portrayed in this set of responses. The dominant impression is, however, that Yvonne and Jonathan McNair were babes in the woods regarding sex – almost unbelievably innocent – during the five years of their marriage that preceded the time of the study.

Yvonne's father was a country doctor. She, her parents, and her grandparents, as well as her husband, were in fact all country people, apparently living in upstate New York.

She was born in 1866 and her mother died – at age thirty-three – six months after her birth. Yvonne had three older sisters. She also had a maternal grandmother who was still living in 1896 at the time of the questionnaire. We do not know whether it was a sister, the grandmother, or someone else who took on the responsibility of raising Yvonne in place of her mother.

After high school, Yvonne went to normal school and became a teacher in the country. In 1891, at age twenty-five, she married Jonathan McNair. He had a Masters degree from Syracuse University, and she gave his occupation simply as "Teacher." This frugal designation occurs many times in the Mosher questionnaires. There are instances in which other information makes it clear that college teacher is meant, but at times, such as in this case, the level is uncertain. Yvonne gave Jonathan's height as six foot seven inches, and she also indicated that he was athletic. Since basketball was not invented until 1891, however, the year of their marriage, we can rule out that he was a basketball star.

Recall that Deirdre Mueller and her husband started out with separate beds because Deirdre thought it was the "right thing" but switched within the first year. Yvonne had the opposite experience. She and Jonathan apparently started out sharing a bed, but it did not last. They had a child, a healthy boy, in 1893, and after that they decided to have separate rooms because the baby disturbed Jonathan and, being a light sleeper who sometimes read during the night, his light disturbed Yvonne. For some reason, Yvonne seemed to feel the need to justify this decision by providing all of the above details. This is one of many signs in her responses that she did not know quite what to think about the intimate relations of marriage – where to put them. One assumes that sexuality

41 Mosher 1980, Blank No. 25, pp. 278-290.

would eventually find a settled place in her view of life, but at that time, after five years of marriage, she appeared still to be bewildered – uncertain what to think or how to manage.

Asked if she had desire for intercourse during her pregnancy, Yvonne answered, "No," underlining the word. The connotation of the emphasis is that this was the last thing in the world she would have thought about or experienced during that time. She indicated in another place that her health was not good for the first year after her son's birth. "I think the cause was over anxiety for the baby." Was intercourse agreeable to her? "Yes," she answered, "but there are times when it would not be." She did not specify what those times were – perhaps during pregnancy, or menstruation, or when tired or nervous – but she apparently had not undergone the disagreeable experience of being pressed to have intercourse on such occasions. The frequency of intercourse for the McNairs was about once per month – in between periods. The baby was, in fact, conceived by accident, fifteen days after menstruation. Intercourse was infrequent considering that they were a recently married couple, but orgasm for Yvonne was not entirely absent. She answered "No" to the question whether she always had a venereal orgasm but showed that "No" did not mean "Never." Asked about the effect afterwards when she did reach orgasm, she wrote, "One of exhaustion & I want to be quiet and go to sleep." When she did not? "Very slight exhaustion." Orgasm, then, was apparently occasional and, in this case as in many others, it was not a life-changing event.

To the question about her knowledge of sexual physiology before marriage, Yvonne answered that she had had a class in physiology in normal school and that during one vacation she had read some of her father's medical books. These sources, she said, gave her a fair knowledge of female sexual physiology, but, "Of the male, I knew but very little if anything." Apparently, classes for women in a Victorian normal school did not cover male sexual physiology, but the information was no doubt available in her father's medical books if she had cared enough or were brave enough to look for it. She did not do so. She kept herself in ignorance by choice – by reticence – as would be predicted by the model of repression. She appeared even at the time of the study to keep sexual knowledge at bay. For example, we know that she did not experience desire for intercourse during her pregnancy, but how about at other times? "Sometimes, but not often, a caress from my husband will cause me to think of it. It is hardly enough to call it a desire." Many women would consider the thought of sexual intercourse upon a husband's caress to be the first stirring of desire, but Yvonne did not see it in quite that way. She was not quick to associate herself with sexual desire. Moreover, she was still, at the time of completing the questionnaire, apparently naïve about some of the facts of life, as were many Victorians. When asked if they had ever used any means to prevent conception, she responded that the only method they had ever used was "for neither of us to have an orgasm." This means that she probably did have an orgasm on the occasion when their baby was conceived. It also means that they practiced withdrawal upon occasion, along with a great number of the other Mosher couples. Lastly, it suggests that Yvonne may have mistakenly considered the female orgasm to be necessary for conception.

If Jonathan had integrated sexuality firmly into his life, especially with some sort of positive orientation, Yvonne might well have found her own bearings within a year or two, as well. It appears, however, that he also was burdened with a notable innocence.

This happens to be one of the minority of questionnaires in which Dr. Mosher included the question about timing of first intercourse after the wedding. In the case of the McNairs, it was two weeks. Yvonne gave no reason, nor did she comment upon any awkwardness. She simply responded, "Two weeks." They were apparently together during that time, sharing a bed, and there is no indication of illness. We will see in a moment that desire was present but they apparently could not quite bring themselves to approach consummation.

Yvonne volunteered one paragraph that was not in answer to any particular questionnaire item but that is informative about the faltering path toward sexual understanding experienced by this couple. It is important enough to quote in full.

> When I was first married a caress or even a touch of the hand from my husband would cause much colorless leucorrhoea [vaginal discharge – a condition Dr. Mosher had asked about much earlier in the

> questionnaire]. The entire lower part of my abdomen became very sore. This continued for two weeks until the first intercourse. A day or so after that the soreness was entirely gone and I was not troubled with leucorrhoea. While I was pregnant & for about six months after there was no trouble or desire for intercourse. As I became strong & well the same symptoms that I had when first married appeared again. For the first two weeks of our married life my husband suffered from soreness even more than I.

This can be puzzling, but there is a fairly obvious interpretation of the symptoms. I was unwilling to accept it until I got the informal advice of several physicians. They were also frankly puzzled at first, but all settled on the same interpretation, namely, that what was going on with both Yvonne and Jonathan was sexual arousal that they did not comprehend. At some early point after the wedding, the bride and groom were all by themselves, joined together in extended privacy on numerous occasions. These were, no doubt, the very first instances in which either of them had ever been in such a situation. Nobody else around to oblige decorum, just all by themselves. As George Eliot put it in *Adam Bede*:

> They were alone together for the first time. What an overpowering presence that first privacy is![42]

The nearness combined with the privacy would have its effect. Her husband's caress kindled a vaginal wetness and the riot of localized physical signs of arousal that Yvonne, never having experienced such a thing before, interpreted as soreness. The arousal was dispelled by intercourse. In the well-known Kinsey report, we are informed that about twenty-five percent of a large sample of women felt ache in the groin after petting without achieving orgasm.[43] Meanwhile, Jonathan had similar feelings. The couple suffered the disturbing physical sensations and the uncertainty for two weeks until they eventually

42 Eliot—Adam Bede

43 Kinsey et al., 1953, p. 281.

found the proper cure. Too bad we do not know whether orgasm occurred for Yvonne on that occasion.

When asked what to her would be the ideal frequency of intercourse, Yvonne wrote, "Not to desire intercourse, except for reproduction." Several of the Mosher women responded to this question with some allusion to behavioral restraint – for example, some variant of "little or no intercourse except for reproduction," but Yvonne put it differently. Her ideal would be no desire. That way, the whole topic would just go away.

It took Yvonne and Jonathan a while, but it had only been five years, and some of their experiences laid a foundation. Clearly, Yvonne was quite prone to experience both sexual desire and arousal. Although these were still bewildering, one has faith that she, and they, eventually would work it out.

Portrait 13: Florence Gibson[44]

We learn very little about Florence's husband, Jonas Gibson. He was born in 1844, the same year as Florence, and went to sea for seven years at the age of fourteen. In answer to the item about his education, which in most cases elicits information specifying a local school or a college, Dr. Mosher wrote "U.S." Therefore, we do not know whether he had a college background or not. This response, however, is one of several inconclusive hints that Florence herself might have spent part of her childhood in another country. For his occupation, Mrs. Gibson apparently told Dr. Mosher nothing more than that it was varied, active, and mental rather than physical. One additional bit of information is that when Florence was pregnant with her third child, most likely in the sixth or seventh year of their marriage, Jonas was ill with melancholia – probably what we would now call depression.

In contrast, we learn a great deal about Florence's mother. We know, for example, that she was a teacher before her marriage and that at some point, for some unknown duration, she was a missionary. Late in life, she returned to teaching. "This child [her mother's seventh] was nursed for 2 ½ years. There were no baby foods in those days. Mother began to teach school. Not enough to eat in those days. Natives paid 25 cents per week. Taught until over 70 years old." The missionary work may have been in a foreign country or perhaps on an American Indian reservation.

A questionnaire item asked about the number of miscarriages the respondent's mother may have had. In this case, the item elicits a full page and a half of sketchy narrative written by Dr. Mosher at Mrs. Gibson's dictation. The tale is a tragic one. Her mother had a total of thirteen conceptions. Of these, the first five resulted in miscarriages and there was another miscarriage between the tenth and eleventh conception, for a total of six. Of the seven live births, the first child was born after fifty-seven hours of labor and died shortly thereafter. The second labor involved a shoulder presentation and again the child died immediately after the birth. Mrs. Gibson's mother blamed both of those deaths on an incompetent physician. The third child, a boy, lived for ten months before being snuffed out by cholera. Shortly after this third tragic death, her

44 Mosher 1980, Blank No. 35, pp. 375-386.

mother received a letter "from home," suggesting that it may have come during the missionary phase, informing her that her father and two sisters were dead. She was pregnant then with her fourth child, and we learn unsurprisingly that she cried during the entire period. Nevertheless, the child survived and was in fact our respondent, Florence, although she nearly died of influenza after three weeks of life. Nearly three years later, when her mother was thirty-five years old, a sister was born. At age two and a half, this new sister contracted measles, then whooping cough, and then dysentery, which she did not survive. At age forty-two, her mother's thirteenth and final conception occurred. A boy was born weighing ten and a half pounds. He was "delicate, sensitive, and nervous" and was nursed for two and a half years, as noted above. Nevertheless, he most happily survived. Thus, of the thirteen conceptions, there were six miscarriages and seven live births, of which only two of the children survived.

Might there possibly be something in this record that is hereditary? It almost seems to be true. Mrs. Gibson herself, who was fifty-five at the time of the study, had twelve conceptions, of which six resulted in miscarriages. The very first conception resulted in one of these miscarriages. Then, a healthy daughter was born after a long labor. The third conception resulted in a healthy baby boy, but he very sadly died of cholera sometime after the age of fourteen months. Next, another healthy boy was born and survived, after which Mrs. Gibson moved to a cold climate. When this child was fifteen months old, the second miscarriage occurred, which Mrs. Gibson said was "brought about by [an unspecified] mental shock." The sixth conception also produced a baby boy, but he died of cholera as well, this time after only six months of life. These cholera deaths, by the way, remind us of the importance of a clean water supply and also of the lack of same even in modernized countries in the nineteenth century. The seventh conception resulted in a baby boy weighing ten and a half pounds and healthy. This son survived. When he was nine months old, Florence's horse ran away with her when she was pregnant once more, causing the third miscarriage. The ninth conception resulted in a healthy, surviving daughter. After that, Mrs. Gibson had three more miscarriages, at ages forty-five, forty-six, and forty-seven. Of the six live births, therefore, two baby boys died of cholera and four children survived – two daughters, one son, and one child whose sex was not specified in the record.

Florence was married in 1869, at age twenty-four. At the time of the study, she had been married for twenty-eight and a half years. She apparently had no formal education beyond high school, but she nevertheless was a teacher before her marriage and, in this unusual case, continued in that job for a while after the wedding – we do not know for how long.

Given that so much of her mother's life was taken up with pregnancies and child-bearing, the parent might possibly have been moved to communicate to the growing child much of the relevant information about the intimate details of married life. Such was not, however, the case. Florence's recorded answer to the question about knowledge of such intelligence before her marriage was:

> Slight from girls. Mother taught her that such things were not only not talked about but also not thought of. School child at 14 told what intercourse was. Was shocked and didn't believe it.

The second sentence could be straight out of training for innocence in English homes. These early experiences might well have prompted an antipathy toward marital sex that could be hard to overcome. Moreover, when she was between five and six years old, her little sister died, piling up reproductive tragedy for her mother, and she herself lost two baby sons to cholera. On the other hand, we seem to be learning from the cases of the Mosher women that adjustment to sex in marriage is complex and can be influenced one way or the other by many factors, including the strength of the sexual hormones, life events having to do with pregnancy and child-bearing, general personality or outlook, and husbands. In this case, happily, Mrs. Gibson's own and her mother's sad reproductive experiences did not have a decisive negative effect.

Throughout the whole of their married life, Jonas and Florence made love about once a week, sometimes a little more often, sometimes a little less. This included the first seven months or so of her pregnancies. I use the term "made love" in the modern sense, by the way, meaning to have sex. There has, however, been a notable transformation. In the nineteenth century, to make love meant to pay amorous attention – always just a verbal action. The expression was used with great frequency in the novels, where, as we have seen, there is precious little overt sexuality.

The couple shared a bed until a few months before the Mosher interview. Florence's feeling was that sexual relations were made to be pleasurable in order that people would take the necessary steps for the reproduction of the species. In the normal course of things, she experienced desire intermittently but frequently. As long as she was not too tired and conditions were right, sexual intercourse with her husband was agreeable to her. On many occasions she did not have an orgasm, but she said that she always did when she desired the intimacy. Afterwards, she felt "sleepy, relaxed, less nervous, good," and the next day she "feels well." When she did not have the orgasm, on the other hand, she was "nervous, strung up, not sleepy," but she tended to get over that by the next day.

Mrs. Gibson's feelings about the role of sex were, in fact, a little stronger than those of most of the other Mosher women. In her view, in spite of being shocked and incredulous at age fourteen by the notion of intercourse, sex had substantial functional importance in life, both for her personally and, in her view, for people in general. To the question whether she felt desire during her pregnancies, Dr. Mosher recorded that Florence had more desire for the sexual relation then than at other times, and she felt that she needed to have sex. Dr. Mosher included a direct quote from Florence: "Nothing would ease my nervous condition but that." Asked whether, in her opinion, sexual intercourse was a necessity for men or women, she answered in the affirmative. Dr. Mosher included Mrs. Gibson's reasoning: "Because many unmarried are too nervous & do not recognize what the cause is." The desire for sex was, she considered, "a normal desire and a rational use of it tends to keep people healthier."

It is impossible to say what bequeathed to Florence Gibson this positive, matter-of-fact attitude toward sex. We do definitely see, however, that neither the offputting information she received about it before she experienced it herself nor the formidable adversity she suffered in connection with born and unborn children was able to turn her against it decisively. We learn and, unlike authoritative physicians in the nineteenth century, can humbly give our opinion that sexual attitudes can be quite unpredictable.

Portrait 14: Barbara Townsend[45]

Barbara was born in December of 1874. We know little about her early life except that she was raised in a small town. Her eventual husband was also a small-town child, but we do not know whether it was the same town. We do know that she went to college, earning an A.B. degree from Stanford in 1895. She then became a young bride in 1896. After about a year, she filled out the Mosher questionnaire – for the first time.

Inexplicably, she filled it out again twenty-three years later, in 1920, or rather she was interviewed by Dr. Mosher, who noted down her responses. She is the only Mosher woman to have responded to the questionnaire twice, and there is no indication that either she or Dr. Mosher ever realized the repetition. The two forms are almost entirely consistent with one another, but there are a few differences, some of which caution us on the accuracy of recall data in the methodology of survey research. One difference is no doubt real: In 1897, she gave her weight as one hundred and thirty-six pounds, and in 1920 it was one hundred and fifty pounds. Her husband grew apace, from one hundred and fifty pounds in 1897 to one hundred and seventy-five pounds in 1920.

Other differences between the two forms have more to do with memory. When asked in 1920 whether she and her husband slept together in the same bed, Mrs. Townsend recalled that they did only for the first three years of the marriage because they did not at that time have an extra room. When asked the same question earlier in 1897, however, she said that they did share a bed because they enjoyed it "from the companionable standpoint" and reported only secondarily that it would have been inconvenient to arrange it otherwise, by which we now know that she had in mind the lack of the extra room. After twenty-three years, the memory of that early enjoyment of marital companionship was not as bright as were the feelings and reactions at the earlier time. Mrs. Townsend forgot, at least for the moment, how much she had liked it.

Dr. Mosher's question about the frequency of intercourse is one that would probably not be asked in the same form by today's survey researchers because it calls for a kind of averaging that can easily be inaccurate. If the true frequency is just about every night, the response is likely to be faithful to reality, but if the

45 Mosher 1980. Blanks No. 30, 33, pp. 330-340, 353-364.

occasions are separated sometimes by three days, sometimes by six or seven, and sometimes by ten or more, the mentally averaged response might be quite unreliable, and the more so the more distant the time of response from the actual events. In 1897, Barbara gave the frequency as once per week. In 1920, however, she gave the current frequency as about once per month and for the earlier days about once every two weeks. There apparently was a fading of the memory of the passion and the youthful desire that actually drove the new Mr. and Mrs. Townsend together twice that often in the early years.

Recall that the question on orgasm was, "Do you always have a venereal orgasm?" In 1897, Barbara answered, "Very nearly always." In 1920, her response was, "Always." Apparently she either forgot about or did not consider it important to recall the early days in which some learning and mutual adjustment was necessary and apparently took place.

The model of repression is supported by Mrs. Townsend's history in one important regard. Asked what knowledge of sexual physiology she had before marriage, she indicated that she had quite a bit, some from her mother (an infrequent source in these data), some from a class in sex hygiene, and some from friends. Perhaps these transmissions had to do only with dry details regarding internal organs and the process of reproduction. In any case, she did not relate whatever factual information she absorbed to herself – her own body. She reported that she had no sexual desire whatever and indeed no personal consciousness of sex at all before her marriage. During the moments when we tend to doubt the possibility of the traditional or repression view of Victorian sexuality, the tendency is to think that young people everywhere have desires that will impel them in the direction of sexual activity. Barbara Townsend and several other Mosher women serve as a reminder that it is quite possible for women, and probably men as well, to be completely oblivious of sex before their first experience of it.

On the other hand, the revisionist or hormones model – the theory that Victorian women were not sexually repressed, as has traditionally been considered, but were ruled more by natural sexual inclinations – is supported by her answers in regard to three of our key dimensions: she did feel desire, she did find sexual intercourse agreeable, and she did quite reliably derive the satisfaction of orgasm. That is not to say, however, that Barbara Townsend was a sex enthusiast, just as there may well be many women in our liberated age who would score the same on these three dimensions and would also not be sex enthusiasts. We will glean from several of her responses that sex simply did not occupy a prominent position in her outlook or thoughts. It was there and agreeable, but she did not have the kind of orientation that would lead her to chime in, with Sally Warren, "Often quite delightful." On orgasm, for example, she did not report any particular effects immediately afterwards whether she did or did not achieve orgasm, nor the next day either, except to agree with Sally Warren that the day after a positive experience she sometimes had a drowsy or "stupid" feeling.

In 1897, a year after her marriage, there had as yet been no conceptions. By 1920, in fact by 1904, there had been three. The stillbirth or later death of a child is important to us in these assessments because it is generally a shattering event – one that, among other things, might well have an impact on future attitudes toward sex. In this case, unfortunately, I do not find Dr. Mosher's notes informative enough to decide whether two of Mrs. Townsend's children lived or died. The middle child, a girl, definitely was healthy and survived. The first, a boy might or might not have survived, the language is unclear. The same is true of the third child, whose sex was not recorded. Mrs. Townsend became a mother, that we know, but what effect the tragedy of infant death might have had upon her we do not know because we do not know whether there was a tragedy at all.

During the sixteen years between 1904 and 1920, there were no conceptions. Asked whether she ever used any means to prevent a pregnancy, she said in both questionnaires that she always used a douche of plain water, and this was the only measure taken. Whatever hygienic results it may have, we know that this particular measure is not an effective contraceptive. The three conceptions in her life were not planned; there was just a "willingness." But Dr. Mosher added the cryptic note: "Plan when don't want." Most probably, when the couple felt that a pregnancy and child were not desired or not advisable, they used some form of abstinence or timing to help implement their wish of prevention. There may have been some physiological reason for sterility during those sixteen years, although nothing like that is mentioned. Otherwise, whatever plan for timing they worked out – while having intercourse once every month to every two weeks – it worked. There was little or no likelihood of a blessed event in the future. Mrs. Townsend reported in 1920 that she was, at age forty-six, in the midst of the change of life.

The conflict that could so easily be created in women during the Victorian era between early and adolescent training on one hand and the experience of marital intimacy on the other is clearly demonstrated in Mrs. Townsend's responses to the question about ideal frequency. In 1897, she wrote a small paragraph inclining toward an ideal frequency of once a month, if both desire. But then she crossed that paragraph out!

In its place, she recorded:

> Since writing the above I have become convinced that the ideal would be to have no intercourse except for reproduction, but it is often hard to live up to such an ideal.

By 1920, twenty-three married years after the first questionnaire, she still had not resolved this same ambivalence. She was still torn between what she thought to be proper and what she felt after a certain amount of personal experience to be both innocent and advantageous. She said she felt intellectually that intercourse should be restricted to the purpose of reproduction, say two to three times a year. Her conclusion, however – on some unspecified basis – was that intercourse should not be restricted to reproduction but should be limited "to times when not pressed with work; when time for pleasure."

Her feelings are amplified by her responses to the question about "the true purpose" of sexual intercourse. Dr. Mosher asked whether intercourse was necessary for men, for women, whether it was for pleasure, for reproduction, and, in general, what besides reproduction was sufficient to warrant intercourse. In 1897, Barbara did not answer the first parts at all (necessary for men, etc.) before finally giving the nod to reproduction as the true purpose. She then amplified with the following paragraph:

> I think the pleasure is sufficient to warrant it provided people are extremely moderate, and do not allow it to injure their health or degrade their best feelings toward each other. This must depend on individual standpoint.

I find that she was groping here to discern in herself a personal outlook that was not quite clear to her. Surely, reproduction was the true purpose. But does that mean that this intimacy was not otherwise warranted? Intercourse gave pleasure, and it seemed to be a kind of pleasure that was somehow important, justifiable. She had not yet, at this early time, put her finger on the exact nature of that value, but she sensed that the quality of the relationship was endangered by seeking the pleasure too often. The experience and pleasure of intercourse could bring out the best feelings of each toward the other, but she sensed that this value could be lost unless there was settled moderation.

Further crystallization came in her 1920 response. Still, the true purpose was considered to be reproduction. No, it was not necessary either for men or for women. How about pleasure? Yes, that was a true purpose, but, she added obscurely, "not necessarily a legitimate one." In other words, she attached a high value to intercourse and it was connected with pleasure, but was not pleasure in and of itself. She amplified when asked what else besides reproduction was sufficient to warrant intercourse:

> A sense of intimacy not to be had in any other way; especially when people cannot be affectionate without going full course. Serves as a bond above even physical pleasure.

For Barbara Townsend, the marital relationship had great value in itself, aside from the purpose of reproducing the species. The quality of the relationship depended in part on affection, but day-to-day affection might not be enough, and some couples (one unavoidably interprets this as applying to her own case) could find it difficult to express or convey that affection adequately during daily life. Sexual intercourse could uniquely produce a sense of intimacy, partly sourced in each seeking to give pleasure to the other. The quality of the intimacy derived in this way would strengthen a bond between husband and wife. That bond represents one of life's highest values.

The Victorian, socialized conviction that sexual intercourse is for reproduction and reproduction only interfered with Barbara Townsend's adjusting to married sex simply, in its own terms, without ideological baggage. However, she discovered that there was potentially a significant element in marriage that went beyond raising a family and supporting one another. There could be a bond between husband and wife that, in its highest character, was in itself a supreme value. That bond was not only uniquely enhanced but in many cases discovered by sexual intercourse, with the caveat that to achieve its purpose securely, the pleasure must be approached in moderation.

V

The Mosher women considered as a group

Our principal aim has been to solve the mystery of the sexual behavior of Victorian women. Was it radically repressed, as scholars have traditionally urged and as many are still inclined to believe, or was it actually more like the behavior of twentieth-century women – in spite of the strict moral code that was apparently in force?

When bringing the discussion to a close in the next chapter, I will succinctly review the primary factors already covered that support the model of repression. It may be said here, however, that these factors make an overwhelmingly convincing case. Given the intense religious and medical advice, the statistics on marriages and births, the data on prostitution, the shortage of effective contraception, the coalition for repression, the evidence from the Victorian novels, and data on the sexual experience of later-born women, it is impossible to believe that a substantial number of middle-class Victorian women were having premarital sexual experience – say as many as thirty-six percent, as the Kinsey Report found for women born in 1900-1910. A very tiny fraction of women having such experience, each with little more than one or two furtive encounters, is much more likely – in other words, a female component of society in the new middle class that was almost unbelievably chaste. In addition to the Kinsey Report, we also keep in mind the Davis study of women born on average in 1882, which found that only seven percent had premarital sex between the ages of fourteen and twenty-five.

On the other side, we have seen examples in the portraits from the Mosher survey of women who did not seem repressed at all. In many cases, it was quite the contrary. They were well aware of the sexual side of their nature and both desired and enjoyed sexual engagement. Their reported experience contradicts the model of repression, and it is this survey, in fact, that constitutes the primary pillar of evidence that advises a marked revision of the traditional view. However, there are only forty-five women in that group, and they were not randomly selected from any particular population. If generalizations are to be made, there must be a defense of making them on the basis of such a small and arbitrary sample. Moreover, up to now we have only looked at the Mosher women as a succession of anecdotes, and we have not even covered half of the forty-five. I hope to make amends in the present chapter by considering all forty-five Mosher women as a group and examining their collective responses. By this means, we will get a good sense of the dominant trends in the group and can also proceed to consider how worthy this particular group might be as a basis for generalizing about all middle-class Victorian women.

We owe the enrichment of information that has come from the Mosher survey largely to Professor Carl Degler, a historian at Stanford University, who discovered the completed questionnaires among Dr. Mosher's papers in the Stanford University archives in 1973, where they had lain dormant for thirty-three years since Dr. Mosher's death in 1940. He wrote a path-breaking article based on the survey during the following year.[1] The major point of his article was that we need to think again about the traditional view – the theory that the sexuality of Victorian women was severely repressed – because the Mosher survey showed a substantial number of apparently typical Victorian women, the great majority of whom were anything but repressed. Their sexual lives were welcome and satisfying. The article sparked a good deal of controversy in the field, with some scholars – I will call them the "revisionists" – agreeing whole heartedly with Degler and others doubting that the Mosher survey should carry a great deal of influence. Some of this discussion will inevitably come up in the following pages, although it is not relevant here to plunge deeply into the academic controversy.

1 Degler, 1974.

A great many treatments of the Mosher survey appeared after Degler's article, some of them picking out brief highlights for inclusion in academic books or articles on broader topics and some focused on the survey itself and the justification of its use as the basis for a revision of the model of repression. The spirited academic discussion was very substantially aided by the publication of all of the survey questions and the original responses in book form in 1980, making the material readily available to a broad community of scholars.[2]

Thus, my own analysis of the Mosher survey is certainly not the first. It differs, however, from previous treatments in several important ways: First, I reconcile the two opposing views: the traditional stereotype and the flatly contradictory revisionist proposals. Second, I take the trouble to gather and present the hard evidence that supports the traditional stereotype of repression, which I think has too often been accepted without critical questioning. Third, I emphasize the human element – helpfully, I hope – by showing the respondents through the portraits as individuals with thoughts, feelings, and reasons rather than primarily as numbers and statistics. Fourth, I defend the Mosher sample of forty-five women as representative of middle-class Victorian women as a whole – in spite of the fact that they were mostly college-educated, which was not typical at all. Fifth, I take up the major published objections to the revisionist view and show that these objections are not valid. Sixth and last, I make the set of data I created from the Mosher survey responses available to all who request it, which has not been done before.

The Creator

We will see that there were two sides to the character of Dr. Clelia Duel Mosher.[3] One was an intellectual side, in which she emerges as highly innovative and highly determined. The other was an emotional side, in which she appears, unfortunately, as solitary and needy.

She was herself a Victorian, having been born in Albany, New York in 1863 – at the height of the American Civil War. She wanted to go to college but

2 Mosher, 1980.

3 This sketch of Dr. Mosher's life is based primarily on Jacob, 1981.

was prevented by her father, a physician, who considered that her health was too delicate to withstand the rigors of student life. Instead, as a consolation prize, he had a small, home greenhouse converted into an educational laboratory and arranged for her to be taught both botany and horticulture. Showing her determined side, however, Clelia turned this training and opportunity into a business as a florist. In 1889, she announced that she had saved two thousand dollars from her earnings, that she had been accepted into Wellesley College, and that her savings would take care of four years' tuition. Thus, the greenhouse gambit became important to her both intellectually and emotionally, for it catapulted her into higher education and also planted the seeds of a lifelong avocation – sophisticated gardening – to which she became deeply devoted.

She did well at Wellesley but, for reasons that are not specified, transferred for her junior year to the University of Wisconsin at Madison. There, in 1892, a seemingly unaccountable event occurred that proved to yield the beginnings of the Mosher survey. For some reason, she was asked by the "Mothers' Club," a group composed primarily of faculty wives, to give a lecture on the "marital relation," which was code in those days for married sexual intercourse. Why on earth would these mature women ask a college junior to give such a talk? No solid information answers the question.

We can put a few facts and conjectures together, however, to come up with a reasonably credible answer. First, they did contact her; they had to know about her somehow and believe that she would be capable of giving a worthwhile lecture on this topic. Also, she was older than most college juniors, being twenty-nine at the time – probably about the same age as many of the women in the club. Third, she was a female science major, in the process of getting her Bachelor's degree in zoology. Lastly, it is highly likely that she had by that time developed an interest in issues concerning women's physiology and its connection to social role. The Mothers' Club questionnaire she developed on which to base at least part of her lecture – the survey questionnaire that is the subject of this chapter – betrays both an interest in topics that she would later follow up with more extensive research, especially the supposed debilitating effects of menstruation, and a knowledge of medical literature concerning other intimate issues of married women. In particular, a series of questions in the questionnaire – poor questions in the light of modern survey technology – is based directly on a book that had recently been published by Dr. Alice Stockham on some of those issues.[4] It is possible that Mosher first read this book and others only to prepare for her lecture after she was asked to give it, but it also may be true that such reading was part of a known, lively interest on her part, an interest that attracted the attention of one or more faculty members and, through them, the attention of the Mothers' Club.

The future Dr. Mosher did not remain long at Wisconsin. She transferred for her senior year to the newly founded Stanford University, where she earned the Bachelor's degree in 1893. She was then offered and accepted a position as Instructor and Assistant in Hygiene at Stanford, whose duties included taking physiological measurements on all incoming female first-year students. She embarked almost immediately on a research agenda centered on exposing error and distortion in common, physiologically based stereotypes of women. First, she attacked what was considered to be an innate difference in the way men and women breathe. Men breathed using the diaphragm; women used the upper chest, which the textbooks attributed to the requirements of pregnancy. Mosher showed that there was no physiological necessity to the way women appeared to breathe, but that it rather was probably caused by constrictive clothing and sedentary living. The findings caused a stir of controversy, but they soon were backed up by other researchers.

Next, she tackled menstruation. We saw in our discussion of the obstacles to higher education for women in Chapter III how formidable a weapon for the male traditionalists was the conviction that monthly periods were incapacitating. Mosher had an innovative insight. She felt that the support for this notion was based largely on the experience of male physicians with pathological female patients. She decided to observe healthy women and collected a mountain of systematic data. The mountain, however, was sobering. She began to see that doing a credible job of capitalizing on these data demanded far more medical knowledge than she possessed. She did not, therefore, give up the project. Instead, she decided to go to medical school. She applied to the School of Medicine at Johns Hopkins University in 1896, at the age of thirty-two, and was accepted, carting the data on menstruation along with her to Baltimore in 1897.

4 Stockham 1911, pp. 150-162.

Mosher, now Dr. Mosher, graduated in 1900 and was selected for an externship in the dispensary of Hopkins Hospital. During that time, she did a preliminary analysis of the menstruation data and published an initial report. The results indicated that there was no physiological reason for incapacity during menstruation but that four factors contributed to the general impression: the debilitating results of lack of exercise; chronic constipation; a purely psychological factor, namely, the expectation that discomfort was inevitable; and, most important of all, constrictive clothing. The Victorian era is famous for the corsets, stays, and tightlacing that not only emphasized but produced an hourglass figure. The text and illustrations in two Wikipedia articles are extremely helpful in appreciating the problem as well as the reasonableness of Dr. Mosher's conclusion connecting this fashion in clothing with discomfort during menstruation.[5] After a year, Dr. Mosher was offered another position at Hopkins, but she declined it and decided to return to California. In 1901, she opened an office for the private practice of medicine in Palo Alto.

During the ensuing nine- to ten-year period, she applied repeatedly for grants to continue her menstruation studies but was turned down. Finally, in 1910, she was offered an assistant professorship in the Department of Hygiene at Stanford, where she would have more time for research, excellent facilities, and an ample supply of subjects. She jumped at the chance. She soon published a major article on menstruation largely confirming the earlier work. A few years later, she published a more general treatise in book form exposing myths of female inferiority and incapacity, urging women to disregard them, and providing specific, inspiring advice on care of the body designed to make women both more competent and more confident. She was then promoted to associate professor. In 1923, she wrote a second book, this one largely devoted to middle-aged women and menopause. The message was similar: that the common deleterious effects were not physiologically necessary and could be avoided, primarily by active interest in pursuits other than the raising of children, which generally came to an end during the middle period of life.

5 *Wikipedia*: History of Corsets; *Wikipedia*: Corset Controversy.

This second book went into six printings and brought Dr. Mosher a much wider audience. Stanford duly promoted her to full professor in 1928, but she held that position for only one year; she retired in 1929 at the age of sixty-five.

Meanwhile, the First World War had broken out in 1914, and America joined the Allied forces a few years later. Dr. Mosher felt a strong need to participate. In November of 1917, she took a position in France as associate medical director of the Bureau of Refugees and Relief. "On one occasion, she led a caravan of sixty anemic children from Paris to Evian, a two-day journey."[6] She remained in France for a year, until the armistice of 1918, and then returned to her academic position at Stanford.

Dr. Mosher began her collection of data on the sexual behavior and attitudes of married Victorian women with the Mothers' Club lecture at the University of Wisconsin in 1892 and continued to have an active interest in the study until 1920. However, when she died in 1940, she had not published any of the findings and had written only a few cursory notes in the way of analysis, which were themselves buried along with the completed questionnaires in the Stanford archives. It was not until the sex survey was discovered over thirty years later that the world, or at least the academic part of it, took an interest in Dr. Clelia Mosher – scientist, teacher, and what one might call "physiological feminist." It remains to look briefly at the personal or non-professional side of the life and character of this remarkable woman.

When her life as a student was finally terminated and she returned to Stanford to open a private practice, her passion for gardening was awakened from its enforced slumber, and for the rest of her life she delighted in the application of her body, her esthetic sense, and her creativity to her beloved plants. Her papers contain warm descriptions of what she grew and how she grew it.

Unfortunately, this was largely a solitary preoccupation, and Dr. Mosher was for a long time distressed about necessarily being so solitary a person. In those days, women did not easily maintain close personal but non-romantic relations with men. With other women, she had very little in common. She was aware that some non-married and often professional women made deep and

6 Jacob 1981, p. 3.

valuable platonic friendships with other women, but this blessing did not, for some reason, fall to her lot. Consequently, she suffered from loneliness.

She never did find a friend, and this lack was felt, and written about, so keenly as to provoke in almost any observer a strong, sympathetic sadness. The price she paid for being a rather peculiar person for her times was enormous. At one point, she began writing intimate, personal letters to her "friend," but it becomes clear after several years' worth of such letters that this friend did not exist; she was imaginary – a deliberate fantasy. This was, however, but one stage; two more were to follow. During 1926, she finally, with forlorn resignation, gave up the dream of finding meaningful companionship. Still later, however, especially in contemplating moving into a new house, she was able to see her situation in a more positive light. She looked forward with joy to her solitary future, seeing in it a trove of riches in the beauty of her surroundings. She began writing, but never finished, the story of her life, entitling it: "The Autobiography of a Happy Old Woman."

Breadth: A View on the Surface

Our aim in this section will be to assess whether there truly is evidence in the Mosher survey to mount a serious challenge to the traditional stereotype – the model of repression. What exactly are the responses and averages from this survey that might prompt us to give up the established idea that Victorian women were essentially detached from sexuality? A first step along this road will be to establish a background in terms of the primary demographic characteristics of the forty-five respondents to Dr. Mosher's survey. They all were married, but were they old or young, urban or rural, highly educated or not?

The age of these women – age when responding to the questionnaire – is not very informative because the questionnaires were administered at a variety of times over a twenty-eight-year period. Two women might have been born on the same exact day but appear in the data with an age difference of, say, fifteen years just because one was interviewed fifteen years later than the other. A more helpful statistic is their year of birth; this would indicate whether the individual might have been influenced either by a lingering, permissive eighteenth-century moral culture or by the gradual loosening of Victorian standards that set in around 1890. The data show that the average birth year was 1863, with a large range extending from 1832 to 1892. The median birth year was the same, 1863, meaning that half of the women were born before that date and half afterwards. Thus, the group can be characterized as mid- to late-Victorian. Given these dates, we see that few, if any, of the respondents could well have been exposed to the loose, eighteenth-century moral culture because it had been replaced by the 1840s, when our early-born subjects were being socialized, but there is some concern about the late-born end. Eleven of the women were born in 1870 or later, so that even the earliest members of this subgroup would have been about twenty years old in 1890 and could conceivably have been affected by the beginnings of a relaxation of moral standards. Six were born late enough that they entered their teenage years during the decade of the 1890s and even into the early years of the twentieth century. Although Queen Victoria reigned until 1901, there might be some question whether these six respondents were really "Victorian" in socialization. In the next section, we will look at the data to see if differences in birth year made a noteworthy difference in sexual behavior and outlook.

Another factor that might be predicted to affect sexuality is urban versus rural in upbringing. The data show that roughly a third of the women were raised in an urban setting, whereas two thirds came from a rural environment or a small town. We can easily examine whether these different micro-cultures made a difference in adult sexual adjustment.

One characteristic of the group of Mosher women that must necessarily occupy our attention is their level of education. The data reveal that out of the forty-one women who answered the question, only seven had *not* gone to college. More than half of the total who responded had a college degree, Bachelor's or Master's. Moreover, of the twenty-one husbands for whom we have the information (Dr. Mosher did not always include questions about husbands), fully seventeen had a college degree. This group of women, therefore, was far more exposed to advanced education than their counterparts in the general population. Putting data together from a variety of sources, only about one percent of all American women went to college in 1890. The figure is so small partly because the great majority of women at the time were working class – much less likely to attend college – rather than middle class. Still, it is plain that the Mosher women as a group were uncommonly highly educated even for the middle class, no doubt reflecting the fact that they were convenient subjects for Dr. Mosher, who spent most of these data-collection years on a college campus. The value of the group as representative of all middle class women therefore depends on whether and how they might have differed in sexual interest from the middle-class majority – their more numerous compatriots who did not go to college. Were they more sexually inclined, or less, or about the same? Fortunately, data do exist to shed light on this question, and we will duly explore the issue once we investigate the evidence relating to sexuality and, in the process, establish appropriate yardsticks to measure sexual attitudes and behavior.

In assessing whether the Mosher survey supports or refutes the model of repression, we are of course limited in our resources to the questions that Dr. Mosher happened to ask, given her own purposes. Many of the questions were neither asked nor answered in ways that would be most helpful to us, but, fortunately, there are numerous others that speak quite directly to our interests.

Prior Knowledge

Dr. Mosher asked what knowledge of sexual physiology the women had before marriage and how they obtained it. The question as worded is not too helpful because it highlights physiology, whereas we would be more interested in knowledge about the sex act itself. It turns out, however, that this question was answered in quite helpful ways. One woman (respondent No. 9, Eleanor Girard), for example, wrote, "Knew what sexual intercourse was, told by others." Another (No. 19) said, "Not the least in the world." (By the way, I gave names only to the eighteen women of the portraits; the others are identified only by the numbers assigned to them by Dr. Mosher.) The responses were such, in other words, that it was possible to score the knowledge question as to whether the subjects were aware of the nature of sexual intercourse before they were enlightened by personal experience in marriage. The repression model would lead us to assume that, as youngsters, these women would very rarely have talked to their mothers, older sisters, or even their peers about sexual matters. The subject was generally taboo, even on the American side of the Atlantic.

Here is a response (No. 41, Maude Eldridge) that is typical of what we might expect, given the religious and medical literatures and the coalition for repression: "Vague ideas from fellow pupils at school. My mother was a physician but refused to instruct me when I asked questions. I remember well the first time I asked a question which showed that I already had the idea there was something shameful about child bearing. Yet, she told me I would read books about it when I was older, and I never asked again."

The results on whether enlightening information was obtained by the respondents are important for two reasons. One is that knowing ahead of time what to expect might affect eventual adjustment. Those who had a pretty good idea what was coming and had time to assimilate the information might adjust fairly readily, whereas those who were completely ignorant might find it difficult or even impossible to recover from the shock of the wedding night. The French novelist George Sand, who did manage to overcome her own innocence and eventually to have many lovers, nevertheless wrote the following:

> Prevent your [future] son-in-law from brutalizing your daughter on their wedding night, for among delicate women many organic weaknesses and painful childbirth have no other cause. Men are not sufficiently aware that this amusement is a martyrdom for us. . . . [Advise him to] temper his pleasure a little and to wait until he has brought his wife little by little to understand it and respond to it. Nothing is so horrifying as the terror, the suffering, and the disgust of a poor child who knows nothing and who finds herself raped by a brute. We bring them up . . . as much as we can, as saints, and then we hand them over like fillies.[7]

In our own study, consider Respondent No. 27, who seems to have reacted as George Sand would have predicted. Her answer to the question about how

7 George Sand, quoted in Gay 1984, p. 286.

much knowledge she had was (as recorded by Dr. Mosher), "None. Ran away 1 mo. after marriage. Sent back by parents & told to behave."

We will check to see if knowing ahead of time what to expect meant greater success in adjusting to the sexual side of married life. The goal of the coalition, of course, would have been that sex should be a nuisance to these women no matter what they knew about it beforehand.

In addition to its possible effect on adjustment, the data regarding knowledge should serve as evidence on the extent to which repression was successful. The model would have young women led to the altar in complete innocence; if it turned out that most of them were fully knowledgeable, repression was not accomplishing one of its major goals.

The data tell us that twenty-seven of the women definitely or very probably did not know what to expect, that is, did not know what sexual intercourse was. That makes sixty percent of the forty-five women. Eighteen of the subjects, or forty percent, did learn the basic facts ahead of time. I would count that 60/40 split as a failure of the forces attempting to repress the sexuality of women. True, they succeeded in shielding most of these forty-five study participants, but the coalition would have hoped for a better record. The important question, however, is what difference knowing or not knowing made in behavior and attitudes. I will give the details in the next section but can anticipate a bit here by reporting that it made no difference at all. The adjustment to the sexual aspect of their new lives was essentially the same whether they knew what to expect ahead of time or not. The portraits, especially, teach us that what counted most heavily was not knowledge of facts but the complex characteristics of personal experience once the initial introduction was well over.

The Mosher survey is unique in its direct application to questions about Victorian women. It is not, however, the only quantitative study with at least some relevance to the topic. In particular, Dr. Katharine B. Davis, an American sociologist, carried out an extraordinarily large study[8] in 1920[9] – about the time that Dr. Mosher was concluding the very last of her interviews. It is not completely relevant because the one thousand married women that constituted

8 Davis 1929.

9 Dickinson and Beam 1970, p. vii.

about half of her sample (the other half were unmarried college graduates) were born much later than the Mosher women. Whereas the average birth year of the Mosher women was 1863, that of the Davis women was 1882. Crucially, a very large proportion of the latter were socialized after 1890, when Victorian moral standards were becoming more permissive; indeed, many were socialized after the First World War, when those same changes in standards accelerated with a rush. With these differences of culture in mind, however, the Davis study can be of substantial value for our purposes. The one thousand married women were not a random sample of the American population. However, the sheer size of the group, together with a method of selection that suggests broad coverage of ordinary, literate, mainly middle-class women,[10] make it a valuable picture of an important segment of American womanhood at the time. If, given the known generational differences in culture, the Mosher results seem to fit a reasonable historical pattern, then they too may be taken at least tentatively as representing a common rather than an offbeat segment of women. In other words, the comparisons would speak to the representativeness of our small sample of forty-five.

Since Dr. Davis had no idea of the existence of the Mosher survey, let alone its contents, it is not surprising that she asked totally different questions (dwelling heavily, for example, on masturbation and on homosexuality, neither of which was touched by Dr. Mosher) and phrased similar questions differently. For knowledge, she asked, "Had you been at all adequately prepared by instruction for the sex side of marriage?" After adjusting for responses that, Dr. Davis thought, might not really indicate adequate preparation, it turns out that the proportion knowledgeable in the Davis survey is close to the forty percent we found among the Mosher women – an encouraging finding in terms of the representativeness of Dr. Mosher's sample.[11] Thus, if preparation for the sexual side of marriage increased at all around the turn of the twentieth century, it probably did not increase by much. More importantly, the fact that more than half of all middle-class women got married with no knowledge of the nature

10 Davis 1929, pp. xi-xii.

11 Davis 1929, p. 64. For example, taking the first ten categories of "instruction" in Table I, minus categories three and seven, yields thirty-nine percent knowledgeable.

of sexual intercourse indicates in both time periods a strong suppression of sex as a subject of discussion, at least partly motivated by the desire to keep young women in innocence so that they would not indulge. If a social system did not care much whether its young women indulged or not, as has gradually become the case in Western culture since the 1960s, there would no doubt be more widespread knowledge of what to expect.

This conjecture regarding freedom to indulge suggests another, potentially prominent source of the knowledge at issue, namely, premarital sexual experience itself. Dr. Mosher did not ask about premarital experience. However, she did ask about knowledge of sexual physiology and how it was obtained. A woman with premarital experience, if she were being fully frank, should have volunteered the information at that point, as in, "Yes, I had the knowledge before my marriage because I had the experience." If she did not, then she was either intentionally hiding the transgression or, perhaps, had managed to persuade herself that sexual intercourse with her soon-to-be husband could be counted as marital rather than premarital.

How many instances of premarital sexual intercourse should we have expected in forty-five typical middle-class women? Davis found that seventy-one of her one thousand married women had had premarital experience.[12] That makes 7 percent. If the Mosher study had yielded the same proportion, we would have expected three cases. We got none. One explanation would be that three Mosher women, although in general the group was strikingly candid, hid the information – or perhaps did not count as premarital an encounter or two with the fiancé. Another and fully credible explanation would be that there were indeed zero instances of premarital intercourse among the forty-five Mosher women and that the modest difference in results between the two studies indicates a change in sexual attitudes and behavior between the respective time periods – a change that would be roughly predicted from what we know of the cultural drift taking place during 1890-1920.

All in all, if having no prior idea of the nature of sexual intercourse is a test of the hypothesis of repression, it does not pass with flying colors. Too many

12 Davis 1929, p. 20.

women somehow found out what to expect, even though more than half still went to the altar with virginal minds as well as bodies.

I will now introduce five items in the Mosher questionnaire that will serve to measure the sexual attitudes and behavior of the group. These items will answer definitively whether or not the group was sexually repressed. The items are: Necessity/Pleasure, Desire, Orgasm, Agreeable, and Ideal Habit. From there, we will go on to question whether we can generalize from this group to middle-class Victorian women as a whole.

Necessity/Pleasure

I turn first to a set of items in the Mosher questionnaire that happens to be technically poor by modern social science standards. Following an analytical scheme advanced by Dr. Alice Stockham in 1883, as previously indicated, Dr. Mosher asked: "What do you believe to be the true purpose of intercourse: Necessity to man? Necessity to woman? Pleasure? Reproduction?" On the face of it, the wording is very poor, making this a difficult set of questions for the respondents to answer. The grammar is twisted because the item asks whether necessity is the true purpose of intercourse, but necessity is not any sort of purpose at all. Further, by asking about *the* purpose, it would seem that only one of the four sub-items should be selected, whereas Dr. Mosher left space for a response to each of the four. Lastly, necessity itself is a hopelessly ambiguous term. What would be meant by answering that intercourse was a necessity? Would people die without it – or perhaps just be uncomfortable? Again, however, as in the case of "knowledge of sexual physiology," the Mosher women came to the rescue. Instead of nit-picking the grammar and syntax, they relaxed and answered in the spirit in which they thought the questions were meant. In a few instances, they showed that they answered the necessity questions as though being asked whether sex were a basic need like food and water, in which case they naturally said, No, it was not a necessity.[13] However, if they simply said No without further comment, one cannot be sure that this "basic need" interpretation is what they really had in mind. In most cases by far, however, it rather appears that the questions they really attempted to answer were: "Do you think that most men

13 See Nos. 4, 15, and 46. Landale and Guest 1986 appear to accept this interpretation as primary.

would suffer injurious consequences if they had no sex? How about women?[14] Is reproduction a significantly important function of sex? How about pleasure?"

The responses vary considerably in style, approach, length, and depth, but as a collection they communicate these women's opinions extremely well and they enable one to score the individuals on an important dimension that I will refer to as Necessity/Pleasure. Recalling the established stereotype and the conservative medical opinion, no Victorian woman should have considered sex to be necessary, either for her or for women in general. Women should be able to get along perfectly well without it. In the same manner, they should definitely not have considered pleasure to be a true purpose or a significantly important function of sexual intercourse. Sex was to be tolerated, not enjoyed. If a respondent answered that sex was not necessary and not for pleasure, or answered No on one of these and left the other blank, I scored her as Low on Necessity/Pleasure, that is, as stereotypically Victorian. If she answered in the affirmative on either one, however, showing quite a radical departure from the stereotype, I scored her as High on this factor.[15] Under the repression hypothesis, we should expect zero Highs. It would truly have been a radical revolt to say that sex was necessary to women or that its purpose was pleasure. If the results showed a great many Highs, it would seem to shatter the repression hypothesis completely. Victorian women cannot have been as sexually repressed as the traditional model would allow if they held liberal views on either necessity or pleasure, showing that they harbored much more modern feelings and no doubt acted on them.

Desire

Dr. Mosher included a question on whether the women felt sexual desire during pregnancy. More importantly, she followed this up with the question, "At other times, have you any desire for intercourse? How often?" A woman was categorized as Low on Desire in this analysis if sexual desire plainly was not a notable part of her life or if it was an infrequent, mild, or negligible occurrence. She

14 See Nos. 5.5, 12, 18, 19, 20, 28, 29, 35, and 41.

15 If she simply answered "Yes" to the question about whether intercourse was necessary, it was assumed that she included women in her response. Many, on the other hand, said something like, "Yes, but only for men."

was categorized as High if desire was declared definitely to be felt, felt twice a month or more, or was sometimes strongly felt.

Dr. Acton and others pronounced that well-brought-up women did not feel sexual desire. They were not interested in sex at all except to satisfy the needs of their husbands and to have babies. This became part of a socialization campaign both to indoctrinate women with negative feelings about the whole idea of sex – once they became aware of its existence – and to keep men from hitting on respectable women. The goals were chastity and, in married women, fidelity. It led to the division of women into Madonnas and Magdalens,[16] the pure and the impure, and encouraged a thriving market in prostitution. However, it is also the case that sexual desire is largely a physiological dimension. True, an intensive, repressive socialization can conceivably succeed in bringing about a psychological blocking or perhaps habitual ignoring of natural urges. Because it is a biological phenomenon, however, even if capable of being influenced by social pressures, we would expect efforts to curb or eliminate it to fail in many cases because the tendency is strong and natural.

Thus, under the repression hypothesis, we might expect our results to show that, say, twelve percent of the Mosher women scored High on Desire, give or take a few points. If it turned out instead that a substantial majority scored High, that would be serious. A lot of female desire means a lot of sex, and a lot of sex would severely threaten the stability of the safe and valuable Victorian social system. To the coalition for repression, a majority scoring High on Desire would mean that their efforts were failing, perhaps disastrously. To us in the present context, it would mean that the traditional stereotype of asexuality might very well not be valid. It would suggest that there was more inclination among women toward sex and therefore a high probability of more actual Victorian sex than the stereotype of repression could tolerate. A revision of the traditional model would apparently need to be considered – exactly what Professor Degler and others proposed.

A word of explanation is in order here on the quantitative yardsticks I am introducing as "expected" results under the working assumption that the repression hypothesis is valid, such as the twelve percent just proposed. These

16 Trudgill 1976.

quantities are not statistically derived. They are rough but I hope reasonable, intuitive benchmarks, as explained in the text in each case. Take, for example, the level of ten percent I will choose in connection with the measure we will call "Agreeable." This choice means that under the repression hypothesis, we might perhaps allow as many as ten percent of the women to find sexual intercourse agreeable, but not many more. If the data revealed that twelve or thirteen percent, or even twenty percent of the Mosher women found sexual intercourse agreeable, that would not necessarily be grounds for rejecting the traditional view of prudish Victorian attitudes out of hand, but it would definitely raise our suspicions and we would look to results on the other four measures to determine how significant such individual results might be for the validity of the traditional hypothesis of repression

Orgasm

This factor is much discussed as an important criterion in the debates between traditionalists and revisionists – perhaps too much from the point of view of our particular goals. I say that because many factors affect whether a woman generally achieves orgasm in her sexual relations. Most of these are of interest to us, but, even so, some have little to do with whether Victorian socialization had its intended, repressive effect, which is our primary focus. For example, many women need more time to come to a climax than their husbands do, so that their regularity of orgasm would depend not on their own attitudes but on whether their Victorian husbands normally took that time. Another factor is the frequency of intercourse. If husbands were insensitive enough to demand sex when their wives were not interested or not yet ready, then female orgasm might occur only rarely. In other words, if only a minority of our respondents achieved orgasm with some regularity, there might be good reasons for it other than Victorian repression of their sexuality.

But what if orgasm were common during this period? Victorian wives were supposed neither to seek nor to find satisfaction in sex, let alone ecstasy. The idea that they would experience the transports of orgasm on a regular basis would have been disgusting to many religious, medical, and social leaders. In this light, regularity of orgasm does have relevance to the testing of the model of repression. If nearly all of the Mosher women were achieving orgasm nearly every time, for example, it would certainly indicate that sex hormones may have been considerably more powerful than Victorian socialization.

The wording of Dr. Mosher's question was unfortunate, even if understandable in view of the rudimentary state of survey technology in her day. She asked, "Do you always have a venereal orgasm?" The reader will easily see that this is a terrible question. To be precisely truthful, the respondent who missed once or twice would have to say no, meaning not always. In fact, a substantial number did say no, and it is difficult on the surface to know whether that meant "not *quite* always," "never," or something in between. However, there are two mitigating factors. The first is that there were follow-up questions, namely: "When you do? Effect immediately afterwards? Effect next day? When you do not? Effect immediately afterwards? Effect next day?" The answers to these probes usually made possible a determination of the regularity of occurrence of orgasm for that respondent. The second mitigating factor was, as before, the inclination of so many of the Mosher women to find the spirit of the question and respond to that rather than to the literal wording. They rescued us once more. Instead of answering just yes or no to the "Do you always" question, they offered a frequency indicator, for example, "Generally, not always," or, "Usually, not so often as my husband," or, "Few times but not often . . . many more times no than yes," or, "Never but once or twice," or, "Not always orgasm, only occasionally," or, "Orgasm if time is taken." With these two aids, the respondents could be scored on the regularity of achieving orgasm either as High, meaning often or even more frequently, or Low, meaning occasionally, rarely, or even less frequently than that.

What should we expect in terms of results? An aspect of the repression theory is that great efforts were made, crowned with substantial success (according to the theory), to cause strong, negative feelings toward sex in married women – innocence followed by disgust, avoidance, and tolerance only as a duty. The great majority of the women should have chorused with Eleanor Girard on married sex: "Usually a nuisance. Never cared much for it." On the rare occasions when she did achieve orgasm, Mrs. Girard said that she felt fatigued immediately afterwards and felt worse the next day. These responses reflect precisely the frame of mind that is scripted by the model of repression. Let us then make a prediction under the repression model that we will find about nine percent of the Mosher women as having achieved orgasm regularly, that is, often or even more frequently than that.

Agreeable

We would not want to depend entirely on either the Desire or the Orgasm factor to measure whether these women were sexually repressed. They both have shortcomings in that light – Desire because it has a biological cause that might overcome socialization, and Orgasm because it can depend so much on the husband rather than the wife. Fortunately, there is an additional item in the questionnaire that is quite clear cut and that, in my view, could almost stand alone as a strong and valuable test. It is also, of course, a very welcome perspective to be taken in combination with the others.

Dr. Mosher asked: "Is intercourse agreeable to you or not?" All of the women provided an answer to the question, and almost all of the responses were short, clear, and to the point. The women could be classified either as High on this factor, indicating that they found sex with their husbands either usually or always agreeable, or Low, meaning that in general they did not find intercourse agreeable or found it agreeable only sometimes.

The hypothesis of the traditionalists would be that we should discover very few Highs. The substantial majority should stand with Mrs. Gerard in finding the duty to have sex a nuisance. Assuming that the Mosher women were sexually repressed, as the traditional stereotype would have us believe, we might predict a total of about ten percent who declared that sexual intercourse was nevertheless agreeable to them.

Ideal Habit

There is one final dimension in the questionnaire that bears directly on our main topic and that should be considered as one of the criteria for measuring the extent of repression in these forty-five women. It would be a great pity to leave it out. From a quantitative perspective, however, it would seem at first glance to be a failure, because thirteen of the women made a special point of *not* providing the quantitative information that seemed to be requested. In this one place, instead of going along with the spirit of the question, they apparently objected to it. They did not want to tie themselves down to numbers. The answers they did provide, however, are perhaps more revealing of true attitudes toward married sex than any other single part of the survey. In one item, Dr. Mosher asked her subjects for their "habit of intercourse, average number of times per week? Per month?" She then followed this up a bit later with the item we are interested in here: "What, to you, would be an ideal habit?" Eight women did not answer this question at all, so we have only thirty-seven responses.

The item can be scored in three categories – an ideal frequency that was Low, Moderate, or High. From the standpoint of the repression theory, the best answer would fit into the principle, "Intercourse to be held only as often as required for reproduction." The women who gave that response or who expressed a preference for having intercourse less often than once a month were scored as Low on Ideal Habit. Those who reported a preference for once a week or more were scored as High. Those who said they preferred once a month or more but less than once a week were scored as Moderate. It is clear that only the Low category fits the idea of repression. Preferring to have sex once a month or more is a transgression. It is too regular and too much! If middle-class Victorian women truly were sexually repressed – absorbing and believing in the conservative medical opinion and advice – they could not assert that their ideal frequency of sexual intercourse was two or three times a month or even once a month.

Omitted from the above scoring rules, however, are the thirteen women who gave a definite answer but not a quantitative one. Their varied responses can be grouped under a category we might call, "Whenever both of us are so inclined," with an emphasis on *both* and with several women qualifying this by indicating that, even when inclined, the ideal would be to refrain at times as the only sure way to guard against unwanted pregnancy. The large number offering this response would seem to spoil the questionnaire item for quantitative analysis. At the same time, it must be admitted that the reaction is certainly a sensible one – and perhaps even more sensible than going by the clock or the calendar. These thirteen women deserve to be included in the analysis; to include them, however, would mean somehow quantifying the non-quantitative.

The actual replies of these participants are important for getting a first-hand feeling for the attitudes of Victorian women toward sex, as well as a feeling for the spirit in which the Mosher women responded to this questionnaire. Here is a sampling:

> What, to you, would be an ideal habit?
> No. 10 (Margaret Osborne): Occasional intercourse, with control over conception, everything to be absolutely mutual.
> No. 12 (Deirdre Mueller): No habit at all, but the most sensitive regard of each member of the couple for the personal feeling and desires and health of the other. In fact, pure and tender love, wide awake to the whole of life, should dictate marriage relations.
> No. 14: Such as I have – Where intercourse is only held when mutually desired, and when no crime will be committed against possible children.
> No. 15 (Lucy Meadows): In general terms the ideal habit would be that which should most perfectly and completely serve as the physical expression of the spiritual union of husband and wife. My husband and I have not found yet what to us is an ideal habit. We believe in intercourse for its own sake – we wish it for ourselves and spiritually miss it, rather than physically, when it does not occur, because it is the highest, most sacred expression of our oneness. On the other hand there are sometimes long periods when we are not willing to incur even a slight risk of pregnancy, and then we deny ourselves the intercourse, feeling all the time that we are losing that which keeps us closest to each other.
> I wish to say that this need is absolutely spiritual so far as we can judge, possibly reacting somewhat upon the physical organization. We do not find health impaired in any way by the self denial.
> No. 16: As often as perfect happiness and union can be and not to affect health detrimentally.
> No. 30 (Barbara Townsend): Not to restrict intercourse to reproduction but limit it to times when not pressed with work; when time for pleasure.
> No. 36: Total abstinence, with intercourse for reproduction only. Until human nature is different from what it is now, it seems as though such a habit

> would not be the most healthful for all people. Persons differ as much in this respect as in others, & it seems as though the only way now, is to gain all possible knowledge on the subject, and then the two persons having equal weight in the decision work out their own habit of life.
> No. 44 (Molly Attenborough): When desired by both.

One thing is very clear from the above, and also very important for our analysis, and that is that these women were not rejecting sex. Read the passages over to be sure. On the contrary, they were embracing it as an important part of their lives and their marriages, but they felt justified in governing its frequency by certain sensible guidelines, no matter what the quantitative result might turn out to be. Their sentiments – translated into practical terms – would seem to exclude both a very high frequency of intercourse and a very low one. On that basis, I feel justified in scoring these women in the Moderate category for Ideal Habit. Again, the critical point to be drawn from their responses is that they were by no means being controlled by sexual repression.

From the standpoint of the traditional stereotype, the ideal response to the Ideal Habit question would fall into the Low category – either just enough sexual intercourse to produce children or just enough to keep a husband from becoming surly. Allowing that some of the latter would fall into the Moderate category (once a month or more but less than once a week) and assuming successful repression, we might expect, say, fifteen percent of these thirty-seven women to opt either for Moderate or for High on the Ideal Habit factor.

That concludes the introduction of the five factors that will serve to measure the extent of sexual repression in this group of women. At the same time, the quantitative results on these factors will test whether it is valid to believe that the Mosher women, and therefore perhaps all Victorian women, were actually sexually repressed.

Before turning to the results, it is necessary to look briefly at one factor that might be considered to be a good test of the competing hypotheses – repressed *versus* modern – but that actually is not. That is the frequency of intercourse. For the record, of the forty-three respondents who provided data on this item, four reported a frequency of once a month or less, sixteen fell into the category of once or twice a month up to three or four times a month, and twenty-three, the largest proportion, reported four times a month or more. On the surface, these results would seem to constitute strong evidence against the repression hypothesis, especially since the great fear of unwanted pregnancy probably held down the numbers. However, to an unknown but probably substantial extent, the frequency would have been determined by the Victorian husband, not the wife. Since the husband's libido and self-concern have little or nothing to do with our focus, the frequency data must be passed over in this context.

Let us begin, then, by displaying concisely the figures I just speculated we should probably find on these five factors if Victorian women were sexually repressed along the lines of the traditional stereotype. "High" means scoring in the categories specified above that indicate being quite favorably inclined on sexual attitude, feeling, or behavior –thereby tending to disprove the repression hypothesis. Of course, at best we would find all zeroes but that would be too perfect a record to expect.

The *expected results* if the repression hypothesis is valid are as follows:

Necessity/Pleasure:	**0** percent High
Desire:	**12** percent High
Orgasm:	**9** percent High
Agreeable:	**10** percent High
Ideal Habit:	**15** percent High

The *actual results* derived from the Mosher survey data are as follows:

Necessity/Pleasure:	**67** percent High – 30 out of 45 women
Desire:	**70** percent High – 31 out of 44 women
Orgasm:	**53** percent High – 23 out of 43 women
Agreeable:	**69** percent High – 31 out of 45 women
Ideal Habit:	**95** percent Moderate or High – 35 out of 37 women

Quoting or paraphrasing from somewhere (I cannot remember where): "We do not need any recondite statistics to tell us that these results are meaningful." It is as clear as can be that the repression hypothesis is rejected, at least as concerns these forty-five American women. In the conservative view of the authorities, no proper, repressed Victorian woman should believe that sex is necessary for women or that an important function of sex for women is pleasure, yet two-thirds of the Mosher women believed exactly that with respect to at least one of these two elements. Similarly, the authorities would have had proper, repressed Victorian women prefer as little sex as they could possibly manage to arrange, yet almost all – not just a majority, but almost all – of the Mosher women who responded declared a preference for having regular or moderately frequent sex – not nonstop sex, certainly, but sex for their own benefit at least in part and clearly in excess of that needed to have babies or placate husbands.

The influential Dr. Acton emphasized that well-brought-up women have little or no sexual desire, but seventy percent of the Mosher respondents to this question did experience desire for intercourse either definitely, frequently, or strongly. Dr. Acton was simply wrong, even for Victorians. The proportions are too great to be dismissed. Further, sexual intercourse should not be agreeable to proper, repressed Victorian women, yet thirty-one of the forty-five Mosher women found their sexual relations to be agreeable either usually or always. In this result, the full set of Mosher women speaks to us clearly: In collectively finding sexual intercourse to be agreeable, the group stands as a denial of the validity of the model of repression. It does not describe reality.

Lastly, I do not recall any church or medical authority as having written that proper, repressed Victorian women should not have an orgasm. Several of what I have termed the "liberal" medical authorities said that they *should* have orgasms, and it is possible that some of the Mosher women read those passages, although there is no sign of it in their survey responses. In any case, having regular orgasms in an active sex life is not a sign of repression. Expression is more like it. More than half of the Mosher women expressed their comfort with marital sexual relations through the medium of regular orgasms; that is: often, generally, usually, nearly always, or always.

I must dwell for one additional moment on the orgasm factor. In a 1985 article, Carol and Peter Stearns pointed out that the results of the Mosher survey show Victorian women to have been more sexually satisfied than modern women, an outcome that is difficult to explain.[17] The implication is that there might be something wrong, something amiss, in the Mosher survey data. They cited a rigorous 1978 study in which sixty-one percent of mid-twentieth-century married women reported having difficulty achieving orgasm.[18] In our data, forty-seven percent were *not* High on the orgasm factor; that is, they achieved orgasm only occasionally, rarely, or never. There is a difference here of fourteen percentage points in favor of the satisfaction of our Victorians. Moreover, there was a greater proportion of "nevers" in the modern study than among the Victorians. The differences are not very large

17 Stearns and Stearns 1985.

18 Frank, Anderson, and Rubinstein 1978.

and can be explained. I relegate the explanation to a footnote for the benefit of those who are interested.[19]

If it were just one or two of our five measures that contradicted repression, there might be the possibility that there were some chance quirks here, but the fact that all five of the items have strong numbers denying the validity of the repression hypothesis indicates the consistency of a true, well-established, and well-rounded state of affairs. From these data, there is no escaping the conclusion that the traditional view of female sexuality in the Victorian age – the model of repression – is mistaken. The revisionists, basing their position predominantly on the Mosher survey, appear to have a sound and convincing case – depending, of course, on the representativeness of this small, non-random sample.

In this section, we have established the criteria for judgment – items in the survey that serve to test which theory of the sexual behavior of middle-class Victorian women is correct, traditional, or revisionist – and we looked at the proportions of Mosher women giving the indicative responses to those key questions. The palm of victory clearly goes to the revisionists; the results emerging from item after item are way too strong to permit any other conclusion. The traditional model is wrong.

That conclusion, however, is starkly contradictory to the one we reached on the basis of the temper of the times, the novels, and statistics from vital records and later surveys. These other sources prove that the traditional model is the correct one, beyond a shadow of a doubt. If we can accept the Mosher survey as representative of middle-class Victorian women in general, that flat contradiction would then have to be explained. Can we generalize from these forty-five women, or were they different, odd, special, atypical, unusual, or offbeat in some way?

---

19 Two factors need to be taken into account. The first is that "having difficulty" achieving orgasm is not the same as reaching orgasm only occasionally, rarely, or never. If several of the women in the modern study who reported having difficulty nevertheless did often achieve orgasm – and were duly subtracted from the total – the two tallies would be closer together. Second, the frequency of intercourse was greater in the modern study than in the Mosher study – 44% as against 33% in the Mosher study having intercourse once per week or more. Frequency can depress satisfaction. The topic is discussed later in this chapter.

Representativeness

Were they typical or not? If not, did their atypical qualities influence their sexual attitudes and behaviors in some way?

The Mosher survey is a very attractive subject of study in part because, as a group, the women are exceptionally appealing. Their responses show so much candor, so much simple honesty, so great a willingness to look inside themselves for the truth even on these intimate matters, so gentle a manner of communication, and at the same time, such variation in background, experience, outlook, and expression that one feels one is seeing in microcosm the very essence of Victorian womanhood. These qualities give one a great deal of confidence that the survey responses are "reliable," that is, that they accurately reflect the reality of the various sexual adjustments of these forty-five women. Unfortunately, these same qualities cannot give us the assurance that the Mosher women accurately represent the sexual adjustments of middle-class American Victorian women in general.

My primary strategy for determining whether we can accept the sexuality of the Mosher women as a reasonably representative sample – that is, as being a faithful picture not only of themselves but of broad, middle-class Victorian reality – will be to find the important ways in which they might be special or different and test whether those ways affected their sexuality. We can never find all the possible ways in which they might be special, nor would we have the data to test whether each of these infinite possibilities might really matter for sexual behaviors and attitudes. We can only try to be as thorough as possible and hope that this is enough to enable both author and reader to reach a confident conclusion.

If one tries to think of what, if anything, might possibly make these women special rather than typical, several leading possibilities happen to be contained in the Mosher questionnaire itself. These factors are: the education of the women, whether they were mostly rural rather than urban, their preparation for the marriage bed by prior knowledge of the nature of sexual intercourse, and whether they used barrier methods of contraception in addition to or instead of timing and withdrawal. In addition, I will look at one promising factor that was included in the questionnaire only indirectly, namely, the possibility that most of these women somehow escaped the strict Victorian socialization altogether and, therefore, were less restrained sexually than we might have expected.

To test whether "special" characteristics of the Mosher women had any influence on sexuality, I will use not just one but all five of the sexuality measures established above, namely: Necessity/Pleasure, Desire, Orgasm, Agreeable, and Ideal Habit. Also, we begin here to examine the relation of one factor to another in the survey data. I set a fairly high statistical standard for relationships to be considered noteworthy.[20] In other words, a relationship had to be fairly strong to command attention.

Surely, the most worrisome factor in terms of the representativeness of these forty-five women is their level of education. In that regard, they definitely appear to be atypical. In the survey data, thirty-four of the forty-one women answering the education question (eighty-three percent) had attended at least some college. In the U.S. population as a whole, less than one percent of women attended college in 1870 and less than three percent by 1900.[21] Given that about eighty percent of nineteenth-century women were working class both in England and America (see Chapter III, footnotes 61 and 62), and making the rough assumption that all women who attended college in that period were middle class, it works out that about five percent of middle-class American women attended college in 1870 and

20 For the most part, I used Kendall's tau-b and tau-c (the latter in the case of non-square tables). It is a stable, conservative statistic and not so sensitive as Goodman and Kruskal's gamma to cells with entry of zero, as frequently occur with such a small sample. My threshold for considering a relationship important was a value of .35 or -.35. In addition, I required a probability of S, the numerator of the statistic, of less than .05 under the null hypothesis. The numerator does fine for interpretation in this context. This second requirement is not the usual test of statistical significance which, for the most part, is not applicable here. There is no question of inference to a population that has been randomly sampled. Also, there are very few cases in which an inference of causality would be pertinent because, in the relationships examined, there is generally the serious threat of pertinent missing variables. These two kinds of inference constitute the two prominent functions of significance testing (see Mohr, 1990 or Mohr, 1995). Instead, I use the .05 threshold for S as another measure of strength. The interpretation would be: If this were a random sample, the observed relationship is so strong as to occur less than five percent of the time by chance; therefore it may be considered to be a strong relationship. The combination of these two requirements seemed to make good sense of the data. The analysis was done using the statistical package, Microsiris, a free download, which is both convenient and lightning fast. I repeat here that the data set and codebook are available by writing to lmohr@umich.edu.

21 American Association of University Women, undated.

fifteen percent in 1900. These numbers are still a far cry from the eighty-three percent of Mosher women who attended college. There is no escaping the fact that the group of Mosher women was atypical on this dimension

The question, therefore, becomes whether or not being college women affected sexuality. The answer is no, it did not. The relationship between attending college and our five measures of sexuality falls short of the statistical standard I set in all five cases. In fact, the relationships are very weak, meaning that those who did not attend college scored about the same on Desire, Orgasm, and so forth as those who did. Furthermore, the Kinsey report had similar findings for a somewhat later period: both the incidence of premarital coitus and the reliability of orgasm for married women were essentially the same for those who had attended college and for the general middle class, indicating that college-educated women were essentially indistinguishable from the average of the middle class with regard to important sexual behaviors.[22]

I should add that for one of the five measures of sexuality, Agreeable, the relationship with attending college in the Mosher survey data did not miss reaching my statistical standard by very much. Still, it is only one measure out of five, and the strength of the relationship is hardly noteworthy. In sum, if most of the Mosher women had *not* attended college instead of the other way round, the sexuality results would have been about the same. As far as generalizing about sexuality is concerned, the fact that so many attended college does not damage the representativeness of Dr. Mosher's sample.

On the rural versus urban dimension, the Mosher sample is not atypical at all. The proportions with urban and rural backgrounds are almost exactly the same in the Mosher survey as in the U.S. population as a whole during the mid-to-late nineteenth century.[23] Representativeness is preserved. Furthermore, this factor explains nothing about sexuality; its relationship with all five of the sexuality outcomes is near zero, meaning that those from urban and rural backgrounds were equally "modern" with notable consistency.

There is no way to check whether knowledge of the nature of sexual intercourse was about the same among our survey respondents as in the United

22 Kinsey, et al., 1953, pp. 337-338, 401-402.

23 *Wikipedia*: Urbanization in the United States.

States as a whole, but again, it makes no difference. The relationships of the prior-knowledge factor with all five measures of sexuality are near zero.

Having looked at three possible reasons (education, rural/urban, and prior knowledge) why the Mosher sample might have been atypical – and therefore a poor basis for making general statements about Victorian sexuality – we find so far that representativeness is preserved.

The last of the items in the survey that I thought might possibly make these women atypical is the use – even just occasionally – of barrier methods of contraception. This factor turned out to be strongly related to one of our important outcomes: Desire. "Barrier methods" refers to the employment of condoms or cervical caps or diaphragms. Charles Goodyear patented the vulcanization of rubber in 1844, thus making possible a material that could be strong, thin, and resistant to disintegration. The first vulcanized rubber condom was produced in 1855. Ten of the Mosher women reported use of the condom. (That precise term never actually appears in the responses; the device is referred to as "the French method" – whereas Dutch or German would in fact have been more accurate – "sheath for male," "cundrum," and a few others.) Three women reported the use of a cervical cap. None name the diaphragm, which was scarcely obtainable before the second decade of the twentieth century and not widely even then. The responses indicate that these methods were utilized tentatively, however, without much confidence and usually together with other methods, especially timing, withdrawal, or some sort of douche. Timing was the dominant tool for contraception. Seventeen of the forty-three women who responded reported depending entirely or in part on the time of the month during which they felt safe in having intercourse – most unfortunate, as we have seen, since mistaken beliefs led them to refrain during or close to menstruation and to indulge around the halfway point in the cycle.

Relation of the use of barrier methods to several of our outcomes could have been important in that it would have suggested that many of the women were pioneers and, therefore, unusual, non-representative. The interpretation would have been that they found sex agreeable, had a high ideal frequency of intercourse, and so forth because they were in general more than commonly open to new ideas and trends, as indicated by their willingness to try these new methods of contraception. But the employment of barrier methods is not related to any of our four other measures of sexuality, nor even to the actual frequency of intercourse, but only to Desire. Even its relation to Desire cannot be seen as hurting the case for representativeness. That is because the direction of causality is suspect. Which is cause, and which is effect? If the extent of use of barrier methods in our group is not typical of the U.S. as a whole, one might be concerned if, in addition, such use influenced Desire. When you stop and think about it, however, this seems quite far-fetched; the use of condoms might affect willingness, perhaps, but not the actual activation of the physical urge. It is more likely to be the other way around, namely, that the frequent experience of desire caused a search for reliable methods of contraception and, therefore, a willingness to try the newfangled "cundrums," and that may very well be most of the reason why the relationship between barrier methods and Desire is observed in the data. Like the first three potential spoilers of representativeness among the survey items, therefore, the use of barrier methods is not a cause for concern.

To this point in the section, we have searched for factors contained in the survey questionnaire that might reveal the Mosher women as being different from the general population and, if such were found, whether those factors affected sexuality in any way. We found no characteristics that both revealed differences and affected sexuality.[24] There remains the possibility, however, that factors not included in Dr. Mosher's questionnaire might account for results so unfavorable to the traditional view of Victorian sexuality. We were limited in the quantitative analysis to the questions she, for her own purposes, happened to ask. Perhaps those who scored in the liberated column happened to be rebellious in other ways as children or early teens. Perhaps their parents were themselves iconoclastic. These are possibilities – albeit dubious ones – and there are no doubt others but, except for one possibility to be considered next, none

24 It might be considered that the analysis by David and Sanderson (1986) supports the above conclusion respecting barrier methods and, indeed, regarding the representativeness of the Mosher women in general. Unfortunately, that is not the case. David and Sanderson compare the Mosher women not to the middle class as a whole, as we do here, but to that narrower segment of women of the period who were urban and married to professional or semi-professional husbands. In addition, their criteria for the comparison are the use of contraceptives and fertility – number of children. These are not adequately similar to our five indicators of sexuality.

spring to mind that, realistically, would be strong candidates for explaining away the compelling results. Nevertheless, to remain conservative, I can only conclude that the attitudes and behavior of the Mosher women were considerably more modern than the repression model would allow and that the primary possibilities for supporting a claim that the Mosher women were different in important ways do not succeed in softening that conclusion.

Here is another possibility. It will be well to cover it because it relates to the issue of whether Victorian women really did absorb and really were influenced by the strict moral code that repression was meant to instill. One might ask whether most of our forty-five women could have been unusual and appear surprisingly modern because, somehow, they escaped being dominated by the standard, starchy Victorian ideas. There are two ways in which this might have happened: either they did not receive the typical Victorian socialization at all, leaving them relatively free to feel and act as determined by natural inclinations, or they were indeed subjected to it and were influenced by it but were somehow able to set it aside. If the former is true (they escaped the socialization), then we would indeed have an unusual and unrepresentative subset of women. However, the analysis that follows demonstrates that this was not the case. If the latter is true instead (they were able to set the socialized restrictions aside), then we must eventually wonder what factors could be responsible for their being able to resist or rise above the moral training that they did in fact absorb. In other words, if repression was applied but they did not end up repressed, how did that come about? We will grapple with that deeper problem, because it is clearly central to our primary issue, but must postpone it until the concluding chapter. Here, we consider the more immediate question of whether or not the Mosher women actually did receive and did internalize the kind of socialization for strict morality described in Chapter II.

They did, but in this case there is no direct questionnaire item on the subject of training or socialization. One has to make inferences based on other hints contained here and there in the responses and therefore cannot hope to get the pertinent information from all forty-five women.

Twenty-three of the respondents showed in a variety of ways that absorption of the Victorian moral code influenced their outlook on sexual relations. They clearly were exposed; they appear to have been subjected to the standard training, and it had its effect. That is more than half of the total number of women, and they happened to reveal their mindset without being asked about it. There is no telling how many more would have shown the basically conservative orientation if there had been a direct question on this, but it is likely that at least several would have been added.

A few of the ways in which responses betrayed a standard Victorian exposure to the code are provided here for illustration.

No. 22 (Mildred Conroy) wrote the following when asked about the reasons for intercourse: "In the married condition my ideas as to the reasons for it have changed materially from what they were before marriage. I then thought reproduction was the only object & that once [conception was] brought about intercourse should cease." In another place she added, "During the first six months of our intercourse I usually felt wearied and 'distasteful' afterwards; even when the act itself had been very pleasant."

Asked what for her would be an ideal frequency, No. 30 (Barbara Townsend) replied in part, "The ideal would be to have no intercourse except for reproduction, but it is often hard to live up to such an ideal." Asked whether pleasure is an important function of intercourse she added, "Yes (?), but not necessarily a legitimate one." [Mrs. Townsend's question mark.]

When asked what were the effects on her of intercourse that resulted in orgasm, No. 11 (Sally Warren) replied, "Very sleepy and comfortable. No disgust as I have often heard it described."

Affirming that she did sleep in the same bed as her husband and asked why, Dr. Mosher's transcription of the answer for No. 19 is, "Had always seen it so, and makes husband happier, duty as wife. When you think about it, no objection in her own case."

To the question about prior knowledge of sexual physiology, No. 35 (Florence Gibson) said, as Dr. Mosher records it, "Mother taught her that such things were not only not talked about but also not thought of."

Lastly, when asked about ideal frequency, No. 36 said, "Total abstinence, with intercourse for reproduction only," although she proceeded to qualify her response because it might not be healthful given the current state of human nature.[25]

The fact that over half of the respondents showed the influence of Victorian morality training without having been asked about it indicates that they were not unusual or atypical as a result of having somehow managed to escape the standard socialization. The conclusion is reinforced by another fact, namely, that Dr. Mosher herself commented upon this as a noteworthy factor. I noted earlier that Dr. Mosher did not carry out an extensive analysis of the data from her survey, but she did make a few notes. One of the notes that she made on a sheet filed with the completed surveys is the following: "Too often her training has instilled the idea that any physical response is coarse, common and immodest which inhibits proper part in this relation."

Among the twenty-three respondents who revealed the influence of Victorian moral training, sixteen nevertheless said that their experience with sexual intercourse was agreeable to them, so we see that they were somehow able to set aside or overcome the training they had received, training whose effects were still strong enough within them to emerge in their survey responses without having been asked a direct question. On top of these sixteen, five more of the twenty-three did not find intercourse agreeable in their own case but scored High on the Necessity/Pleasure factor, so that in spite of their training they now believed either that sexual intercourse was necessary for women or that pleasure was one of its important purposes.[26]

In sum, one sees over and over again as one reads through the surveys that these were women who grew up in quite a different moral atmosphere from children of the present day and, in fact, who developed and matured very much as prescribed by the conservative authorities reviewed in Chapter II. Two inferences are made possible by this analysis.

---

25 Besides these six, the other seventeen respondents betraying their exposure to the strict moral socialization were Nos. 1, 4, 5.5, 6, 10, 12, 13, 15, 17, 23, 24, 25, 32, 38, 41, 42, and 47.

26 These five were Nos. 19, 22, 35, 42, and 47.

First, we saw in Chapter II that there were many authorities, especially medical authorities, who taught that women did feel desire and did derive pleasure and satisfaction from sexual relations. There was, therefore, a question whether the conservatives or the liberals had most influence over the outlook of ordinary Victorian women. The above analysis provides good evidence that the conservatives had a strong impact; the preponderance of Mosher women showed clear signs of Victorian socialization in the traditional view. They were able to set many of the sexual aspects aside, to be sure, but there is no evidence in the survey responses that this was because they believed the liberal authorities. They may very well have; it is doubtful that we will ever know. I do suspect, however, that if many of the Mosher women had an authority to justify their "immodest" feelings and sexual responses, mention of such authorities or other traces would have been found in the data. In the meanwhile, I will propose that there were different reasons – persuasive ones – for their being able to act contrary to their prudish training. I will present this explanation in the final chapter, in its proper place. In any case, we see that the conservatives had their influence.

Second, based directly on this finding and with close relevance to the issue under scrutiny in this section, we have seen that one cannot explain the liberated attitudes and behavior of the Mosher women by supposing that they might somehow have escaped the expected Victorian socialization. Twenty-three respondents showed in their responses that their sexual outlook was indeed influenced by what is traditionally considered to be Victorian socialization. The real total may in fact be more than twenty-three because there was no direct question on this subject. Additional respondents may have had a similar outlook but happened not to reveal it in these indirect ways.

Having covered questionnaire items that would be considered good candidates for branding the Mosher women as atypical, one can go further and consider whether there are other items in the survey that might not be suspected to be good candidates but that nevertheless happen to relate well to the measures of sexuality. If they do, and if they also are not typical of the general population, they would seriously threaten the claim of the revisionists that the traditional stereotype should now be rejected. The Mosher survey would be flawed as evidence of the general picture. Social scientists sometimes refer to this procedure as a "fishing expedition" – just looking through the data for noteworthy relationships and then trying to make something out of them.

I fished and found only two items worthy of consideration or comment. One is the year of the woman's birth, which turns out to be strongly related to her indicating that intercourse was agreeable, thereby suggesting a cultural trend. The later she was born, the more likely she was to find intercourse agreeable. Simplifying a bit, the data show that those born in 1860 or later were much more likely to find intercourse agreeable (eighty-three percent High) than those born before 1860 (forty-three percent High). [27] Recall that we are looking for factors that might reveal the Mosher women as having been unusual or special in some way and therefore not representative. We find that the year of their birth appears at first glance to be one such factor, at least as far as their considering intercourse to be agreeable is concerned.[28] Defenders of the traditional view, the model of repression, might want to use this finding to claim that the Mosher survey is flawed as evidence because it only applies to late Victorians, and we already knew that standards loosened a bit in the late-Victorian years. It is not big news. The repression model, they might continue, is still valid because mid-Victorian women were less likely to find sexual intercourse agreeable.

This possible attempt to invalidate the Mosher survey as evidence would fail for two reasons. The first is that even the figure of forty-three percent – those who found intercourse agreeable among the respondents born before 1860, when repression was most stringently applied – is much too high for the repression model to tolerate. The goal would have been zero. Five or ten percent

27 Tau-b=.41, P(S)<.007. The birth years from 1860 to 1865 were critical: using the latter as a dividing line, the relationship is no longer noteworthy (tau-b=.21, P(S)>.17), meaning that the "before" group now contains a majority who find intercourse agreeable, so that it looks much like the "after" group. Using 1870 as the dividing line, the trend is even more pronounced (tau-b=.14, P(S)>.34).

28 Year of birth is unrelated to all other key outcomes – desire, orgasm, ideal frequency, and even actual frequency. It might be considered that, given that year of birth using the 1860 break point is related to whether intercourse is considered agreeable, it ought also to be related to a similar attitude, namely, whether intercourse is considered to be either "necessary" or for pleasure. Using our adopted statistical standard, it is not, but this is due to volatility in the responses for each particular year of birth. If we combine and group the years in order to have a series of larger subsamples, we find that for those born in 1830-1859 the percent scoring High on Necessity/Pleasure was 53%; for those born in 1860-1869 it was 68%; for those born in 1870 or later, 73%. These results provide a modicum of support for the expectation that birth year should affect the two attitudes similarly.

finding sexual intercourse agreeable could be explained away as resulting from women who were depraved, or not well brought up, or freakish, but forty-three percent is unquestionably a demonstration that repression largely failed. It is not a number that could be used to advocate holding on to the traditional stereotype of repressed Victorians. In essence, a substantial proportion even of mid-Victorians found sex agreeable in spite of stringent repression. Hormones prevailed over socialization in a great many cases, and the revisionists would seem largely to be vindicated.

Secondly, not only did a large proportion of the Mosher women find sexual intercourse to be agreeable in both the earlier and later periods, but, *both early and late*, around seventy percent affirmed that they often felt sexual desire, over half achieved orgasm often or even more reliably, more than fifty-seven percent gave their opinion either that pleasure was an important function of sexual intercourse or that intercourse was necessary for women, and well over ninety percent expressed a preference or inclination towards having sexual relations at least moderately often.

The well-known loosening of standards over time may be reflected here in the data on the Agreeable factor, but that does not mean that the Mosher women were unrepresentative, nor does it decrease the pressure on the repression model. They were representative of the normal trend over time, and even the mid-Victorian women, according to these data, demonstrated liberalized attitudes and behavior that cannot well be accommodated by the traditional view.

But why would sexually liberated behavior as measured by our five factors emerge as normal rather than special and atypical in straitlaced Victorian times? Why would the moral code and its violation so easily coexist? That is both an intriguing and an extremely important question. It has an answer that will become clear with the examination of love letters in the following chapter.

Before continuing, we should take note of what might well be considered a puzzle in the data just reported. Only forty-three percent of the Mosher women born before 1860 reported that they found sexual intercourse usually or always to be agreeable. If, then, the remaining fifty-seven percent did not consider intercourse to be agreeable, or found it agreeable only sometimes, why would over ninety percent declare an ideal frequency of at least once per month, as shown in the data? The interesting solution to this apparent discrepancy pertains closely to the discussion of the frequency of intercourse that follows immediately; I will therefore return to the topic in that context.

There is one potential cause of the major outcomes that was not looked for but that advanced quickly to the forefront as part of the fishing expedition. This was the frequency of intercourse (not ideal, but actual). Whereas other factors were related to none of the five major outcomes or at most to one, the frequency of intercourse was strongly related to three: considering intercourse agreeable, the experience of desire, and the reliability of orgasm. At first glance, it would seem to be a powerhouse of explanation. Perhaps these women were unusual in that, on average, they had high frequencies of intercourse, and that explains their more modern-appearing sexuality. A second look, however, shows that, surprisingly enough, all of these relations were *negative*! That is, the greater the frequency of intercourse: the lower the score on desire, the lower the tendency to find intercourse agreeable, and the lower the reliability of orgasm. In fact, the data show that of the fourteen women who indicated that they did not find sexual intercourse agreeable, twelve scored high on the frequency dimension; that is, they reported a frequency of four or more times per month. Moreover, of the eleven women who scored low on our measure of desire, eight were high on the frequency dimension. And lastly, six of the nine respondents who rarely or never reached orgasm also were high on the frequency dimension.

The incidence of undesirable consequences from frequent intercourse must have struck Dr. Mosher in her interviews because she commented on it in one of those brief notes: "Lack of consideration of the woman by too frequent coitus destroys psychologic sex impulse."[29] The notably important suggestion from the systematic analysis of the data is that if the husbands concerned had been more considerate of these particular wives, the survey results would have been even more strikingly damaging to the traditional hypothesis. Almost all of the women, in that case, might well have reported that they experienced desire, found sexual intercourse agreeable, and reliably achieved orgasm.

Return now to the puzzle considered above, in which substantial portions of the Mosher women did not find intercourse to be agreeable, yet over ninety

29 Mosher 1980, p. 5.

percent avowed an ideal frequency of intercourse of once a month or more. Might the apparent discrepancy be explained by the adverse effects of the frequency of intercourse just reviewed? Indeed, it can.

Among the total of thirteen Mosher women (eight born before 1860 and five later) who scored Low on the Agreeable dimension, eleven reported an actual frequency of four or more occasions per month, many considerably more than four.[30] Nine of those eleven declared an ideal frequency in the category of once a month or more but less than once a week. For women who tended not to find intercourse agreeable, that ideal need no longer be seen as surprising but rather as an expression of a preference for relief from too-frequent intercourse while still doing one's Christian duty as a wife.

Still, two of the eleven opted for an even higher ideal of once a week or more. Why would this be so, given that they did not find intercourse agreeable? Again, the same logic is found to apply. One of the two was respondent No. 43. She reported a frequency of two to three times per week for most of her married life. Moreover, while her reported ideal did fall into the category of "once a week or more," her particular answer was specifically once per week. This might still be considered high for most, but in her case it no doubt signified a better option than two to three times. The other woman was respondent No. 22, Mildred Conroy. Mrs. Conroy reported a frequency of intercourse of twice a week, then a hiatus for her pregnancy, then nearly every night. A careful look at the data therefore not only helps to explain why women who did not find intercourse agreeable might well report an ideal frequency of once a month, or even once a week, but also sheds light on why many of those women did not consider intercourse to be agreeable in the first place.[31]

These results on the possible negative effects of the frequency of intercourse are valuable for what they reveal about Victorian marriages and the experience of Victorian women. They also have relevance for extended intimate relationships in any age and will no doubt always warrant attention, but they are probably not as worrying now as they were in Victorian times. The standing of women

30 There were actually fourteen such women, but one lacked the information we need on the ideal frequency of intercourse.

31 A potential connection between the reported puzzle and the frequency of intercourse was suggested to me by Karen Lystra. She was right.

has changed. Kinsey and his associates found that: "The mean frequencies in the sample . . . had dropped . . . This means that there were fewer individuals in the younger generation who were having coitus with such extreme frequencies as sometimes occurred in the older generation. Various factors may have contributed to this situation, but the data confirm our impression that many of the males of the older generation were less often inclined to consider the wife's desires in regard to the frequencies of coitus and were less often interested in seeing that she reached orgasm in that coitus. It is our impression that today [the 1940s] the males of the younger generation more often limit their contacts to the frequencies which their wives desire."[32]

We are, therefore, left with no particular explanation for the surprisingly liberated behavior displayed in the survey data – but this is no bad thing. It indicates that the Mosher women, as far as we can tell, were not unusual for their time in any discernible way; they were apparently normal, everyday women. Not being unusual, there is no reason yet encountered to disqualify them – and their liberated behavior – as a good, representative subset of middle-class American Victorian women in general.

Of course, the only technically sound way to generalize would be from a "probability sample," such as a random sample of the U.S. and British populations, but it is way too late for that. In this case, however, I believe a random sample is not really needed. I said at the beginning of this section that we can apparently rely on the truthfulness and accuracy of the Mosher women's responses. Their sexual attitudes, feelings, and behavior, although perhaps surprising, are established. We also have now seen that these women were not part of some special subgroup that had unique, atypical characteristics which damage generalization about sexuality – such as artists might be, perhaps. For our purpose, which is to evaluate the repression model on the basis of this survey, we do not need to have confidence that the proportions and relationships in the Mosher study are very close estimates of the same quantities in the general population. The possibility of being off by several percentage points one way or the other is not a problem because the quantities involved do not hover modestly around twelve or fifteen percent but are dramatically high. All we really need

32 Kinsey, et al., 1953, p. 359.

to know is that this group's experience is real and that it is not unique or highly special. The latter, like the former, is now also established to a high degree of confidence. We see vivid examples of unrepressed women and have confidence that they were not unique. It means that there must have been many thousands of women with a similar range of sexual adjustment in the Victorian population. That is all that is necessary to doom the model of repression. The conclusion on the basis of Dr. Mosher's survey must be that the revisionists are justified. The stereotype of repression is not to be believed.

Two Challenges

It is important to grapple with some plausible challenges that scholars have raised against the revisionist conclusion, that is, against the conclusion that the Mosher survey results demand the rejection of the broadly accepted stereotype of repression. If these challenges were valid, meaning that the evidence from the Mosher survey must be seen as weak or flawed, there really would be no contradiction to be explained. The stereotype of Victorian repression would remain undented.

Not all scholars have been willing to accept the Mosher survey as a sound basis for overturning a century of belief in repressed Victorian sexuality. A new model, what I have been calling the revisionist model – depicting middle-class Victorian women as sexually knowledgeable, interested, and active – has not been firmly established, and I believe that there are at least two reasons for this. One reason – a very good reason – is that it denies a significant component – the sexual component – of the known, obsessively respectable tone of the period. The archetype of a Victorian woman, without any doubt, was an extreme example of respectable chastity and modesty. It is hard to come over to the belief that she actually was sexually vibrant. The image does not fit in well with the pervasive respectability that was both demanded and practiced. The other reason is that there are a few academic objections to the revisionist interpretation of the survey. Given the above analysis that finds strong support for the revisionists, I would be remiss if I simply ignored those objections. I will therefore consider them briefly.

The sociologist S. Seidman writes: "I wish to cast doubt on this revisionist interpretation."[33] To characterize the interpretation he has in mind, he refers to passages from C. Degler and P. Gay in part as follows: "Among these women, sexual relations were neither rejected nor engaged in with distaste or reluctance. In fact, sexual expression was for them a part of healthy living and frequently a joy." And also: "The Mosher survey . . . persuasively suggests that many educated bourgeois women in the nineteenth century valued – some even craved – a sexual commerce that brought an equal measure of gratification to both parties."[34] But a close reading suggests that Seidman does not really cast doubt, as intended, on such interpretations. He is more interested in showing that, around the turn of the twentieth century, sexuality began to be viewed to a greater degree than before as an expression of love and spiritual union.

His primary difficulty with revisionist analyses of the Mosher survey is that they fail to notice a change in outlook from those subjects responding before 1900 to those responding afterwards. For evidence, he points to certain attitudinal information volunteered by some of the respondents plus the responses to the item asking whether sexual intercourse is a necessity.[35] First, many more women interviewed before 1900 than afterward volunteered the word "primary" (or a synonym) in regard to reproduction as a purpose of sexual intercourse. This indicates a conservative outlook. Second, many *fewer* women interviewed before 1900 volunteered expressions, in one place or another, to the effect that the meaning of intercourse is love, bonding, or other spiritual emphasis, again indicating a conservative or pre-modern outlook in Seidman's view. Third, many fewer women interviewed before 1900 provided the response that intercourse is a necessity for women – yet again indicating a more conservative outlook in the pre-1900 group. All three of these findings, then, show the post-1900 group to be relatively liberated or modern and those interviewed before 1900 to be more classically Victorian, indicating a cultural change toward a more liberated outlook around the turn of the century.

33 Seidman 1990, p. 60.

34 Seidman 1990, pp. 59-60.

35 Seidman 1990, pp. 60-63.

I do not believe that Seidman's analysis damages the revisionist interpretation. He does not claim that any part of the survey shows truly repressed attitudes and behavior, nor does he deny that the survey reveals a generally modern or liberated outlook.[36] He apparently feels, however, that those interviewed before 1900 show somewhat *less* of a liberated outlook – an outlook somewhat closer to the traditional Victorian image of repressed sexuality – than those interviewed afterwards.

There are two kinds of evidence in the survey itself that undermine Seidman's concern. One is that there are credible reasons for the stated differences between the two subsets – participating before and after 1900 – other than a general cultural shift in sexual attitudes. It happens – presumably by chance – that the women who participated after 1900 were eight years older on average and had been married ten years longer than those who participated before 1900. Both of these factors have been known to affect sexuality in a positive or favorable direction.[37] There is, in fact, strong statistical support for the proposition that the apparent effect of the 1900 break point is due, in part, not to a cultural shift but to the age of the respondents and the number of years they had been married, so much so that once the effects of those two factors are subtracted statistically, what is left of the effect of the 1900 break point no longer meets our standard for recommending attention.[38] In a similar light, recall that Dr. Mosher's recruitment of subjects before 1900 mostly took place when she was in the Midwest and the East, whereas after 1900 she was in California. That

36 He does say (p. 60) that the results on whether intercourse is considered agreeable should not be taken at face value because the word "agreeable" is ambiguous. He suggests, for example, that intercourse may have been agreeable to the women only because it pleased their husbands. However, of the 30 respondents who scored High on the Agreeable dimension and also provided data on the Desire and Orgasm dimensions, 26 scored High on either Desire or Orgasm, with 17 of those scoring High on both. This is a good indication that in addition to pleasing their husbands, intercourse was most likely agreeable to the respondents themselves.

37 For example, see Kinsey, et al., 1953, pp. 353-354, 375-378; Landale and Guest 1986, p. 162.

38 I used the combined variable "considered intercourse to be necessary for women *or* considered pleasure to be the true purpose (i.e., an important function) of intercourse." The tau-b for the 1900 break point is 0.37, $p(S)=0.018$, so that Seidman's hypothesis is firmly upheld using this dependent variable. Corroborating with regression, the standardized beta is $\beta=0.37$, $p<0.02$. Controlling for the respondent's age, beta is reduced to $\beta=0.30$, $p>0.06$, and controlling for both age and number of years married it is reduced to $\beta=0.27$, $p>0.11$.

difference in micro-culture, which has little or nothing to do with time, might also have had some influence.[39]

We know that the strictness of Victorian morality began to ebb around 1890 or even earlier, but that did not necessarily have the particular influence emphasized by Seidman. The effect of the break point in this survey probably lies substantially in the age and geographic characteristics identified above, which just happen to have differed for the women participating before and after 1900. In this light, a large share of the apparently conservative responses of the pre-1900 group on these few items is part of chance variation and not the effects of an influential cultural development. In other words, if those participating before 1900 seem more repressed by Seidman's measures, it could be largely because they were younger, married a shorter time, and not from California rather than their being more classically Victorian.

The second kind of evidence against the proposed meaning of the pre- and post-1900 subsets lies in the extremely important similarities between the two rather than their differences. In terms of sexuality, the respondents in the two groups are strikingly similar in key respects. They are about equally likely to feel desire, to find intercourse agreeable, to reach orgasm with some regularity, and to prefer at least a moderate frequency of sexual intercourse. There is, therefore, a very great deal to be said in favor of their being about equally liberated sexually and relatively little to support a significant difference between them. Moreover, this equality is at a high level: for the *pre*-1900 participants, fifty-seven percent regularly achieved orgasm, sixty-eight percent were high on both the desire and agreeable factors, and ninety percent favored at least a moderately high frequency of intercourse (once a month or more). Therefore, the pre-1900 group alone in these terms, seems quite forcefully to deny the validity of the repression model and does not differ sexually in any notable way from those interviewed later.

There may very well be truth and value in recognizing a shift taking place around 1900 by which sexuality was seen more than before in terms of love and spiritual union. As for sexuality itself, however, strong evidence of a cultural

39 I could not subject this proposition to regression analysis because of lack of within-group geographic variation.

shift in attitudes and behavior around that date is absent. In this regard, the revisionist interpretation of the Mosher survey and its implications for historical theory stand undiminished.

The other primary objection that has been raised to the revisionist interpretation of the survey has to do with the frequency of intercourse. The actual frequency reported by the Mosher respondents is lower than is the case for more modern women. More important, the ideal or preferred frequency declared by the respondents is in many cases even lower than the actual, which would seem to indicate repression; that is, their true, underlying attitudes, especially their preference for a very low frequency of intercourse, are close to the classic Victorian expectations of modesty, chastity, and godliness.[40] The critical analysts do not explicitly claim that frequency and a few other problems disprove the revisionists and vindicate the traditional model of repression. In indicating that the revisionist interpretation of the survey is flawed in certain respects, however,[41] and that the frequency data show the Mosher women not to be very modern in their sexual behavior after all,[42] there is the suggestion that the survey does not provide a strong basis for revision of the traditional perspective on Victorian sexuality.

Frequency of intercourse is indeed low in the Mosher survey by modern standards, but that should not indicate that the survey is a weak basis for revision. First, the low levels are readily understandable in terms other than the effects of prudish Victorian socialization. Second, the basis for revision does not depend upon frequency of intercourse.

As almost all analysts and critics freely acknowledge, it was extremely dangerous to have a baby in the Victorian era. In nineteenth-century England and America, the probability of a woman dying in or as a result of childbirth was forty to fifty times greater than it is now. The records show that in the latter part of the nineteenth century, the prospective mother perished once in every

40 See, for example, Degler 1980, pp. 295-297, Seidman 1990, p 60, Landale and Guest 1986, pp. 157-159, and D'Emilio and Freedman 1988, p. 176. While many scholars draw attention to the low actual and ideal frequencies of intercourse in the Mosher survey, they do not necessarily suggest that these indicate the kind of repression hypothesized in the traditional model.

41 Seidman 1990, p. 60.

42 Landale and Guest 1986, p. 166.

two hundred births. That is a drastically high rate. For many women, it was little short of terrifying. Imagine the ambivalence – wanting a family but being deathly afraid of what might happen in the process. Consider these two excerpts from letters written during the period:

> I was awfully scared . . . because something was a few days late –. . . . You miscalculated a certain matter – it was due on the 16th but was as usual several days late – I became very uneasy and uncomfortable . . . when my mind was set at rest by the arrival. . . . I suppose it is cowardly of me to shrink from any suffering or death, but I know that you would think the penalty too great – I do think that you value my life more than any other that is or that might be, – don't you dear?[43]
>
> Poor fellow you do want a boy so bad and so do I but oh I dread it so I dont know what to say hardly – I want to satisfy you and I want your name perpetuated as well as you do, and I feel as if there was something wanting yet to our happiness. I *do* want a son *just as bad as you do* – and I feel a sort of yearning come over me some times to feel a pair of baby lips close to me once more and a little pair of soft baby arms and hands groping in my bosom once more. I know I would be happier than I am now if I had already a little *baby boy*. But I feel so frightened when I think of it – I am afraid to risk my life. I am afraid I will die and I am afraid it would be a girl after all and then I would have nothing to pay me for my long suffering and suspense. But Oh dear I *do* wish I would have a boy. Would you love me any better Frank for being the mother of a son? than you do now? I have thought perhaps I wouldent be so sick again as I was the first time. I tell you what I will do Frank when Nita gets to be five years old I will consent to have another baby.[44]

Most unfortunately, the relevant death rate in cities and in hospitals was even higher than the average. In those cases, physician-attended births, often in busy quarters, were the norm. It has been shown conclusively that most of the

43 Lystra 1992, p. 83.

44 Lystra 1992, p. 78.

maternal deaths were due to puerperal fever and that most of the agents of the spread of the infection were physicians themselves, going from a patient or an autopsy to another patient, very often with bloody clothes and hands. At the time, the germ theory of disease was barely known and certainly not accepted. Physicians were furious at the suggestion that they themselves were responsible for the death toll and refused to take the antiseptic precautions that had been shown by one or two researchers to be effective in keeping new mothers alive.[45]

Recall that if the size of a Victorian family were to be limited, the only method of contraception most husbands and wives could consider to be truly safe was abstinence, that is, restricting the frequency of intercourse. It is also true that married women were gradually acquiring more power over their sex lives during the period. They had been put on a pedestal of purity. One of the consequences was that this image could be used to curtail sexual indulgence.[46] It is for these reasons one can say that the low frequency of intercourse in the Mosher survey, and indeed the low birth rate in the statistics of the era, can be attributed to causes other than Victorian prudery. The following evidence from the survey suggests, in fact, that very little of it should be attributed to prudery.

The low frequencies of intercourse in the Mosher survey do not, of course, contribute to a basis for revising the model of repression. At first glance, they appear to do just the opposite, to reinforce that model, because rare married intercourse can be taken as a sign of repressed sexuality. Other elements, however, do form a solid basis for revision and at the same time they demonstrate that the low frequencies should not be attributed to Victorian socialization. How to interpret a low frequency of intercourse should depend on the feelings and attitudes that go along with sexual practice when it is held, even if that is relatively infrequently. If a woman generally feels repugnance, that is one thing, but if she often feels sexual desire, if she quite reliably attains orgasm, if she finds her sexual activity agreeable, and if she would opt to have sex not just for reproduction but moderately often, say two or three times a month, it is impossible to claim that her sexuality is severely repressed, whatever the actual frequency

45 The description and data are based on Loudon 2000 and Chamberlain 2006.

46 For example, see Smith 1973a, Cott 1978, pp. 233-236, Degler 1980, pp. 279-297, D'Emilio and Freedman 1988, pp. 171-180.

of intercourse. Perhaps the unusual combination of low frequency with these other, more positive factors can best be grasped anecdotally, by the example of Lucy Meadows quoted above: "We believe in intercourse for its own sake – we wish it for ourselves and spiritually miss it, rather than physically, when it does not occur, because it is the highest, most sacred expression of our oneness. On the other hand there are sometimes long periods when we are not willing to incur even a slight risk of pregnancy, and then we deny ourselves the intercourse, feeling all the time that we are losing that which keeps us closest to each other."

One would not want to say that Mrs. Meadows was sexually repressed because "we deny ourselves the intercourse." That would be ridiculous. She apparently had a beautiful relationship – including a whole-hearted and deeply fulfilling sexual relationship – with her husband. It is in this sense that one sees the low frequency of intercourse in the Mosher survey as a natural part of the new (revisionist) theory of Victorian sexuality rather than as a challenge to that theory. The better and the more valued the sexual relationship, the more likely one would be to feel the need to curtail it in order not to spoil it by too many unwanted pregnancies, let alone by a maternal death. Curtailing the frequency would be due not to prudery but to the desire to preserve happiness and fulfillment, prominently including sexual fulfillment, in a relationship like that of Lucy Meadows.

The other thrust of the objection based on frequency of intercourse is that the ideal or preferred frequency declared by many of the Mosher women was lower than the actual frequency of intercourse they reported. On the surface, that would be consistent with the proposition that repression prevailed and therefore the ideal was low, but that these Victorian women had to please their husbands, therefore the actual frequency was higher.

This difference between actual and ideal does occur in the data, but it is not true for the majority of the women. The statistical relationship is actually strongly positive, meaning that, in general, the higher the actual frequency of intercourse, the higher the ideal. True, there are several cases in which a lower ideal is preferred, but those cases are overridden statistically by the majority, whose ideal is about the same as or higher than their actual frequency. In this sense, evidence for the repression model, if it were to hold up, would apply only to a minority. I wish to propose now that, upon closer scrutiny, it does not even apply to the minority. Their ideal may be lower than their actual, but that does not imply repression.

Almost all of the cases in which the ideal is smaller than the actual are those in which the actual frequency is reported to be four or more times per month, and the ideal would be one or more times but less than four. Recall that the Ideal Habit factor was scored as Low, Moderate, and High. If we include in the Moderate category the group of women who basically subscribed to what I will call the Molly Attenborough principle – "When desired by both" – in their response to the question on Ideal Habit, we find a total of thirteen women whose ideal frequency was less than their actual out of the thirty-six who supplied data on both dimensions.[47] I find that the group of thirteen contains two kinds of cases that help explain why these particular women preferred less sexual intercourse than they were actually experiencing. In both subgroups, the reliability of orgasm is the critical factor in the analysis.

Of these particular thirteen who were having intercourse four or more times per month, seven reported that they achieved orgasm often or more reliably and six reported that they did not. Take the latter group first, the six who did not often reach orgasm. Having intercourse once a week or more and very frequently being cut off before attaining full satisfaction can certainly make a woman feel that less might well be more. Recall Dr. Mosher's own observation: "Lack of consideration of the woman by too frequent coitus destroys psychologic sex impulse."[48] Recall as well the observation of Kinsey and his associates: an important difference between the earliest- and the latest-born respondents was that the needs of the woman with respect to the frequency of coitus were less honored in the former group.[49] That seems to be the essence of the preference for less sexual intercourse here: too frequent coitus and not enough satisfaction – a matter of the relationship between inconsiderate Victorian husbands and frustrated Victorian wives, and not prudish attitudes instilled by Victorian socialization.

47 If we omit the women who responded with the Molly Attenborough principle, as most other analysts have done, the numbers are of course smaller, but the purport of the results is exactly the same. See note 49.

48 Mosher 1980, p. 5.

49 Kinsey, et al., 1953, p. 359.

Now turn to the remaining seven women in the category of preferring less, namely, those who were regularly achieving orgasm but would have preferred less frequent intercourse anyway. Why? We cannot know for sure, but here is a strong possibility, stronger, I propose, than socialization to Victorian prudery. Bear in mind the difficulty of preventing childbirth except by abstinence. Of the seven in this subgroup, five already had multiple children at the time of the interview: one woman had three children, two had four, one had six children, and one had eight.[50] It is highly likely that this concern for repeated pregnancies crept into the responses on Ideal Habit and to the extent that it did, especially considering the regularity of orgasm, the responses do not reflect repressed sexuality. Rather, they reflect the subordinate status of women, existing for the convenience and pleasure of their husbands even to the point of multiple unwanted pregnancies – a grim reality of the Victorian era.[51]

I conclude that the second objection (that the data on frequency and ideal frequency show the survey to be a weak basis for revision) is not significant. The relevant data show .that the sexuality of the women was not repressed; Among those reporting a low actual frequency of intercourse by modern standards (less than four times per month) and those for whom the ideal was less than the actual, scores on our main outcome dimensions – Desire, Agreeable, and so forth – indicate the same modern or liberated outlook seen in the group as a whole.[52] Therefore, concerns about the danger of childbirth, family size,

50 The mean number of children for the group as a whole was 2.4; the median was 2.2.

51 If the group responding with the Molly Attenborough principle is excluded, there were nine women whose actual frequency was four or more occasions per week and whose ideal was fewer. Of these nine, five achieved orgasm often and four did not. For those who did not, the analysis is the same as in the text; the frequency of coitus was too high for their physical needs. For the five who achieved orgasm often, four had multiple children: one had 3 children, two had 4 children, one had 6, and one had 8.

52 For those reporting an actual frequency of less than four times a month (n=22), 77% were high on Desire, 91% found intercourse Agreeable, 65% achieved orgasm often or more reliably, 64% felt that intercourse was necessary or for pleasure, and 89% had an ideal frequency of once a month or more when the Molly Attenborough response is included; 78% with that response excluded, (n=9). For those reporting an actual frequency of four times a month or more and a lower ideal frequency with the Molly Attenborough response included (n=13), 58% were high on Desire, 69% did not find intercourse agreeable (the source of most of the negative relationship between frequency and the Agreeable dimension), 54% achieved orgasm often or more reliably, and 69% felt that intercourse was necessary or for pleasure. With the Molly Attenborough response excluded (n=9), 50% were high on Desire, 67% did not find intercourse agreeable (the source of most of the negative relationship between frequency and the Agreeable dimension), 56% achieved orgasm often or more reliably, and 67% felt that intercourse was necessary or for pleasure.

and physical needs and tolerances explain the low actual and ideal frequencies of intercourse better than the effects of socialization for repressed sexuality. Again, the case for revision stands.

In this chapter, after an introduction to the survey and its creator, we have covered three bases. First, we saw that, as a group, the Mosher women were far more interested in and accepting of sex than the traditional view of Victorian attitudes and practice would have predicted. Second, we searched for ways in which these results might be explained by the respondents' being atypical and therefore collectively poor as a representation of middle-class Victorian sexuality in general. The conclusion was that they were not atypical in ways that affected their sexuality insofar as we could discern but with the reservation that more will be said about this in the final chapter. Third, we examined scholarly reservations about the validity or at least the strength of the Mosher survey as a basis for needing to revise the traditional model. The conclusion of the analysis was that the objections are not telling and that the survey should stand as a solid basis for revision.

However, we also have a solid basis in Chapters II-IV for maintaining the model of repression unaltered and undiminished. After one last interlude for portraits, we come to the final chapter, in which we examine love letters in the hope either of reconciling the two proven but conflicting analyses or somehow choosing between them.

Fifth Interlude: Portraits 15 – 18

Portrait 15: Margaret Osborne[53]

Margaret's father fought in the Civil War and was married during the course of that war at the age of twenty-one or twenty-two. This is the only mention of the Civil War in the entire body of the Mosher responses. It had ended almost thirty years before the first Mosher questionnaire was completed and, in spite of its huge impact on the psyche of the country, plus the fact that at least twenty-two of the respondents or their husbands were old enough to remember it personally, that lapse of time was evidently enough to subdue consciousness of the war in a context such as the present one.

Margaret had some colorful forebears. Her maternal grandfather was a ship's captain, and, after the war, her father became an inventor as well as a tradesman.

Margaret was a city girl while her husband, Jacob Osborne, was a country boy. He became citified enough, however, to earn a PhD from Johns Hopkins University, and he eventually undertook a career in teaching, although we do not know whether it was at the college level. Margaret was born in 1868, four years after the war ended, taught kindergarten for a while after high school, and married Jacob in 1891, at the age of twenty-three. At the time she filled out Dr. Mosher's questionnaire in April of 1894, two and a half years later, both of her parents were in their fifties, still living, and in good health.

Dr. Mosher asked about knowledge of "sexual physiology" before marriage, with a follow-up on how obtained. The answers were generally full enough, however, to allow me to score them on the more interesting issue of knowledge that marriage entailed sexual intercourse. Margaret's answers were "Very slight" and "Mostly from *Tokology*." The latter is a book by the American physician Alice Stockham, first published in England in 1883. The title refers to the science of midwifery. One can readily agree that Margaret's knowledge of the relevant physiology and certainly of the idea of sexual intercourse must have been slight because, as with so many of the other books on this subject available at the time, the language in *Tokology* relating to activity in the marriage bed

53 Mosher 1980, Blank No. 10, pp. 103-114.

tends to be scientific, vague, and quick. "Coitus" is referred to several times but not explained. In her most informative passage, Stockham writes, "The vagina serves as a passage for the menstrual fluid, for the foetus at birth, and for the reception of the male organ in copulation and in a state of health assists the perineal muscles in sustaining the uterus."[54] There is nothing about erection, lubrication, pleasure, or emotional involvement. It is not easy in any era for a young woman to learn enough about sexual intercourse to approach her first experience with confidence, but Margaret was apparently not very well informed at all and less so than many of the other Mosher respondents. There is no information on Jacob's prior knowledge and experience, a factor that can potentially make all the difference in the world, so the question of adjustment to marital reality is left entirely for other items in the questionnaire.

This adjustment in the case of Margaret and Jacob is rather startling and, at the same time, illustrative of the profound potential effects of both knowledge and experience – even brief experience. First, it is well to be aware that the couple shared a bed – for reasons, Margaret said, of "Preference." As far as we know then, they slept together for the whole duration of their marriage up to the time of the questionnaire – a little more than two and a half years. They had two children, the first born about fourteen months after the wedding and the second about sixteen months later, just a month or so before the survey. The first child, a healthy boy, was conceived by choice, whereas the second, also apparently healthy but whose sex is not given, was an accident. Asked if they ever did anything to prevent conception, Margaret replied, "Sulfate of zinc," and added sardonically, "It is not infallible."

An initial surprise is that Margaret and Jacob's first intercourse took place five months after the marriage. We do not know why, but there is no indication, as there is in other cases, of the husband's travel or of serious illness. Apparently, although sleeping in the same bed right along, it took that long to get used to the idea, to work up the courage, or, very possibly, to feel ready to have a child. Apparently also, this first experience resulted in a conception. Margaret reported that the second intercourse did not take place until sixteen months later – seven months after the birth of their first child (she indicated

54 Stockham 1911, p. 26.

poor health for the first six months after the birth). However, once the ice was decisively broken, intercourse took place about twice a week for most of the eleven months leading up to the time of the survey – including the first six months of the second pregnancy. Asked if she had any desire for intercourse during this second pregnancy, she responded, "Yes, at times," and asked whether she felt desire at other times she answered simply, "Yes." Whether out of restraint or ignorance or diffidence then, the couple was long in taking up the marital custom, but once practiced, or rather twice, it seems to have become as natural as would be expected of any young married pair. Was intercourse agreeable to her? "Yes." Did she always have a venereal orgasm? "No, but usually." (Margaret was not as forthcoming with extra words as were some of the others.)

Although her sexual experience was not extensive up to the time of the survey, Mrs. Osborne had developed views about the role of intercourse in a marriage and in the life of a woman. She did not feel that intercourse was necessary either for men or for women. She in fact wrote, "No," and underlined the word. Nor did she feel that pleasure was a true purpose. Ideally, intercourse should take place occasionally, "everything to be absolutely mutual," with care exercised to prevent unwanted children. Philosophically, she considered sexual intercourse to be an expression of love. "I think to the man and woman married from love [presumably the case for her and her husband], it may be used temperately, as one of the highest manifestations of love, granted us by our Creator." Her underlining shows her feeling that indulging much more often than their twice a week average would undermine the significance and value of sexual intercourse as an exalted expression of that eminent romantic icon – love. Whether this happens to be true just for Margaret Osborne, or just for her era, or would be true for almost any intimate couple in any age can only be a guess, but one that would seem to merit thought.

Portrait 16: Angela Kohler[55]

After seven years of marriage, Mrs. Kohler hardly knew what to think or feel about sex. Her responses betray a predisposition against it, but like Mildred Conroy and Barbara Townsend, her experience made dents in this predisposition and inclined her at the time of filling out Dr. Mosher's questionnaire to be ambivalent. She was then on the whole positive, but not strongly positive, and there were cautionary reservations.

There was one very important source for the weakening of the negative predisposition toward sex that she brought to the marriage. This source was the fact that she had been in love these seven years. Her own avowal was, "I have been very much in love with my husband." When a person is in love, we expect a certain amount of abandon, perhaps unaccustomed abandon – not just sexually, but in much else in life. Angela, however, seems to have been "very much in love" while remaining quite straitlaced and consciously proper at the same time – the opposite of abandon. "Personally", she said, "I prefer to sleep alone always," although she had not been sleeping alone except when pregnant. She had been inclined to think that reproduction was the only true purpose of intercourse and was finding the process of softening that position difficult. She probably had quite a good idea of what the events of the wedding night would be, gained from reading three quite scientific books, which she characterized as learning "in a pure and sacred way." Asked if her husband used tobacco, she answered, "NO!" – in capital letters and with an exclamation point

There is no reason whatever to doubt that she was in love. In fact, we will see the signs of it in her reactions to sex, but the passion was not diffusing unhindered over the rest of her being.

Angela was a city girl while her husband, Arnold Kohler, was raised in the country. Both her father and her husband were of German descent. She was born in 1862 just two and a half months after the birth of her future husband. Both she and Kohler attended the University of Indiana, and, given that they were the same age, it is probable that they met there and fell in love. Meanwhile, Angela's mother had died at age 32, probably when Angela was about ten years old, and there is no indication that her father ever remarried. When asked what

55 Mosher 1980, Blank No. 24, pp. 265-277.

her occupation was before marriage, she replied that she had, "An old fashioned training in housewifely arts and too-practical use of same, lasting nearly through my nineteenth year." It seems, then, that after her mother's death she was enlisted in the care of the home and bore those responsibilities through school and until she went off to college. She had three sisters. We do not know their ages, but it is likely that one or more of them also participated in the housewifely duties and took over completely when Angela left for the university. She also taught school for a while, as did so many of the other Mosher women. Angela and Arnold married in 1886, at age 24, and Angela filled out Dr. Mosher's questionnaire seven years later.

Just as love and marriage did not transform her completely, neither, it appears, did a great deal of grief. She had setbacks, but nothing in her words or her tone indicates that they put her into a chronically low state of spirit. The setbacks had mainly to do with children. The Kohlers had three up to the time of the survey. The first born, a son, was, at the time of the survey in 1893, healthy and happy. The second child, a daughter, did not seem to develop properly. They attributed it to transient causes but finally faced the fact that it was apparently systemic. They went to a specialist in New York who showed them that their daughter was both mentally and physically retarded – from causes, he thought, that could be corrected. He operated, but the child tragically died in surgery at the age of three years and three weeks. Meanwhile, a third child was a boy, "A large child (12 lbs.), proclaimed the finest new born child ever seen by doctor, nurse and alas! undertaker. He had an obstruction in breathing and lived only 10 hours."

Another factor that clearly bothered Angela, because she referred to it several times, was weight gain. When married, she was five feet, four inches tall and weighed around one hundred and twenty pounds. By the time of the survey seven years later, she had gained fifty pounds, to about one hundred and seventy-one. Twenty to twenty-five pounds were gained after the birth of the first baby and then another thirty pounds in just three months' time after the birth of the third. Worry and grief probably did not help. A little over a year after the birth and death of that third child, the daughter succumbed in the operation, after months of anxiety and concern.

Angela had an orgasm on the occasion of the conception of her first baby, but the experience was repeated only very rarely over the next five years. A factor in this might have been that their primary method of contraception was withdrawal, robbing the woman both of a little time and of the close experience of the male orgasm. Over the year or two before the questionnaire, however, orgasm occurred for Angela about half the time. Since intercourse had always taken place three or four times per month (fewer during pregnancy), this means reaching orgasm in that period about once or twice a month. Asked whether intercourse was agreeable to her, Mrs. Kohler did not specifically answer. In the questioning about orgasm that followed, however, she indicated that when she did achieve orgasm it "makes intercourse in a sense more agreeable." In a sense! Only in a sense? One would think that there would be little vagueness or uncertainty or qualification about it, especially in that when her feelings were intense and she did not achieve orgasm, she was bothered the next day by headache and disturbance in the lower regions. But this cautious phraseology is in keeping with Mrs. Kohler's ambivalence, her lack of readiness as yet to let herself go. We should note that "in a sense more agreeable" indicates that intercourse was agreeable to her at other times as well, but apparently less agreeable than when full satisfaction was achieved.

Angela reported that the couple had intercourse less frequently during her pregnancies and that she had less desire for it at those times, as well. Otherwise, she fairly frequently felt sexual desire. Thus, if one looks only at the quantitative scoring of these questionnaires, Angela Kohler emerges as perfectly well adjusted to the marital relation and as sexually fulfilled. She commonly felt desire, found sex agreeable, and frequently reached orgasm. One must say, however, as we did in the case of Irene Morrison, that she does not appear to have been a sex enthusiast. In answering the questions about finding sex agreeable and reaching orgasm, she said that she had "rather cultivated the passion," meaning that she was not inclined towards it spontaneously and promoted it in herself in order to effect a necessary "compromise." (Quotation marks hers.) That is, she knew that her husband wanted this, and, loving him as she did, she tried and at least partially succeeded in feeling positively about it in her own heart. Certainly, it must have helped that she often felt desire. Similarly, although she would generally have preferred to sleep alone, she slept with her husband when she was not pregnant for the sake of, as she phrased it, "getting along." Something, perhaps her Victorian upbringing, rendered her rather apathetic when it came to sex, but she was in the process of seeking to conform constructively to her new circumstances – "constructively" in terms of enjoying a close and healthy marriage. One must add that her partial success in this must surely have been due in some measure to her having a husband who did not make oppressive demands.

Angela Kohler believed that marriage must focus on children and the institution of family. Children to her, however, meant wanted children – children conceived in love and choice. Too much sex meant too strong a risk of accidents, that is, unwanted children. On the other hand, she began to feel that there can also be too little sex. It is true that she believed at first that marital sex was for reproduction only. She said, however, that her "ideas have undergone some modification through experience." She came to see that married sex could beget "a certain bond of love and sympathy" between husband and wife when it was "mutual" (her emphasis) and when they were "happily mated." Furthermore, this valuable bond could be forged and maintained only by sexual communion – what she referred to as the "marital relation." She realized this, and the feeling seems quite obviously to have been genuine, but it had not yet taken over the control of her spontaneous orientation by the time of the survey. It is a tone of non-engagement rather than enthusiasm that emerges from her written responses. However, she was barely into her thirties when we met her. Additional time may have brought change toward greater conviction – one way or the other.

Portrait 17: Dorothy Farnsworth[56]

We cannot be certain exactly what it was, but something was wrong, and deeply wrong, in the relationship between Mrs. Farnsworth and her husband. There is a question toward the very end of Dr. Mosher's questionnaire that reads: "What other reasons besides reproduction are sufficient to warrant intercourse?" It was quite often answered in terms of the personal functions or effects of the sexual relation. We have already seen that many of the women responded with thoughts about a bond between husband and wife or about the importance of intercourse for maintaining the quality of the relationship. Mrs. Farnsworth's response was quite radically different. She said (or rather Dr. Mosher transcribed her response as):

> Shock and destruction of all ideals: When a pure woman is treated by her husband as he has treated the prostitute he has been to before marriage, it becomes loathsome.

"Loathsome" is a strong term. Mrs. Farnsworth had bitter feelings of injury and resentment. The ideals she speaks of as having been destroyed no doubt refer to love, along with the marriage vows of "to honor and to cherish." She indicated that her treatment by her husband was a violation of her purity. It may well be that she and Dr. Mosher knew from the conversation just what sort of treatment she referred to, but we can only guess that his sexual behavior must not have been loving at all but offensively brusque, self-oriented, and uncaring. Did she say something to him about it? There is nothing in the survey to indicate that she did. It would not be characteristically Victorian to do so, although no doubt some women would. Another version of the legendary advice to prospective brides cited early in Chapter I – aside from "Lie still and think of the empire" – is: "Suffer and be still."[57] That is apparently what Mrs. Farnsworth had been doing for the twenty-three years of her marriage.

Yet not even that is the whole story, for at the same time as she was apparently treated in the textbook Victorian fashion as a second-class being, Mrs.

56 Mosher 1980, Blank No. 42, pp. 418-423.

57 Vicinus 1972.

Farnsworth was also a biological woman. When asked what would be the ideal habit, she said, "When both had desire." This means that there probably were times when both did have desire and that it was appropriate, in her opinion, to have intercourse on those occasions – in spite of the fact that her treatment in the act was highly likely to be spiritually injurious.

When asked if she had a desire for sex during her pregnancies, she said, "No." How about at other times? "Occasionally." When? Before her period, she indicated, and when there was a "feeling of well-being and harmony." One would think that there would never be occasions characterized by feelings of well-being and harmony between Mr. and Mrs. Farnsworth, but apparently there were, in spite of the treatment in bed. In modern times, many women would choose divorce. In the Victorian period, when that was next to impossible, many would have been enduringly bitter and would never have allowed intercourse if they could possibly have avoided it. Another factor to remember, however, is the strong Victorian injunction to do one's duty as a wife – often thought of as one's Christian duty as a wife. Feeling under the charge of this duty, Mrs. Farnsworth apparently made the best of it, recognizing her own occasional desire, glad to have children, and willing to have closeness with her husband if it appeared at all likely to be rewarding.

Dorothy was born in 1863. All we know about her education is: "Private school." In addition, for the response to the question about occupations before marriage, Dr. Mosher wrote, "None." She married in January of 1891, at the age of twenty-seven, so there is a considerable period about which we have no information. The survey took place for her in December of 1913, just shy of twenty-three years after the marriage, when Mrs. Farnsworth was fifty years old.

The early years after the wedding were filled with child bearing. Dorothy reported that the marriage was consummated "immediately." She had had no prior knowledge of what Dr. Mosher tended to call "the meaning of marriage," even though she was twenty-seven years old. During the first year, she unfortunately had a miscarriage when two months pregnant, due to a fall. Children were then born in 1893, 1894, and 1897. This last was a birth of twin boys, but one of them was stillborn. The Farnsworths therefore had three healthy children, two girls and a boy. A year after the last birth, Mrs. Farnsworth had another miscarriage – in her fourth month. This one was brought on by a shock, but we do not know its nature. We do know that there was frightful hemorrhaging for two days and that her hair turned white. She said that this was during the Spanish-American War (1898) and that she had an incompetent doctor.

Apparently, none of the conceptions were planned. When asked, "Did conception occur by choice or accident?" the response was, "Accident." The only method of contraception mentioned in response to the relevant questionnaire item was: "Cold douches." Yet, between 1898 and the interview in 1913, there were no further conceptions. One might think to attribute this to a regimen of very rare instances of intercourse, but Dorothy indicated that intercourse took place three or four times per week. During the pregnancies, the frequency was not reduced to zero but to two per week. Why with this frequency there were no conceptions in fourteen years must remain a mystery to us and was perhaps a mystery to the Farnsworths as well.

Dorothy indicated that intercourse was not always agreeable to her and that she had an orgasm only occasionally. When she did achieve orgasm, she felt more relaxed afterwards and better the next day. When she did not, she indicated that she was "more nervous." We have seen that the wife's syndrome of only occasional desire, occasional orgasm, and intercourse that often was not agreeable might be due to some combination of too-frequent intercourse and mismatched timing, that is, when the time to climax for the man was significantly shorter than for the woman. It would usually take some caring and some discussion to work these things out. For the Farnsworths, that apparently did not occur.

Mrs. Farnsworth volunteered nothing about a bond between husband and wife or about a role for marital sex in maintaining a good relationship, as many other subjects did. We do not know for sure, but it seems that the relationship in this case was in fact not very good. The survey gives us two possible causes, and they may be closely related, namely, an inconsiderate husband and a frequency of intercourse that was too great for the desire and readiness of the wife.

Portrait 18: Nancy Wright[58]

Mrs. Wright was interviewed by Dr. Mosher rather than filling out the form herself. The information supplied was even more sparse than in other such cases, perhaps because it was one of the last of the interviews to be carried out, sometime in March of 1920.

Nancy was born in 1889, making her the second-youngest among all the Mosher women. Still, she would have graduated from high school in about 1907, well before the change in sexual attitudes that came with the First World War. Although she lived in the country at the time of the interview, she was raised in the city. We know that she attended Stanford University, completing not only the A.B. degree but an A.M., as well. She did not indicate the field or fields of her study. After college, she was a teacher for three years and was then married in about 1915, at the age of twenty-six. Thus, she was thirty-one years old at the time of the interview.

Mrs. Wright had two children, one born in 1916, ten months after the wedding, and the second in 1918 or perhaps early in 1919. We do not know the sexes of the children in this case and can only surmise that they were living and healthy at the time of the study because there is no indication to the contrary, which there probably would otherwise have been. Asked if the conceptions were by choice or accident, Mrs. Wright replied that in the first case they just allowed themselves to take a chance and that the second child was actively planned. These responses suggest that Nancy was fairly confident in her methods of birth control, but she probably should not have been. She said nothing about withdrawal or even timing. What she did say is that she used a "pastile suppository," probably beforehand, and that she always took a douche of cocoa butter and cold water afterwards. "Pastille," as it is now spelled, refers only to the lozenge shape of the medication. Thus, we do not know the ingredients. However, neither cocoa butter nor water nor anything else likely to have been available in that period could have had a high rate of contraceptive effectiveness.

Nancy knew what to expect in terms of sex in marriage. She said that she learned about it in part from her mother and in part from Dr. Cowan's book.

58 Mosher 1980, Blank No. 17, pp. 194-199.

Recall that Dr. Cowan's book, in addition to having a very small amount of detailed information about the sex act, was vehemently negative on the subject of frequent marital intercourse. It is uncertain whether the knowledge gleaned gave her a positive or a negative initial attitude, but for Nancy, somehow, the outlook soon became definitely positive. Here we have a living example of a subject just discussed in this chapter. Mrs. Wright was exposed to Dr. Cowan's radically conservative views but was able somehow to set them aside. How? We will see more such examples and an explanation in the next chapter.

She indicated that their frequency of intercourse was about once per week, "oftener at first," but that they stopped altogether after four months of pregnancy until the first child was two months old. (She said nothing about stopping during the second pregnancy for a reason I will soon report.) She indicated that she had no sexual desire while pregnant.

During normal times, however, she did experience desire. It might crop up at just about any time of the month, with no particular relation to her menstrual cycle. Sex with her husband was not only agreeable to Mrs. Wright but she "wants it." Does she always have a venereal orgasm? "Always." As noted, she regularly took a douche afterwards, but she then felt relaxed and went to sleep. The next day she felt "rested and refreshed." She made a point of saying that this was a "normal, natural function." As to the true purposes of intercourse, she said that it was "physically necessary to the woman as well as the man for a complete life." Is pleasure a purpose? Yes, she indicated, if not too frequent. Reflecting on her experience, she concluded that coitus supplied a "sense of completeness, a spiritual completeness which is not gained in any other way." Lastly, Mrs. Wright made a point of saying that it was she who regulated the frequency. She always determined when intercourse was held, and she believed that any woman could do the same.

I would say that holding onto the repression model of Victorian sexuality in the face of Nancy Wright's experience would have to be extremely difficult.

There are a few notes about Nancy's husband at the end of her interview. We learn his height and weight and the fact that he was a civil engineer, a "U.C. man" (University of California). In the very last line, we make the unprepared discovery, with immense dismay, that he died of influenza before the second child was born – most likely in the great and virulent, world-wide influenza epidemic of 1918, which affected fully twenty-five percent of the American population. Thus, the rewarding sexual aspects of Nancy Wright's marriage were cut tragically short by her husband's untimely death.

VI

Conclusion: Evidence from love letters and solution of the mystery

Our principal aim has been to solve the mystery of the true sexual behavior of middle-class Victorian women. In this chapter, we will not only wonder whether they undertook sexual activity of various kinds but what it meant to them. Did they talk about it? If they had desires, did they admit it to themselves? We saw in earlier chapters what came down from sermons, books, and parents, but what were the orientations of the relevant individuals themselves? Our interest extends to how they felt about what they did and did not do. And also, why? What were the motivating forces behind their attitudes and actions?

I will aim for as complete an understanding of their positive or negative engagement with sex as possible. This can help us a great deal in inferring their likely behavior and that of others in their social milieu. The evidence considered to this point has been starkly conflicting, but it has also been superficial. Statistics and vital records tell us nothing about states of mind. The novels are of little help in this because of the strong taboo against dwelling on sexual matters, except to direct proper attention to the occurrence of sin. The Mosher survey comes closest, but most of the responses tend to be matter-of-fact rather than deep, emotional, and expansive.

What we need are letters and diaries – the private outpourings of the soul written both with love and with candor to oneself or one's lover. As it happens, there is precious little of this sort in the published record from Britain.

Historians have, however, researched and published a fair measure from the American side. What we have is not sampled scientifically enough to constitute statistical evidence, but the collection from several sources does serve well, I believe, to give us the insight into states of mind that we seek. Although not scientific, the record will nevertheless constitute valuable evidence in our quest to choose between the traditional and revisionist perspectives. An appreciation of *why* a smattering of individuals did or did not behave in certain ways will show us the tenor of the times as actually experienced by individual women. This will provide support for conclusions regarding the extent of various sexual behaviors, but the understanding in itself is almost more important than the counting up of instances of desire, coitus, and so forth. I propose, finally, that the letters and diaries serve admirably in conjunction with the quantitative evidence to settle the issues that we investigate.

Thus, the aim is to use the letters and diaries in such a way as to constitute rigorous evidence toward the solution of our central mystery – in spite of the fact that, without probability sampling, the writings are essentially anecdotal rather than statistical. The method will be to quote excerpts from the letters and diaries in several key categories – unmarried lovers, illicit lovers, and married lovers – to show the thoughts and feelings of the writers about their actual and potential sexual activities. I will make the case that the letters and diaries do contribute in a major way to resolving the conflict that has been our main preoccupation.

Recall the definition of romantic love that was widely utilized in the nineteenth century and still serves well today: strong, unselfish affection blended with desire. For people in love, such as the writers of the love letters and diary entries that fill many of the following pages, it is difficult to separate these two components. They are individually recognizable in the passages to be cited, but we rarely encounter one without the other. Still, in order to capture the emphasis that the "romantic" part of romantic love received in the age of Victoria, it is well to begin by examining a few excerpts in which the carnal component is relatively subdued. The extravagant expressions of affection, more akin to old poetry than to modern speech, indicate the deep meaning and extraordinary importance of romantic love to those involved. Victorian sexual expression cannot be understood without it. The term "romantic love" has been analyzed in substantial detail by several scholars,[1] but there are certain aspects that stand out boldly as they are portrayed over and over again in the Victorian novels, especially but not exclusively during courtship. There is a massive intensity to the feeling. The soul soars; a giddiness besets the lover. The relationship is more important than anything else in the world. The beloved is put on a pedestal as a paragon. The beloved is nearly deified, even tending to displace religion as a source of inspiration and wonder. Love is considered to be permanent, fated; the beloved is the one and only. The happiness of the beloved is more important than possessing her – or him, as the case may be. The highest gratification of the lover lies in aiding the beloved. No sacrifice can be too great.

In almost all of the excerpts that follow, the couples are soon to be engaged or already engaged and soon to be married. Several toward the end of the section are already married. We begin with a very brief quotation from Nathaniel Hawthorne, who left a copious record of letters to his beloved Sophia. Hawthorne was a major American novelist, author of *The Scarlet Letter* and *The House of Seven Gables.* Writing would be natural to him and no doubt pleasurable. In fact, we will see that many of the love letters and diary entries in the published record are authored by wordsmiths – individuals whose careers were bound up with writing and speaking. This is one reason why the sampling cannot be considered objective and impartial. Numerous other included examples, however, come to us from non-professionals, some of them well educated and some not. With such differences in mind and sensitive to their possible effects, we seek an understanding derived from the documentation as a whole.

The reader will note many vagaries of spelling and grammar, as well as great liberties taken with punctuation. Again, these were left intact in the published record and I continue to adhere to the originals here. The italics in the quoted passages represent underlining in the source documents. This was a common and very freely sprinkled practice in nineteenth-century letters.

1 See especially Lystra 1992. Romantic love is a major theme in her treatment of the letters. The concept is analyzed and exemplified in numerous contexts throughout the book.

> Now good bye, dearest, sweetest, loveliest, holiest, truest, suitablest little wife. I worship thee. Thou art my type of womanly perfection . . . Thou enablest me to interpret the riddle of life, and fillest me with faith in the unseen and better land, because thou leadest me thither continually.[2]
> *Nathaniel Hawthorne, 1841*

Hawthorne refers to Sophia as "wife" here, but in truth, they did not marry until the following year, 1842. They had three children and lived happily together, through many ups and downs, until Hawthorne's death in 1864.

The time of the century in which the letters and diary entries in this chapter were written seems to make very little difference in the way the sentiments were felt and expressed. They all seem to be quite interchangeably Victorian. The following excerpt from a letter by Robert Burdette was written late in the century, in 1898. Burdette was also a writer by profession, as well as a Baptist minister and one of the most famous lecturers of his age. He was a humorist, but that side of him, with one exception recorded below, did not noticeably find its way into his love letters. Romance, on the other hand, is very much in evidence, both in the manner of address and in such details as the capitalization of key words.

> I open this letter once more – this is the second irresolute time, and even now I do not know what I want to say. It is as though I held you in my arms sweet My Own, saying good bye. At every movement of yours to disengage yourself, I hold you the more closely. And every time my arms relax themselves, of their own motion they tighten their grasp upon you. It is a lover's good night, only. Not a good bye. Come what may dear, dear Clara, you are My Sweetheart, My own dear Love, my Darling – my darling – my darling. And always and always, fond, and loyal and true, I am your Lover.[3]
> *Robert Burdette, 1898*

2 Nathaniel Hawthorne to Sophia Peabody, 1841. Quoted in Lystra 1992, p. 41.

3 Robert Burdette to Clara Baker, 1898. Quoted in Lystra 1992, p. 175.

Lyman Hodge, author of the following excerpt, was a Yale graduate but a merchant and not a professional writer.

> And now love, you with the warm heart and loving eyes, whose picture I kissed last night and whose lips I so often kissed in my dreams, whose love enriches me so bountifully with all pleasant memories and sweet anticipations, whose encircling arms shield me from so much evil and harm, whose caresses are so dear and so longed for awake and in slumber, making my heart beat faster, my flesh tremble and my brain giddy with delight, – whose feet I kiss and whose knees I embrace as a devotee kisses and embraces those of his idol, – my darling whose home is in my arms and whose resting place my bosom, who first came to them as a frightened bird but now loves to linger there till long after the midnight chimes have uttered their warning, – my life, with your generous womanly soul, my heart's keeper and my true lover, – Good night: a good night and a fair one to thy sleeping eyes and wearied limbs, the precurser of many bright, beautiful mornings when my kisses shall waken thee and my love shall greet thee.[4]
> *Lyman Hodge, 1867*

The next, very brief entry is from the journal of Mabel Loomis Todd, written when she was pregnant with Millicent, her only child. It emphasizes the vast importance to her of her love for her husband, at least at that time.

> I know I shall love this little one – yet not . . . with the strength in that sort of love which I put in my wife love – the one is not necessary to me – the other is my air & food & water – without it I should perish.[5]
> *Mabel Loomis Todd, 1898*

Crossing to England, our last entry in this introductory series is from a letter of Walter Bagehot (rhymes with "gadget"). He was a well-known writer on

4 Lyman Hodge to Mary Granger, 1867. Quoted in Lystra 1992, p. 68.

5 Mabel Loomis Todd, Journal 1898. Quoted in Gay 1984, p. 88.

academic topics, especially economics and politics, and was an early editor-in-chief of *The Economist* magazine.

> No one can tell the effort it was to me to tell you I loved you – why I do not know, but it made me gasp for breath, and now it is absolutely pleasure to me to tell it to you and bore you with it in every form, and I should like to write it in big letters I LOVE YOU all across the page by way of emphasis. . . . I go about murmuring, "I have made that dignified girl *commit* herself, I have, I have," and then I vault over the sofa with exultation. Those are the feelings of the person you have concerned yourself with. *Please* don't be offended at my rubbish. . . . Yours with the fondest and deepest love, Walter Bagehot.[6]
> *Walter Bagehot, 1857*

Unmarried lovers

Two entries follow that suggest women who may not have needed the moral code to keep them chaste before marriage; they simply did not experience sexual arousal. How they felt about sexual relations after their marriage is not part of the record. The first is from an ordinary (that is, not famous) middle-class woman. The second is from Harriet Beecher Stowe, author of *Uncle Tom's Cabin*, written to her husband after his revealing information to her regarding the licentiousness of certain clergymen. Note that she uses the term "love" in a sense different from our definition: it does not include the carnal component. Moreover, this is not an isolated example; there are other cases in the relevant published literature of deep, unmarried love that explicitly avoided, even rejected the carnal component.[7] Mrs. Stowe clearly preferred another Victorian definition of love, one that derives in part from the body-soul or appetite-reason duality discussed in Chapters II and III. In this sense, which I will consider to be secondary, romantic love is an intense spiritual affinity between two people. Both definitions seem to have been in common use even though they are ap-

6 Walter Bagehot to Eliza Wilson, 1857. Quoted in Gay 1999, p. 33.

7 Seidman 1991, pp. 42-50.

parently conflicting. We will see later in the chapter, however, how a trick of perspective could essentially erase this conflict. Note as well by Stowe's use of the word "astray" that she internalized the code: sex before marriage would have been morally wrong.

> I learned to hunger for your tender words and caress . . . but I never wanted extremes.[8]
> *Lu Burlingame, 1853*
> What terrible temptations lie in the way of your sex – till now I never realized it – for tho I did love you with an almost insane love before I married you I never knew yet or felt the pulsation which showed me that I could be tempted in that way – there never was a moment when I felt anything by which you could have drawn me astray – for I loved you as I now love God . . .[9]
> *Harriet Beecher Stowe, 1845*

The following are three similar excerpts, that is, the women involved have apparently not fallen in love – by either definition – and therefore have little difficulty in keeping their suitors at a safe distance; they do not have to fight down their own feelings. However, we see that they are very much concerned with their chastity, their reputations, and their adherence to what appears to be an accepted moral code governing this kind of relation. In a sense, this observation is old hat; we know that women even into the 1940s were aware of strict rules about sexual relations and were expected to obey them. What is important here is the presentation of hard evidence to support such impressions. The social and religious authorities promulgated the code, but did the women internalize it? Did it actually govern their behavior?

> I told him that he might call another night soon if he'd leave very early and not expect me to stay on the porch alone with him when he leaves. He says, if I loved him as he loved me I wouldn't care for the whole

8 Lu Burlingame to Will Adkinson 1853. Quoted in Rothman 1987, p. 136.

9 Harriet Beecher Stowe to Calvin Ellis Stowe, 1845. Quoted in Cott 1978, p. 234.

> world to know that he held me in his arms and kissed me good-night. But I told him it was highly improper.[10]
> *Maude Rittenhouse, 1882*
> When you come up again, we had better sit on the piazza and be dignified. . . . there will be lots of things I will tell you "you mustn't do."[11]
> *Florence Hemsley, 1889*
> I didn't think that you thought me that sort but now you know that I'm not. . . . Everyone has impulses now and then and I think . . . you probably had one and gave way to it without thinking. I haven't any doubt that girls have the same feelings at times but being girls can't give way to it the way a fellow can.[12]
> *Emma Lou Story, 1906*

One sees from these latter excerpts that the Victorian code governing relations between the sexes appears to have achieved widespread awareness, that it was internalized by young women, and that it had a pronounced influence on behavior. These cases furnish excellent examples in support of the traditional theory. However, we now cross over into new territory. From here on, the women are in love. Therefore, they have to do something about the sexual urges, even quite vague ones, that are part of that state. They might give in to them, or they might resist. Or, they might allow desire to govern their behavior to a certain distance but then draw a line when they sense a danger to something highly valued: chastity, reputation. What they do and how they think about it should give us an even better indication of the extent to which the Victorian moral code was either a powerful governor of behavior on one hand or a set of relatively feeble principles on the other.

In the first of the two excerpts that follow, Gertrude Foster is clearly in love and derives gratification from the physical nearness of her beau, but at the same time she is in no doubt that she will adhere to the path of virtue, as the repression model would predict. Madeline Doty, the young New York

10 Maud Rittenhouse, Diary 1882. Quoted in Rothman 1987, p. 232.

11 Florence Hemsley to William Wood, 1889. Quoted in Rothman 1987, p. 232.

12 Emma Lou Story to George Bellows, 1906. Quoted in Rothman 1987, pp. 232-233.

lawyer in the second excerpt, is intensely in love and is impelled to linger long in physical communion with her lover, the investigative journalist and novelist David Graham Phillips. But he did not believe in marriage for himself. She made her choice, and the agreement they reached was kept; the relationship did not continue.

> I want to feel absolutely certain that when you promise me anything, I can rest, since it is kept. . . . I made up my mind that if I allowed things I knew I should regret that I should not allow you to come out for two weeks as punishment for myself. . . . The only thing we can do . . . is to practice and learn self control & self denial.[13]
> *Gertrude Foster, 1893*
> He remained until 3 AM without the ultimate union. Such a state of affairs could not go on. We agreed not to see each other.[14]
> *Madeline Doty, 1908*

In the next pair of excerpts, the women experience strong inner conflict. Their own hormones as well as their desire to please their lovers make it extremely difficult for them to keep on the right side of chaste behavior. In both cases, they go further in sexual exploration than they would cerebrally have preferred. They both did, however, manage to draw the line before actual intercourse. What is important to us is their strong sense of the moral code, its general acceptance, and its influence on themselves. They internalized the code; they did not ignore it or dismiss it. These examples leave the repression model intact, but with the qualification that engaged couples will sometimes take more liberties than the ultra-conservative authorities would prefer.

> Keep your hands just to hold me to you *nothing* else . . . I cannot resist your love, . . . but if you take it away, the strong kind that for the last week has frightened me, and made me so weak, and replace it by the protecting love then I shall be able to work and wait for you. . . . Even

13 Gertrude Foster to Raymond Brown 1893. Quoted in Rothman 1987, pp. 236-237.

14 Madeline Doty, 'Autobiography' 1908. Quoted in Rothman 1987, pp. 240 241.

> your unmanageable hands seem so dear. . . . I'm glad they're way off though. They're going to be very good and mind me after this, aren't they?[15]
> *Francis Crane, 1894*
> I did not feel so quiet a part of the time last night as I appeared & you supposed. Although I love you dearly & trust you so perfectly that I am perfectly willing and glad to make you happy by those favors which no one else in the wide world could obtain, yet even toward you I can not resign all the feelings which nature and education have fixed in my mind – I *was glad* afterwards when you seemed so sincerely pleased & happy – so *satisfied* with *me*. . . . I did not feel unpleasantly or unwilling. No, it was a *pleasure* and yet women so naturally guard such treasures with jealousy & care, that it seems very "strange" to yield them even to the "best loved one" who has a claim to such kindnesses.[16]
> *Mary Butterfield, 1848*

Next we examine the contents of several exchanges between two individuals who suffer doubly. They are tormented to distraction by frustrated desire. There is sheer desperation in their language. At the same time, they are greatly troubled by the issue of the compatibility of their deep mutual affection and strong sexual longing with their religious ideals. Samuel Francis Smith was a theologically conservative Baptist minister, and Mary, soon to be his wife, was a young woman of profound Christian piety. They tried to view their love as furnishing opportunities for reverence and gratitude to Christ. They tried, often with little success, to love Christ more than each other. They felt themselves making gods of one another. They feared the strength of their love as a snare to lead them away from true Christian observance. Until marriage, their love affair was a great trial in two senses of the word. The mutual physical yearning was torture, inflicting pain comparable to lashes. It also severely tested their religious values and moral strength. There was never any question of giving in completely to desire; it was only a question of suffering until the day of holy

15 Frances Crane to Frank Lillie 1894. Quoted in Rothman 1987, pp. 238-239.

16 Mary Butterfield to Champion Chase 1848. Quoted Rothman 1987, p. 126.

union. They looked forward explicitly to the sexual aspect of that impending union and even to the children that would result. The strong, conscious sexual attraction between Samuel and Mary Smith should not occur under the traditional theory, but perhaps they are an unusual couple. At any rate, the model is ultimately vindicated by their attitude of assured self-denial as regards intercourse. It was never a possibility.

> Your letters my dear Mary be assured do give me unmingled gratification. I trust they are not merely causes of pure delight in my own heart, which is comparatively of little importance, but what is more to be desired, occasions of gratitude and prayer to the Father of Spirits. . . . Surely our correspondence then will not have been in vain, if it leads us to send up but one more burst of praise – to feel but one more thrill of humble yet adoring gratitude in our daily devotions. . . . I hope I shall by and by learn to love you more rationally and less passionately. . . . While therefore we love, and must still love each other with a pure heart *fervently*, May we have grace to love Christ more. . . . It would greatly cheer me, beloved, if you could but be here today, tomorrow, *every* day – For every day, I see some new reason to long for your presence. If I could at all times so strongly anticipate communion with God, and if the anticipation were so sweet of being with him as is the anticipation of being with yourself, I should charge my heart to leap and sing for joy. . . . indeed I am beginning to be almost seriously afraid I shall put you in the place of God as the guide and the object of all I do. . . . We shall do no wrong, dear one, by loving each other with our *whole hearts* if only we love each other "in Christ."[17]
>
> *Samuel Francis Smith, 1834*
>
> It is to me a rich consolation to know that I have your prayers. I need them – *indeed*. I *do need* them. I desire to be more holy – more heavenly: more weaned from earth. I am in *continual* danger of doing wrong – my affections too strongly fix upon things [that] "must perish

17 Samuel Francis Smith to Mary Smith 1834. Quoted in Lystra 1992, pp. 242-246.

with their using." . . . If I am not with you my friend, in "presence" I am often (alas!) I fear too often with you in "heart". Oh pray for me that my affections may not dwell *too* much upon earthly *treasures*; but may be strongly, most strongly placed upon Him "who is worthy of them all." . . . There dwells not *one* on this earth who possesses so entirely, so unreservedly – my whole affections as yourself . . . Tis not the cold passion which the passing crowd call friendship – it is something more – yea nothing less than a deep settled permanent lively ardor – would lead me to offer every thing, all I have, at its shrine. As *well* as I love my parents – as well as I love my connections to friends – yet all *all* could I resign most willingly – most happily for *your* sake. My affection for them dwindles into comparative insignificance when I think of what I bear toward you. Cast me not from your bosom, I pray, I beseech – love me trust me still and believe me when I say all I have is *your own*. To use a borrowed expression which speaks my heart "had I as much proof that I loved Jesus Christ as I have of my love to you I should prize it more than rubies?" . . . *It is* my "*sweet*" love *in the honest sincerity of my whole soul, that I solemnly pledge to you my heart and hand.* And *most* happily, yea, triumphantly *do I accept yours as the richest earthly boon*. . . . Why *why is it* my dear Francis that I love you as I do? Is it to be a snare to me – a source of unhappiness through my short pilgrimage? I *pray not*. But is there no danger. I am sure there is – for our heavenly Father will surely chasten us if we make an idol of any one of his merciful gifts. . . . "I would fain love earthly beings less" – or *one* at least. I would not make you an idol – indeed I *would* not. But oh – if I ever had one you *are that one most certainly*. . . . Oh I do feel it such a luxury to hide myself a little time in my own room and think of God and heaven and your precious self! But what would you think dearest of my piety – if I should tell you that you engage the chief of my thoughts and attentions even then? But it is thus And what *shall* I *do?*[18]

Mary Smith, 1834

18 Mary to Samuel Francis Smith 1834. Quoted in Lystra 1992, pp. 242-245.

I am looking forward, my dear, with anxious longing to the day of our union. The thought that it is so near unsettles my thoughts and almost wholly unfits me for the performance of any duty whatever. . . . I cherish the hope that all will be joyously and happily, yea, and to our eternal joy and happiness, consummated.[19]
Samuel Francis Smith, 1834
Though I would fain be all loveliness yet while I feel so much of evil rioting in my bosom how *can* I conceal it? . . . And might we not anticipate blessed results from the sweet union we are now so ardently longing to be consummated?[20]
Mary Smith, 1834

We cross the Atlantic again to consider a relationship that had some evident similarities to that of Francis and Mary Smith. Charles Kingsley was a university professor and widely read novelist, but he was also an Anglican minister who served in part as chaplain to Queen Victoria. His bride-to-be and lifetime partner, Fanny Grenfell, was also a devout Christian. There is a difference from the Smiths, though, in that this couple rather celebrated their sexuality, even before marriage, as here, and had no trouble seeing it as consistent with their faith. Fanny had to pluck up her courage to face the nebulous, impending first encounters with the institution of married love ("admirable mystery") – not so much the mechanics of it, it seems, as the uncertainty concerning her reactions, the effects that it would have upon herself. The vagueness shading the experience of the sex act, however, was not enough to prevent her from ardently looking forward to it. Charles and Fanny were extremely impatient, but they did wait. The code was stronger than desire, and the repression theory is ultimately supported. Kingsley begins his letter with a daydream:

This morning I awoke at 5, & as I lay, white limbs gleamed before me, & soft touches pressed me, & a wanton tongue – yet chaste & holy!, stole between my lips! . . . What is sensuality! Not the *enjoyment* of *holy glorious matter,* but blindness to its spiritual meaning! . . . How

19 Samuel Francis Smith to Mary Smith 1834. Quoted in Lystra 1992, pp. 70-71.

20 Mary to Samuel Francis Smith 1834. Quoted in Lystra 1992, pp. 70-71.

> much more delicious when in each others' arms, the flesh and the spirit shall tend the same way, increasing each other's delight! Bless God Bless God! . . . Will not these thoughts give us more perfect delight when we lie naked in each other's arms, clasped together toying with each other's limbs, buried in each other's bodies, struggling, panting, dying for a moment. . . . Do I expect to marry an *angel*, passionless, unsympathizing? – No! My wife must be a woman – subject to like passions with myself![21]
> *Charles Kingsley, 1843*
> Once with you . . . I will drop all false dignity, mock modesty, & I will entreat you to hurry our wedding day, that we die not in the interval – Darling! . . . Oh! that God wd have pity on me, tormented in this flame! . . . Pray for me! How can *I* pray, when every tho't of my heart, every Aspiration of my Soul proclaims me an Idolator and *you* my God! . . . I *did* pray for patience today, and oh! Darling! I prayed so much for you . . . My idea of *perfect bliss, perfect repose, perfect security* is *sleeping in your arms* – can I be *afraid* of you? . . . Darling, Darling, . . . *I do love you perfectly* – but I am a woman & I don't know what it is yet. . . . when married Man & Woman are *one flesh* (admirable mystery!) . . . Beloved! If she shrank not, why sh'd *I*? If Holy Eden was the scene of Marriage & Married Love, why should I fear to leap into your arms to realize one of Eden's blessings or taste an Enjoyment wh: *must* be pure if it was *tasted there*! I will trust & not be afraid!! . . . To the Pure all things are Pure! . . . Oh! How pure that Institution must be wh: He Himself gave the man whom He had just created in *His Own Image*! I thank GOD and take courage![22]
> *Fanny Grenfell, 1843*

Like the Smiths and the Kingsleys – although not, perhaps, with as much candid ardor – many couples looked forward to the time of union, of release from

21 Charles Kingsley to Fanny Grenfell 1843. Quoted in Gay 1999, pp. 308-309.

22 Fanny Grenfell, Diary 1843. Quoted in Gay 1999, pp. 304-306.

the constraints of unmarried virtue. The first of the following excerpts is from Nathaniel Hawthorne, the next two from uncelebrated middle-class Americans.

> Even the spoken word has long been inadequate. Looks – pressures of the lips and hands – the touch of bosom to bosom – these are a better language. But bye-and-bye, our spirits will demand some more adequate expression even than these.[23]
> *Nathaniel Hawthorne, 1842*
> Never mind, one of these days when I have a right to be "that sweet name" I will lose my reserve and let my words as well as actions, show how very dear you are to me.[24]
> *Eliza Trescott, 1864*
> I felt that just to know that you loved was happiness enough, even if we were never married, but now I do not feel *exactly* so about our marriage, and know that choicest boon of love is yet to be ours.[25]
> *Mary Granger, 1866*

We now progress to a string of excerpts in which the couples indulge in highly charged sexual behavior, either in thought or in deed or both. We wonder how far they will go.

We begin with two passages from David Todd and Mabel Loomis, certainly among the most colorful of all the couples treated in this chapter.[26] Mabel Loomis was conscious of her attraction to men almost from puberty and felt strongly sexually inclined thereafter. We know this because she kept a diary almost all her life and candidly recorded in it both her sexual exploits and her feelings about them as well as her feelings about the men with whom she became romantically involved – mainly two. She was not what you would call movie-star beautiful, but I concur in the opinion of many that she was unusually sexually attractive.[27] In 1879 at the age of twenty-two, she married the suc-

23 Nathaniel Hawthorne to Sophia Peabody 1842. Quoted in Gay 1984, p. 457.

24 Eliza Trescott to Eldred Simkins 1864. Quoted in Lystra 1992, p. 69.

25 Mary Granger to Lyman Hodge 1866. Quoted in Lystra 1992, p. 67.

26 Gay 1984, pp. 71-108; *Wikipedia*: Mabel Loomis Todd.

27 See the photo in Gay 1984 following p. 182.

cessful astronomer David Todd, who was as passionate as she. We saw from the excerpt above, when she was pregnant with Millicent, how powerful she felt her love for Todd to be and how supremely important to her was their mutual adoration. They remained close all of their lives, in spite of adultery on both parts.

In 1881, they moved to Amherst, Massachusetts, and it was there that Mrs. Todd met Austin Dickinson, the married older brother of the poet Emily Dickinson. They fell in love and pursued a highly passionate affair until Dickinson's death in 1895, a death that was devastating to Mabel. During the fourteen years in which the affair was carried on, David Todd not only knew about it, as did most of the relevant people in Amherst, but aided it in active ways. After Emily Dickinson's death in 1886, when hundreds of her poems were discovered, Mabel, with the Dickinson family's permission, edited a volume of the poems for publication. It is uncertain whether Emily Dickinson ever would have become known to the world as a great American poet had Mabel Todd not undertaken this task. She later edited several more volumes of Dickinson's poetry and letters. Mabel Todd died in 1932; David outlived her by seven years.

I include here two brief excerpts from the period of the premarital relationship between Loomis and Todd. In spite of her passionately sexual nature, all evidence indicates that Mabel Loomis was a virgin when she married Todd in 1879.[28] There could hardly be more convincing evidence of the sovereignty of the Victorian moral code and thereby the validity of the model of repression. Further passages from her diary from after the marriage are included later in the section.

> Drive in buggy with "accommodating horse." . . . Home about 9. Mabel will remember with pleasure the new sensation I caused her this evening. We may call this our engagement night.[29]
> *David Todd, 1878*
> We walked, and walked & walked, & had a most congenial time. . . . walked up and down the room, and, – and he – well, I couldn't help it. . . . I woke up the next morning very happy though, & feeling not at all

28 Gay 1984, p. 81.

29 David Todd, Diary 1878. Quoted in Gay 1984, p. 79.

> condemned. . . . His letters have a truly *physical* effect on me . . . I am going to tell something which I ought not to – I *know* David is necessary, not only to my happiness, but his presence is absolutely essential to my physical health.[30]
> *Mabel Loomis Todd, 1878-9*

Here is James Hague looking forward to a visit to his beloved. Although the actions contemplated are innocent enough, the intense desire is evident, as is the recognized necessity for restraint.

> Well, I hope I shall have my arms around the old girl herself before many weeks and if I don't behave with great impropriety then it will be for better reasons than I can now foresee. I'll just squeeze her and hug her, and kiss her forehead and eyes – yes I'll kiss them again and again, and when I have looked at them to my heart's content I'll kiss them again, and her cheeks and lips and throat, and I'll take liberties with her back hair and pull out her hair pins, and tousle and tumble her up generally until she boxes my old ears and goes up stairs to set herself straight. Won't that be nice old Loveliness? glorfied, exalted, ecstatic, radiant; and don't I wish I was there now.[31]
> *James Hague, 1872*

Elias Nason and Mira Bigelow had a long engagement and were apart a great deal of the time. The temptations were severe; chastity, however, was preserved.

> O! I really do want to kiss you. . . . How I should like to be in that old parlor with you. . . . I hope there will be a carpet on the floor for it seems you intend to act worse than you ever did before by your letter . . . but I shall humbly submit to my fate and willingly too, to speak candidly.[32]
> *Mira Bigelow, 1831*

30 Mabel Loomis Todd, Diary 1878-9. Quoted in Gay 1984, p. 79.

31 James Hague to Mary Ward Foote 1872. Quoted in Lystra 1992, p. 64.

32 Mira Bigelow to Elias Nason 1831. Quoted in Rothman 1987, p. 53.

> Oh Mi how intensely do I long to see you – to *feel* you – to put these hands that hold this pen upon you. Yes in your bosom – that soft delicious bosom. . . . I shall tear you to pieces. . . . I cannot restrain my passions when I see my own loved girl . . . How is it, Mi, that you can bear so much from me? How can you *love* me after *all*? … My passions are terrible and none but you could master them. And you forgive me all and love me still.[33]
> *Elias Nason, 1833*

The two couples in the following excerpts are skirting very close to the line. Lester Ward, whose diary provides the first two passages, was an early American sociologist who is still required reading in the profession. He indicates that his beloved, Lizzie Vought, gave him her body. That does not mean what it might seem to mean. They did not go all the way, at least not yet. The third is from a letter by Robert Burdette – lecturer, Baptist minister, and humorist – whom we met above and will consider again further on. He fantasizes a tender encounter that is meant both to relieve his own tension and frankly to arouse his beloved Clara, at which he was quite successful. It should be understood that at the time of the initiation of this correspondence in 1898, Robert Burdette was fifty-three years old and Clara Baker forty-two.

> I did not plan to remain more than two hours, but O, the charms of love! She had never before been so sweet. She looked at me so gently and spoke so tenderly. "I love you," she said, kissing me on the mouth. . . . We lay with our faces together. I unfastened my shirt and put her tender little hands on my bare breast, and . . . she gave me her heart and her body, asking nothing more in exchange than my own.[34]
> *Lester Ward, 1860*
> The girl and I have had a very sweet time. I kissed her on her sweet breasts and took too many liberties with her sweet person and we are

33 Elias Nason to Mira Bigelow 1833. Quoted in Rothman 1987, p. 53.

34 Lester Ward, Diary 1860. Quoted in Rothman 1987, p. 128.

> going to stop. It is . . . a very fascinating practice and instills very sweet, tender and familial feelings in us, and consequently makes us happy.[35]
> *Lester Ward, 1861*
>
> And I stoop to cover the soft warm lips with a lover's kisses – many and long – and lingering – a Lover's kisses, dear. And you can only get them of one man. Only one. No one in all the world – no one else, can kiss you as I do. My darling; My darling. . . . Come here then, sweet. No, your head isn't in the way – you know I love the scent of your hair – I love to touch it with my lips, and feel it upon my face. See, I kiss it here on the moonbeam that marks its parting; and I lay my face into its coiled masses as one might smell a mass of clustered violets. And my lips follow it down to the dear white neck, which again and again I kiss – can you feel my breath playing upon it, dear heart? . . . How warm and soft your lips are, dear. There is no laughter on them now – not with that love-light softly glowing in the dear blue eyes. A soft love-born dew is on the tender lips, like the honey-moisture on a dawn-kissed rose. . . . Holding you closely and more closely still, yet with all gentleness, I smooth the silken hair back from the temples, with caressing hand and many kisses. Softly I press the dear, white, beautiful breasts that rise like snowy mounts above the heart I love – the heart that throbs for me. Sweet and white, balmy and fragrant – my lips in loving homage lay their loyal service upon them so tenderly, softly pressing their swelling grace, lingering in the sweet warm valley that divides these twins of snow and warmth and clinging with loving compression on the dainty tips of soft October tint. And all the time I am whispering your own dear name.[36]
> *Robert Burdette, 1898*

The excerpts from diaries and love letters that we have considered so far would seem to constitute good evidence. They come from a variety of types of individuals from across the United States and, in one welcome case, from England. In

35 Lester Ward, Journal 1861. Gay 1984, p. 129.

36 Robert Burdette to Clara Baker 1898. Quoted in Lystra 1992, pp. 96-97.

every instance, they reveal the existence of a reigning moral code. The subject individuals themselves have internalized the code, and it is seen to have strong influence over their behavior. The code universally prohibits premarital sexual intercourse and acts to inhibit behavior that risks drawing too close to that line – even if the exact nature of the activity that lies on the other side of the line is not perfectly clear to the participants. There is variation in what is considered risky. Some individuals permit nothing at all, some allow hugging and kissing but little else, and some go further, but the necessity for restraint is everywhere in evidence. Sexual inclination, as for example the strong desire to touch, is in plentiful supply in the group. For that reason, we cannot say that a severe version of the repression model – under which women will never even have a sexual thought – applies to the couples concerned in the above passages. However, if we admit a version of the model under which engaged couples will sometimes take moderately advanced liberties, the attitudes and behaviors we witness here are consistent with the theory of repression. The restraint under the influence of the Victorian moral code is stronger than the pull of the sex hormones. In other words, and critically important for our investigation, the documents we have considered to this point provide good support for the traditional model of Victorian repression. Is the mystery then solved? What about the contrary evidence from the Mosher survey? As of now, the contrary results of the Mosher survey would seem to be some sort of aberration – but we have not finished yet. We will turn next to exceptions – to the breakdown of restraint – but they are few. By and large, premarital intercourse was effectively curbed.

Illicit lovers

We follow the lives of two couples of our acquaintance into forbidden territory and add two more. The aim is not only to document what they did but how they felt about it. In all four cases, the relationship was of long standing and marriage was desired and intended by both parties. We begin with a brief excerpt from the diary of the sociologist, Lester Ward. There is unfortunately no record of how Lizzie Vought felt about this forbidden experience, but Ward's own reaction was "felicity."

> When I arrived at the house of the sweetness, she received me in her arms of tenderness and pressed me to her form of honey, and our lips touched and our souls entered Paradise together. . . . Her mother was ill, but her sister had gone away and all was well. That evening and that night we experienced the joys of love and tasted the felicity which belongs to married life alone.[37]
> *Lester Ward, 1861*

I present next four passages from the pens of Robert Burdette and Clara Baker. Whereas the activity in Robert's letter is imaginary – in this courtship, he delighted in fantasizing – it goes further in what is fancied than his previous creations, even to evoking the joint sexual climax. The liberties are the result of having tasted the experience, as Clara (also known between them as Violet) unmistakably indicates in her own letters. Recall that at this time Robert Burdette was fifty-three years old and Clara Baker forty-two. Robert had been widowed many years earlier, and Clara had in fact been widowed twice. Neither was a stranger to married love. Here, the playfulness of Clara's tone contrasts with Robert's romanticism, but both the deep affection and the desire shine through in both cases. There is no remorse, guilt, or fear and trembling. They were happy, and within a year they married and stayed married for fifteen additional years, until Robert's death in 1914. The last of the four passages shows Robert's humorist side but also betrays the intimacy of the new level of their relationship.

> There can be no woman's passion slumbering in such a tenderly affectionate nature as this – this is pure child love. But by and by, when my own caresses and kisses – given at first, under this child-influence of your own . . . as they quickened into the fire of passionate desire by their repetition, as they became amorous and eager, as I forced my way into your arms, upon your breast, stifling your protests with my kisses, struggling into the snowy smother of your skirts, – I cannot go on dear – I saw the new light dawn in your blue eyes and transfigure your beautiful face, and lo, My Little Girl was gone, and My Lady – My

37 Lester Ward, Journal 1861. Quoted in Gay 1984, p. 129.

Lady Violet . . . lay panting in my enraptured arms. . . . Which wants the most? We'll make a little "match" some day. I will draw your dear white warm throbbing body into my arms and nestle you up to me until swell and dimple, muscle and hollow fit into each other, and every breath and heart throb feels the other – and I will crush you to myself and fasten my lips to yours, and see who can lie there the longest and do the most petting. Your petting Sweet Violet, will be prettiest, with the cooing of my Dove, but mine will be the stronger. From your sweet brown hair to your dainty instep I will kiss you, love, and I'll murmur a thousand impassioned words with every kiss. I will cling to your perfumed breasts with my passionate lips till mother and sweet-heart love will throb together in your heart as it upholds the weight of your lover-husband. I will bury my face in your fragrant hair and praise its silken beauty till your heart is aflame with love. I will clasp my arms around the dear rounded waist and belt it with a girdle of kisses. The swelling thighs shall taste my lips until you can stand no more of it, and then I will kiss your dimpled knees to rest you, while I laugh with an overflow of joy and love. My Little One – ten kisses to your one I will give you – long – sweet – lingering kisses. We will love each other My Beautiful Betrothed, until love itself cries out in an agony of bliss, in the very pain of ecstasy –"My Violet!" "Oh, Robert!"[38]

Robert Burdette, 1898

Want to see Violet? Want to kiss your sweetheart? Want to play with your Little Girl – she's spoiling for a little romp – and much kissing. . . . Good night, sweetheart – oh! For a good night such as has been – but the memory of it is very sweet. . . . "Violet wants to be loved . . . and kissed and petted – ." . . . Such a lover! . . . Tho we shall begin where we left off at parting – tho it will seem the most natural as well as sweetest thing in the world for you to take me in your arms and love me and kiss me and talk to me as only my Robin can. . . . My heart beat[s] a little faster and I wish it was to be tomorrow – oh to night and *now.*[39]

38 Robert Burdette to Clara Baker 1898. Quoted in Lystra 1992, pp. 97-98.

39 Clara Baker to Robert Burdette 1898. Quoted in Lystra 1992, pp. 97-99.

> *Clara Baker, 1898*
>
> You haven't been kissed in a long, long time except "on the side" as they say of some course dishes – and you just deserve to be now – kissed until you struggle for breath – kissed until you think you are Hobson – kissed every way, every where – every second until Violet yields to Robin and together they rest.[40]
>
> *Clara Baker, 1899*
>
> But my arm is all right, dear love. I'll go to the dentists and have it pulled, and send it to you. Then you can tie it around your waist –"cinch it" . . . Tie it on tight dear, or sure as love it will slip down. I know that arm.[41]
>
> *Robert Burdette, 1899*

Charles and Dorothea Lummis (her maiden name is not recorded) had a difficult time of it, or at least she did. Charles was a highly influential journalist in the West. Dorothea was a medical student at Boston College, eventually graduating and practicing homeopathic medicine in Los Angeles. Their relationship was strained and did not last; hints of this, and Dorothea's distress, are discernible in letters presented further along. At the beginning, however, their love was strong, and it led them to cross the line. Unlike Lester Ward and Robert and Clara Burdette, Dorothea was deeply troubled by the transgression. The guiding beacons of chastity and purity were potent in her heart, but her love for Charles, including very prominently the component of sexual desire, was overpowering. Her classmates whispered about her. She hoped for the cleansing effect of marriage, which soon did occur. Few excerpts show the permeation and sovereignty of the Victorian moral code more forcefully than this one.

> Nobody would or could believe, but our own hearts, how much of purity or passion was in our love then. . . . I shall never care or regret it, if some day we can hold our own before everybody. . . . What do you think they say of you and me. That the sheriff visited you and gave you the choice

40 Clara Baker to Robert Burdette 1899. Quoted in Lystra 1992, pp. 75-76.

41 Robert Burdette to Clara Baker 1899. Quoted in Lystra 1992, p. 99.

> of three girls all needing marriage and you chose the one with the most money. . . . Ah tell me that you at least believe that it was only lack of wisdom not of purity that laid me open to all this insult. . . . A man can never know the deadening feeling of utter despair that a woman knows at the shadow on her fair name. . . . I did not wisely, but too well, perhaps in not asking you to give your legal name before giving you myself, but *you* cannot hold me less pure, Carl, for that.[42]
> *Dorothea Lummis, 1884*

Annie Cox was also very deeply troubled. She tried to be philosophical about her lapse, but she suffered for it and blamed herself severely. Both her love and her respect for Winan Allen, however, remained intact. Repeating here from Chapter III:

> When temptation to wrong suggested itself from natural passions and opportunity, 'twas my mission to have been *fine*, giving you a kind refusal and leading your mind away and beyond. In the first instance, I failed in the full possession of my reason & judgments thus giving strength to your desire and weakening my better nature. We made firm resolves and the next opportunity showed how they were kept. . . . God only knows how I detested myself. You meanwhile . . . kept your old standing place in my estimation. . . . I own I think you to blame in some degree. That is, for not accepting my first denial. . . . We have both done wrong. I having done much the greater because I should have acted the part of a true, noble, Christian woman. . . . If I have not injured you dear one, fear not for me . . . Tis only for you I weep for the sorrow I have caused when you think of me. . . . [But I do] not feel, strange as it may seem, any the less pure *now*. I shall stand at the altar with you, only humble and for that reason better. I know this experience will be for my good, though it would have been better if it could never happen.[43]
> *Annie Cox, 1863*

---

42 Dorothea to Charles Lummis 1884 (before their marriage). Quoted in Lystra 1992, pp. 74-75

43 Annie Cox to Winan Allen 1863. Quoted in Rothman 1987, p. 130.

These are the major instances of illicit premarital coitus in the published record for Victorian America and Britain. In numbers, they are overwhelmed by the numerous couples who did restrain themselves, but one cannot read too much into numbers when the sampling cannot with confidence be considered representative. Recall in this connection that part of the potential bias in sampling would lie in the probability that love letters and significant diary entries would be written by individuals who are passionately in love and that those who are passionately in love would be the most likely to yield to desire. What is more important here than numbers is the further evidence of intense feelings in almost all of the cases reviewed so far in the chapter that to proceed too far along the sexual path was wrong. Even Lester Ward, though he and Lizzie eventually succumbed, had previously expressed the determination to exercise restraint lest they "offend against the laws of virtue."[44]

Married lovers

One characteristic of the four specimens from the correspondence of Robert Burdette and Clara Baker just offered is the openness of these lovers, their candor, their exultation regarding the fact of their ultimate sexual experience and its details. This is wildly contrary to the strictures of the model of Victorian repression. Nobody was supposed to behave like that. Accepting the traditional model as valid, such behavior is almost impossible to believe. It is enough to give heart to the revisionists. But might this perhaps be just one isolated example? In fact, it is not. There are many others in which sex is celebrated, some earnest, some playful, and I present a sampling of them now. But there is a crucial difference. The couples to be considered in the remainder are married.

We begin by revisiting several old friends and observing the progress of their love.

Here is Lester Ward speaking of his Lizzie in the year following that in which their souls entered Paradise together:

44 Lester Ward, Journal 1861. Quoted in Gay 1984, p. 129.

> All men who can are going to war, and all is excitement. But one more event is needed to crown the catalogue, and yesterday was the day. Wednesday August 13, 1862. I had to register my marriage! What? I, married? True enough. The cherished of my heart, whom I have loved for so long, so constantly, and so frantically, is mine. . . . O how sweet it is to sleep with her! I paid $3.00 fee.[45]
> *Lester Ward, 1862*

Sophia Peabody Hawthorne considered coitus to be a "miraculous form" and a "wondrous instrument." For shame! This would seem to be a violation of chastity, virtue, and modesty – but consider that she is now married. We see here the kind of revelation and change after marriage – the opening up of a significant aspect of life – that was plainly detectable but not quite so explicitly expressed in the Mosher survey.

> Ah, yes – also I suppose some persons are the den of the archfiend, through such has this miraculous form [i.e., sexual intercourse] come into disrepute. Before our marriage I knew nothing of its capacities, & the truly married alone can know what a wondrous instrument it is for the purposes of the heart. . . . The profane never can taste the joys of Elysium – because it is a spiritual joy, so they cannot perceive it.[46]
> *Sophia Hawthorne, 1843*

From all we know, Sophia Peabody was a perfectly chaste and thoroughly respectable young woman, a model of Victorian femininity. Yet, we now find her frankly and without embarrassment extolling the virtues of sex. There is a hint here that the information and advice of physicians and other authorities regarding lack of female interest in the marital relation – sex for procreation only – may not have carried a great deal of weight once women, especially women in love, experienced that relation.

45 Lester Ward, Journal 1862. Quoted in Gay 1984, p. 130.

46 Sophia Hawthorne, in Nathaniel's diary 1843. Quoted in Gay 1984, p. 457.

The following is a further excerpt from a letter by Charles Kingsley. Given the passionate and impatient ardor of Charles and Fanny Kingsley before their marriage, it is not too surprising that he could write to her so candidly, we might even say immodestly, about their celebration of the marriage bed. He apparently does not offend her, far from it. Yet, there is nothing in the repression model that would lead us to expect this variety of happiness in a Victorian couple. Nothing at all.

> My hands are perfumed with her delicious limbs, and I cannot wash off the scent, and every moment the thought comes across me of those mysterious recesses of beauty where my hands have been wandering, and my heart sinks with a sweet faintness. . . . Oh! to be once again with you – to lie once more naked in your arms . . . you will once more unrobe with utter delight those lovely limbs, & come to me a bride again! . . . Shall we the first night we meet re-enact our marriage night?[47]
> *Charles Kingsley, 1843*

The following, from Dorothea Lummis, is even more candid and less tightly bound by Victorian fetters, though not free of personal concern for the marriage. Whereas after sleeping with Charles in the premarital state she was sadly worried about "the shadow on her fair name" in true traditional-model fashion, she is now able to give herself up to a sweet and eager sexuality. Her attitude is so distant from anything envisioned in the theory of repression as essentially to deny its validity. This, clearly, she owes to marriage.

> I like you to want me, dear, and if I were only with you, I would embrace more than the back of your neck, to be sure. . . . I guess its the cherishing that I miss. You know I never had any real petting or tenderness until I had it from you, and I have missed it more than I can ever tell you. . . . Love me sweet, and try to want me. . . . Now I won't think of anything but sweet things and will study a bit and then go to

47 Charles to Fanny Kingsley 1843. Quoted in Gay 1999, pp. 306-307.

> bed to dream that your arms is about me, and your nice sweet body sort 'o warm and close to me. . . . And . . . it brought up a great wave of sweet memories and longings and the touch of clinging warm lips, and the still magnetic thrill of your warm body, and I was all lost to the present. Let us be very tender and careful of this physical bliss, which in its entirety means more – and not abuse it, but keep it sweet and clear through the years of our young strong life, at least if we can. . . . Pretty soon we can begin to think of nice naughty things cant we. . . . I want you tonight sort 'o awful badly! I want you to kiss me and say Thea! I love you. Would you if I was there eh? I shall like it a lot when the train get[s] into the depot a[t] C. and you come out of the dark to meet me, and then we go off up to your room a little minute and stop a bit for just one kiss, that makes us hungry for more. . . . If we only could be happy, not miserable once . . . *and not mind anything but love, and not think anything was naughty that made us happier.* Ah, I can't write of it. . . . How can I wait![48]
> *Dorothea Lummis, 1883*

Within a year, however, Dorothea felt Charles slipping away. Her insight in the following letter is profound, and the sophistication of her philosophy is worthy of the late twentieth century. The topic and the high value placed on sex do not fit within the traditional model of Victorian behavior, especially from the pen of a woman, but it begins to be evident that marriage may have a great deal to do with this level of openness.

> Say, Carl dear, tell me something. Did you like me as well as you used to, and were you just as happy as you used to be – in bodily ways I mean – because I though[t] maybe you didnt so very much, and I dont want you to get too used to me, or tired of me, so soon. We were happy, but it didnt seem to me we were as nice as we used to be. Not that the happiest minute wasn't as nice, but we sort 'o hurried Love all up, didn't we. Don't let's us, will you. Because even in this, habit tells, and I want that to

48 Dorothea to Charles Lummis 1883. Quoted in Lystra 1992, pp. 72-73.

> be the very last thing to become commonplace. I spect its partly because you are so busy, that you dont have time to be hungry for happiness, but its better to wait a long while, and then take time for love, isnt it, than to lose half the sweet from haste.[49]
> *Dorothea Lummis, 1884*

After her marriage to David Todd, Mabel, now Mabel Loomis Todd, continued to write regularly in her diary, with many entries chronicling the happiness of their sexual relations. The following three passages display a gaiety in her sexual gratification that, again, would be both shocking and repulsive in the perspective of the traditional model. Formerly, she was indeed open about her sexual feelings and explorations, but now there is a higher level of delight to match the more advanced stages of sensual experience, especially sexual intercourse.

> Every night . . . he undressed me on the bright Turkey rug before the fire, & then wrapped me up to keep warm while he put hot bricks in the bed. Then he took me in his arms & tucked me safely in bed, & kissed me over & over, while he went to his desk & studied an hour, or two longer. And after parties, when I came in cold, he did first the same for me – & loved me so! . . . [In the morning] he would get up and brighten the fire, & spread all my clothes around it until they were warm, when he would come for me, & taking me in his arms, set me down on the rug close to the fire, where all my "toasting hot" garments were awaiting me. Then would come the grapes or figs or apples on which he always regaled me before breakfast.[50]
> *Mabel Loomis Todd, 1881*

The following is a sequence of very brief excerpts from a series of different dates over four years:

---

49 Dorothea to Charles Lummis 1884. Quoted in Lystra 1992, p. 74.

50 Mabel Loomis Todd, Journal 1881. Quoted in Gay 1984, p. 82.

> Ice cream on the way home –, and the most rapturous and sacred night of all our love.
>
> David . . . it is just dreadful to sleep alone. . . . I want you very much, dear, very much.
>
> The night of the fourth is our time, darling, and I am anticipating it with joy.
>
> Last night was almost too happy for this world.
>
> This night, from 9 P.M. until about 12, was the happiest of my whole happy life, so far.
>
> The last was such a happy night! Oh! Oh!
>
> We retired at seven & had a magnificent evening, David and I. I shall never forget it, so I'll not write about it.[51]
> *Mabel Loomis Todd, 1879-1882*

A final entry from the writings of Mabel Todd documents intercourse during pregnancy:

> The night brought us very near to each other. The physical effect of our close communion was unlike anything I ever experienced – it was enjoyment, and yet it was very hard for me to feel the same kind of intensity as before – it was a thrilling sort of breathlessness – but at last it came – the same beautiful climax of feeling I knew so well, yet even in its intensity different from the spring's rapture. . . . Through all these happy weeks, . . . all the time our lively intercourse – more, I think upon every occasion than the last, though we indulge but rarely and try

51 Mabel Loomis Todd, Journal 1879, 1881, 1882. Quoted in Gay 1984, p. 83.

> to be particularly careful about the time in each month when I should have been ill, were it not for my little one.[52]
> *Mabel Loomis Todd, 1879*

One might want to explain the un-Victorian delight of Mabel Loomis Todd by saying that she was just a different sort of person, but the truth is that most of the women in this last, extended set of passages are equal to her in their enthusiasm for sexual relations, even if not quite so effervescent about it. They are most probably not all just a "different sort"; rather, what they have in common is that they were married.

Nathaniel Wheeler expresses the sentiment well in the following. (He is writing, by the way, to Clara, the woman who became the wife of Robert Burdette; Nathaniel was her first husband.)

> Dreadful state of mind (and body) . . . such a powder-magazine as I'm discovering myself to be, especially when there's no waterworks or any patent extinguisher within reach. . . . How much longer before I see you, feel you, look at you all over, Kiss you, hug you, put my arms around that soft little waist, draw you up close to me, closer, closer, forget everything but our two selves, then hold you off and look again, and so to sleep with my own wife in my arms, which ache with emptiness these long, long nights? . . . Oh the sacredness of wedded love. I begin to realize its depth and strength, and its purity, its frank surrender, its implicit confidence.[53]
> *Nathaniel Wheeler, 1880*

There follow now four passages containing excerpts from letters written by Victorian women from a variety of social backgrounds. They have two additional things in common: one, they unabashedly enjoy and look forward to sex, and two, they are married. The first is from an Iowa frontierswoman, writing

52 Mabel Loomis Todd, manuscript, "Millicent's Life" 1879. Quoted in Gay 1984, p. 84.

53 Nathaniel to Clara Wheeler 1880. Quoted in Lystra 1992, pp. 79-80.

to her husband who is off in the Civil War. The three that follow are also written by uncelebrated, ordinary Americans.

> Do you ever wish you had me for a bedfellow? . . . I have wished you were here more than once when I would get ready for bed. But I feel in hopes that we can have that privilege before long, don't you?[54]
> *Unnamed, 1853*
> I am almost crazy to see you – This being away from you is torture. Do tell me everything darling. My own sweet Wellie. My dear precious love. How long are we to be separated must it be much longer, I want to sleep in your arms again.[55]
> *Jane Burnett, 1857*
> Now beloved – one of my heart – embrace me – and love me as I do desire – kiss me over and over again – while I say beloved one – good bye – . . . . I wrote you darling one a little messenger yesterday but on the arrival this morning of another song of Love, from thee, I could not help saying a few words . . . would that I could *kiss you all over* – and then *eat you up*. . . .[56]
> *Emily Lovell, 1862*
> Aunt Mary . . . said you asked her advice about it you didn't know whether to marry her or me. Mr. Frank D. Baldwin, if I had known you was in such a quandry I would have settled the matter at once by giving you the mittens. I felt real queer and strange when I heard you had half a mind to marry another girl. I thought I held *undivided* you[r] love. Well its too late now. Nellie Smith dont know what she escaped. She would have been killed at one nab: of your old long Tom!!! . . . I got your letter last night . . . so you have been casting sly glances at Mrs. Sowters Bubbies . . . You ought to be ashamed. I intend to show mine to somebody before long. . . . How are you this hot day? I am most roasted and

54 Unnamed Iowa frontierswoman to husband 1853. Quoted in D'Emilio and Freedman 1988, p. 78.

55 Jane to Wellington Burnett 1857. Quoted in Lystra 1992, p. 62.

56 Emily to Mansfield Lovell 1862. Quoted in Lystra 1992, p. 63.

> my chemise sticks to me and the sweat runs down my legs and I suppose I smell very sweet, don't you wish you could be around just now.[57]
> *Alice Baldwin, 1873*

We close with two exchanges, in each case husband to wife first and then the reverse. The last excerpt in the first passage shows again the revelation to an individual of the potential value of a marriage. The fact that two souls were permitted without guilt, in the privacy of their bedroom, to revel in the marital relation was a precious boon, so much so that it could easily take on a sacredness in the romantic Victorian outlook. For better or worse, such feelings would be rare in our more permissive sexual culture today. The first exchange is between Alfred and Emma Roe:

> I see now how much more right you were & I not only respect you more but you have lifted *me* above my former self. . . . I feel even now that I am learning much, much from you. I am stronger, wiser, better for your influence over me. There is that in you which calls me out, makes me more of a man & urges me on to reach out ever more from day to day to-wards the pattern of the standard man in Christ Jesus. . . . These letters much as I loved them from you & loved to send them to you always worried me lest they should get under other eyes. . . . I miss the little notes we used to send to & fro & though I do not think it perhaps wise to write quite in the same way we did *very often* I want the privilege of writing something in the way we would talk when we lay so happily together with your head resting on my shoulder & my arms about your dear person & hands on your sweet breasts. . . . With you sexual intercourse and desire is holy and pure. . . . There can be no harm in my recalling to mind how sweet & fair your dear person appeared to me those nights when you came entirely naked to my arms. How fair & soft your breasts were & how sweetly one restless and weary reposed his cheek there & felt truly *at home*. How pleasant to feel your arms around

57 Alice to Frank Baldwin 1873. Quoted in Lystra 1992, pp. 61-64.

> & dear limbs pressed against mine. How sweet & how precious a thing is true & pure wedded love.[58]
> *Alfred Roe, 1860*
> I was never in my life in so excitable a condition. . . . Ought we to write again reserved as of old. Would it not be wiser. Yet perhaps there is no harm I know there is no sin in it – but Gods dear word permits and encourages our love. . . . I had little Mamie most weaned . . . but now she nurses day & night a great deal – As I lie awake with her at my breast I think of you. Sometimes if I remember the exciting letters you have lately written or imagine what our pleasure shall be when side by side again I get so excited that I sometimes fear lest it unfavorably affect Mamie. . . . I did mean Alfred not to allude again to the matter of our future sexual relations . . . but since you say so much and hope you are not *too free* in doing so, let me assure you that you can not give me more pleasure until you can come your very own dear self to my arms – than by writing *just what* you did. . . . I am perfectly and forever content to do what despite *all men* can *invent* to say – I *know God allows. You are right – all* right and *never* shall I call on your forbearance to practice that severe self denial that is rather sinful than pleasing to him who united us and made us *"one flesh" no* more *twain*. . . . Yes I think we shall lie many a night in sweeter intimacy than we ever yet have known body & soul knit in former bonds. . . . No *bride* adorning for her husband – can burn with a passion so *pure* and so *ardent – to be pleasing and attractive – to the man she* loves. May the *bearing matron* be as precious in your eyes as ever a virgin to her first possessor. *All my desire* is to my *Husband* – and I can not think of greater worldly pleasure than to have him joy over me. Yes and rule over me – so God ordains and not less for *my* pleasure than *yours*.[59]
> *Emma Roe, 1864*

The brief, concluding exchange is between Joseph and Laura Lyman:

58 Alfred to Emma Wickham Roe 1860, 1865. Quoted in Gay 1999, pp. 128-131.

59 Emma to Alfred Roe 1864. Quoted in Gay 1999, pp. 129-30.

I anticipate unspeakable delight in your embrace . . . feel close around me the caressing hands & be soothed by the voluptuous touch! But soon we will have it – all – full measure. . . . I love you ver---y much indeed my dear wife . . . How kindly you would put your white arms all around me and make me sink to sleep sweet as asphodel with the exquisite contact of your smooth body. How the dreams would be of summer winds.[60]
Joseph Lyman, 1865
Oh how I love you . . . How I long to see you . . . I'll drain your coffers dry next Saturday I assure you.[61]
Laura Lyman, 1853

Conclusion: The married, the unmarried, and the code.

At first glance, it would seem that the evidence in this chapter is as conflicting as it was in those that came before – we found women who resisted sex and others who welcomed it – but now we understand the primary reason and, as the reader has no doubt concluded, the mystery is solved.

Both models are correct, and both are wrong. Each is correct in that it applies with validity to a certain important segment of Victorian sexual behavior, but the theories have been too ambitious. Each is wrong to the extent that it seeks to apply to all such behavior. The repression model correctly characterizes the behavior of unmarried women. The revisionists do not succeed in disproving that portion of the traditional view. They do, however, succeed in disproving the repression model with respect to married women. It is the solid, compelling evidence on married women that makes a revision of the traditional theory necessary.

The statements I have just made are, in fact, a bit too categorical. They need some qualification that will become clear in the following explanation, beginning with the case of married Victorian women.

60 Joseph to Laura Lyman 1865. Quoted in Gay 1984, pp. 125-126.

61 Laura to Joseph Lyman 1853. Quoted in Gay 1984, p. 126.

The Mosher survey, which is a survey of married women, is widely used as evidence to show that a revision is required of the traditional model of Victorian sexual behavior. Therefore, one would expect, and correctly so, that the traditional theory has ingredients which conflict with Dr. Mosher's results. Let us take a convenient overview of those ingredients by quoting a few citations of earlier works taken from the original article by the historian Carl Degler, written shortly after he discovered the Mosher survey in the Stanford University archives.[62] In order to urge a revision of the traditional model, he had to include some characterization of what he took that traditional model to include, both in its prescriptions and its outcomes. The following show his view of the traditional, or repression theory through his quotes from the writing of others:

> The majority of women (happily for them) are not very much troubled with sexual feelings of any kind.
> I do not believe one bride in a hundred, of delicate, educated, sensitive women accepts matrimony from any desire for sexual gratification; when she thinks of this at all, it is with shrinking, or even with horror, rather than with desire.
> For the sexual act was associated by many wives only with a duty.
> In the whole Western world during the nineteenth century and at the beginning of the twentieth century it would have been not only scandalous to admit the existence of a strong sex urge in women, but it would have been contrary to all observation.
> Many women came to regard marriage as little better than legalized prostitution. Sexual passion became associated almost exclusively with the male, with prostitutes, and with women of the lower classes.
> The audience should be informed that, in the present state of society, the sexual appetites must not be fostered; and experience teaches those who have had the largest means of information on the matter, that self-control must be exercised.

62 Degler 1974, pp. 1467, 1468, 1477-1479.

> There will be many . . . who will not bring their minds to accept the truth which nature seems to teach, which would confine sexual acts to reproduction wholly.
>
> Others, while equally opposed to the excesses . . . [would] limit indulgence to the number of months in the year.

The results of the Mosher survey show that a model with these characteristics cannot be supported. Far from it. By substantial majorities, the Mosher women experienced both desire and orgasm, found their sexual relations to be agreeable, and wanted to have at least a moderate amount of sex in their lives. When the data on the negative effects of the frequency of intercourse were explored, we found that the majorities would probably have been even greater if some of the husbands involved had been more considerate. Degler's own conclusion was: "It seems evident that among these women sexual relations were neither rejected nor engaged in with distaste or reluctance. In fact, for them sexual expression was a part of healthy living and frequently a joy."[63]

The letters from married women presented in this chapter cannot bolster the Mosher survey statistically because, as noted, the writers cannot be considered a representative sample. They do, however, strengthen the revisionist case in one important way. The repression model would have it that women would act in certain ways and refrain from acting in others because of absorbing a strict moral code. If they transgressed, it would be with fear, guilt, and regret, as was the case for several of the unmarried lovers reviewed above. The letters and diaries involving married women show us, however, that in them this sense of wrong was absent.

I do not refer to the fact that no guilt was ever specifically confessed but rather that the language that actually was used demonstrates not just the absence of a sense of doing wrong but its complete opposite. The letters and diary entries cause us to doubt that the moral code was effective with respect to married women. The passages are in fact strong examples of the code's being ignored – and ignored by a set of women with quite a variety backgrounds. The evidence is only anecdotal, not statistical, but the instances of total rejection of

63 Degler 1974, p. 1488.

the code vividly display the *possibility* that married women could conduct themselves without interference from the received moral wisdom. When we explore why and how this could come about, we may well be in a position to infer that it came about commonly. Here are examples showing utter freedom from the moral code, consisting in a line or two taken from several of the letters and diaries of married women already quoted above:

- The truly married alone can know what a wondrous instrument it [i.e., sexual intercourse] is for the purposes of the heart.
- I like you to want me, dear, and if I were only with you, I would embrace more than the back of your neck, to be sure.
- It brought up a great wave of sweet memories and longings and the touch of clinging warm lips, and the still magnetic thrill of your warm body.
- Every night . . . he undressed me on the bright Turkey rug before the fire.
- It is just dreadful to sleep alone. . . . I want you very much, dear, very much.
- How long are we to be separated must it be much longer, I want to sleep in your arms again.
- Would that I could *kiss you all over* – and then *eat you up.*
- How are you this hot day? I am most roasted and my chemise sticks to me and the sweat runs down my legs and I suppose I smell very sweet, don't you wish you could be around just now.
- If I remember the exciting letters you have lately written or imagine what our pleasure shall be when side by side again I get so excited that I sometimes fear lest it unfavorably affect Mamie.
- How I long to see you . . . I'll drain your coffers dry next Saturday I assure you.

Where in the language of these letters is the oppressive hovering of the moral code? Where is the inclination to participate only out of duty to husband, the sense of a base, animal function, the distaste, the shrinking, the horror, the inhibition, the self-control, the reproduction wholly, the not-for-pleasure, and above all, where is the Victorian modesty? Apparently, out the window. Certain biological ideas and moral precepts were the backbone of the intention to restrain married sexual behavior; if they could be ignored or sidestepped, there could be little hope of keeping sex in check. But we see here several examples in which they were indeed passed over as if they simply did not exist. The instruction just was not a factor in the lives of these few. Understanding how this might come about will enable us to see that these examples are probably not unique but were most likely repeated often in the Victorian social system, even if not always celebrated in love letters. Based on the evidence, I propose that the women writing these letters and diary entries were able by means of two devices to sidestep or ignore the instruction we are presuming they did receive.

The first device is the spiritualizing of sex. As background, bear in mind that women have sex hormones; they are impelled at times towards sexual activity. Also, women who do engage in sexual activity would most likely prefer to do it without being encumbered by a nagging guilt. We have seen that in the nineteenth century, love was considered to be a function of the soul or spirit, whereas sex was seen as animal, a function of body or appetite. In this sense, sex would always be a threat to true love.[64] There is no doubt that this was a major philosophical strain in Victorian times and that it had important influence in several areas – for example, in prostitution to divert the sex impulses of men away from women who would more properly be objects of purely spiritual love. But while dominant in theory, this duality did not necessarily prevail in all areas of practice. In fact, we have excellent evidence from the Mosher survey and the diaries and letters that couples in love managed to turn this philosophy on its head, and they did so to their immense advantage because it enabled them to enjoy sex without guilt.

Instead of sex as cause threatening love as effect, it was love as cause that spiritualized sex, which otherwise, without love, would truly have been seen as base in nature. Love was not only an exceptionally strong force in Victorian times but a salient one. A great many of the women – women in love – *felt* that

64 This is a major point in the treatment by Seidman 1991; see especially pages 78, 82, 26-32, and 40-42.

what they were experiencing in their sexual relations was beautiful, exalted, spiritual – a reaction that is not at all surprising. They resolved their divergence from the prevailing philosophy by seeing that there were two kinds of sex, that which was an integral expression of love and that which was practiced outside of love. As between love and sex, love was the more powerful force. Sex was not a threat because, as an expression of love, it was transformed from a function of appetite into a function of soul.

In this perspective, the two definitions of love that I pointed out earlier – the one that includes a carnal component and the other that is strictly spiritual – no longer conflict, for married sex now becomes spiritual. Sophia Peabody Hawthorne captured the reasoning perfectly in the quoted passage above, where her contrast between the "truly married" and the "profane" essentially translates into with and without love: "The truly married alone can know what a wondrous instrument it is for the purposes of the heart. . . . The profane never can taste the joys of Elysium – because it is a spiritual joy, so they cannot perceive it." A few additional excerpts from passages already offered from the letters and diaries plus several from the Mosher survey show how this reasoning toward the conclusion of spirituality could well have been common – among men as well as women – and suggest as well that lovers may not have needed the writings of authorities[65] to arrive at it but came to it spontaneously, on their own, each out of his or her own feelings in the context of love (first and foremost), sex, and a Victorian perspective.

- What is sensuality! Not the *enjoyment* of *holy glorious matter,* but blindness to its spiritual meaning! . . . How much more delicious when in each others' arms, the flesh and the spirit shall tend the same way, increasing each other's delight! Bless God Bless God!
- If Holy Eden was the scene of Marriage & Married Love, why should I fear to leap into your arms to realize one of Eden's blessings or taste an Enjoyment wh: *must* be pure if it was *tasted there*!
- With you sexual intercourse and desire is holy and pure. . . . How sweet & how precious a thing is true & pure wedded love.

65 Relevant authorities did exist. See Lystra 1992, pp. 101-119 and Seidman 1991, p. 209.

- Oh the sacredness of wedded love. I begin to realize its depth and strength, and its purity, its frank surrender, its implicit confidence.
- I know there is no sin in it – but Gods dear word permits and encourages our love.

The similar survey responses that follow are by no means the only examples in the data of the spiritualizing of sex through the medium of love but are all in answer to just one of Dr. Mosher's questions, "What other reasons besides reproduction are sufficient to warrant intercourse?"[66]

> No. 3: It seems to me to be a natural and physical sign of a spiritual union.
> No. 8: Ideal marriage – spiritual.
> No. 10 (Margaret Osborne): I think to the man and woman married from love, it may be used temperately, as one of the highest manifestations of love, granted us by our Creator.
> No. 12 (Deirdre Mueller): I think it is only warranted as an expression of true and passionate love.
> No. 15 (Lucy Meadows): The desire of both husband and wife for this expression of their union seems to me the first and highest reason for intercourse.
> No. 17 (Nancy Wright): A spiritual completeness which is not gained in [any] other way.

---

66 Recall from Chapter V that Seidman (1991) urges that there was a cultural shift around 1900 by which the sexual relation began to be considered as more of a spiritual behavior than one attributable to animal appetite. The eleven extracts that follow in the text bear loosely on that claim. Since they all tend to spiritualize sex, the great majority of them should have been recorded after 1900. However, the data show that five of the eleven women were interviewed before 1900 and six afterwards. (Seidman 1991, p. 95, claims twelve after 1900 but I cannot find these responses in the data.) As to the extracts just above from the love letters, all were written well before the 1900 break point. Seidman's claim might well be valid; it would be an unwarranted digression to explore it here. However, I do not find support for it in the evidence pertinent to the particular issues in this volume, which indicates that the spiritualizing of sex prevailed throughout the Victorian period.

> No. 22 (Mildred Conroy): But in my experience the habitual bodily expression of love has a deep psychological effect in making possible complete mental sympathy & perfecting the spiritual union.
> No. 38: Love – a spiritual experience.
> No. 44 (Molly Attenborough): Oneness uplifting like music. Very little that is animal about it.
> No. 45: One man & one woman spiritual significance most vital.
> No. 46: A phase of expression of love. . . . Natural, pleasurable, because you love the man.

We see, then, that perceiving sex as an expression of their love, thereby making it a spiritual experience, Victorian women were enabled to discover that the critical biological ideas and moral precepts to which they had been exposed did not apply to them. Their love put their sexual relations into an entirely different category, far removed from the baseness of lust and sensuality. By this means, the strictures of the code became irrelevant, natural inclinations were fulfilled, and guilt was obviated.

We turn now to the second device by which our married writers of love letters may have avoided being affected by the relevant aspects of the Victorian moral code. It consisted simply in not being made to feel that those aspects were important and therefore not taking them seriously. For one, the efforts exerted to restrain married sex must necessarily have been half-hearted compared to the parallel efforts directed towards unmarried sex, and in addition, in the case of married women, those efforts had no teeth.

We have seen that to claim that women were passionless might possibly serve well as a deterrent both to premarital sex and to adultery. It is therefore easy to see why authorities interested in controlling behavior would convince themselves of and promulgate the notion that married women were uninterested in sex, as we see in the quotes above claiming shrinking, horror, only as a duty, and so forth. This claim would seem to be rather foolhardy; it would clearly bump into the actual sexual experience of individual married women and therefore risk being exposed as invalid.

Take Sally Warren, for example. Asked how she felt after intercourse with orgasm she replied, "No disgust, as I have often heard it described." She was exposed to the propaganda, in other words, but her personal experience taught her that the propaganda was not true, or at least not true for her. Her reaction to married sex was quite far from disgust. When asked if it was agreeable to her, part of her answer was, "Usually very delightful." But the propagandists could get away with this because Sally and others like her were not about to publicize their sexual feelings, impressions, or behavior. They would be highly unlikely even to talk about such matters to close family members or friends. Only to husbands, perhaps, and people like Dr. Mosher. Talking about sexual relations was not done in Victorian times; the bedroom was strictly private. Therefore, there was no real chance of the propaganda being exposed as a fraud. By the very same token of reticence and privacy, however, the authorities were not about to investigate to make sure that there was not too much married sex going on or overly much enjoyment of it by women. They put the propaganda out there and probably believed it themselves but were apparently content to leave the corresponding realities muffled in obscurity.

Why would they be content with the obscurity of actual behavior? Because few if any would be likely to care very much about the realities of the marital bedroom. There could be but little interest in these aspects of the code – much less interest than in the applications to unmarried women. Consider, in this connection, the coalition for repression. The church was interested in memberships, the example of women for their husbands, and the training of children, none of which was likely to be threatened by more or less married sex. As long as they did not interfere with domesticity, godliness, or public modesty, and there is no reason why they should, the church would not consider the quantity and quality of married sex to be vital interests. The middle class as a member of the coalition was interested in adultery, but adultery was not likely to be made more probable by a responsive wife and a satisfying sex life; if anything, quite the opposite. Contraception was also an issue, but as long as married couples did not make positive views towards contraception public, which of course they did not, there was no danger that such views would encourage premarital sex. Parents were pretty much out of the picture. Husbands also were concerned with adultery. Here there is an interesting Catch 22. If husbands sought to lessen the probability of female adultery by standing for passionlessness, shrinking, horror, and so forth, they would only decrease their own chances of a sexually satisfying marriage – quite substantially.

Consider feminist leaders as members of the coalition. Our purpose here is to understand how the married women concerned in the love letters and diaries managed so completely to escape the Victorian moral code as it applied to them. We see that the application of the code was half-hearted on the part of members of the coalition because they did not have much stake in its impact. Married couples could thereby perceive that nobody really cared what they did in their bedrooms; the code could be safely ignored. Feminist leaders with a concern for the self-esteem and power position of wives, on the other hand, clearly did have a stake. They wanted reform. If individual wives did not understand the motives of feminist leaders in supporting the code (self-esteem and power position of ordinary wives attained through purity), then they might well be affected by its provisions. This is the one credible source of pressure towards restraint that might have influenced some of the women concerned in our love letters. It apparently did not have influence, probably because feminist leaders who held these views were few and limited in fame. On the other hand, those wives who understood the motives but did not feel needful of increasing their self-esteem or power position in the home could simply disregard the advice as not applying to themselves.

Moreover, the code as applied to married women had no teeth. It could not be enforced, and for that reason, wives were able to feel safe in ignoring it. An unmarried woman who violated the code ran the terrible risk of losing her reputation, her parental family, and her chances of marriage and children. Furthermore, if the violation included sexual intercourse, she might easily be found out – and totally ruined – by becoming pregnant. Married women who welcomed sex rather than shrinking from it, however, ran no risk at all. They were only doing what they were expected to do, and nobody need know that their feelings about it were positive. Pregnancies were not only normal but praiseworthy. There was really nothing to lose in following where both love and hormones palpably led.

A significant discovery in these letters and diaries is that the married women concerned were so unworried about the code that they seemed oblivious to it.

Are these women unique in that respect, or was such an orientation common? Understanding that they were able to ignore the code because of the spiritualizing of sex through love and because the code's enforcement was both half-hearted and toothless helps us to see that the orientation might very well have been common – that there are likely to have been a great many more married women in the Victorian system just like most of Dr. Mosher's respondents and the wives concerned in our letters and diaries.

Let us turn now to unmarried women.

In the ways just described, the published love letters support the Mosher survey in requiring that the traditional or repression model of Victorian sexuality be revised: that model does not apply with validity to married women. Their story is entirely different, and the difference needs to be appreciated. But the revisionists would seem to demand the overturning of the traditional model in its entirety. They do not mention any restrictions. Is that position valid? It is not, for the repression model does correctly characterize the sexual position of unmarried middle-class women and must continue to be accepted as valid in that critical respect.

To the best of my knowledge, no writer has characterized the traditional model of the sexuality of Victorian women in its totality and with precision. Most are content to paint an impressionistic picture with such statements as, "Everyone knows that Victorian women were sexually repressed," "It was considered improper to put books by a male and a female author side by side on a shelf unless the two authors were married to each other," "Victorian women not only covered their own legs out of modesty but the legs of their pianos," "One serious slip and the Victorian woman was ruined for life," or, "No line in a novel could appear if it were likely to bring a blush to the maiden cheek."

One gets the general idea – and perhaps that is good enough. In fact, it is probable that no single traditional model exists. There are many, depending on the analyst, and they vary both in scope and severity. That conceded, it is best for our purposes to have something definite in mind as we consider whether "the traditional model" is valid as it applies to unmarried women. Accordingly, I propose that, purely for purposes of exploration and discussion, we consider the traditional or repression model pertinent to unmarried women to consist in the following: By instilling a strict moral code that included both biological "facts" and moral precepts, a preponderance of relevant, influential Victorians sought to prevent unmarried middle-class women from having any sexual thoughts, feeling desire, having or hearing any sexual conversation, or indulging in any sexual behavior, with the primary aim being the prevention of all premarital sexual intercourse, and further, that the authorities succeeded in achieving all of these outcomes.

It does not matter that the model as stated cannot possibly be correct in its entirety. What matters is in what aspects and to what extent it can or cannot be supported, and why.

Insofar as the crucial primary aim is concerned – the prevention of premarital sexual intercourse – Chapters II through IV demonstrated that this goal was achieved to such a great extent that the model can be considered as definitely supported in this aspect. The demonstration was not based on one single source or argument but the convergence of several:

1. The prebridal pregnancy rate in America (birth less than 8 ½ months after the marriage) in the period 1841-1880 was under ten percent. Since this included the working class, which was the great majority of the population and in which intercourse between engagement and wedding was common, the rate for the middle class would have been even lower.
2. The major Victorian novelists, who wrote mainly about England, were permitted by the publishing norms to write about illicit sexual intercourse in their works provided that they observed the restrictions of necessity, faithfulness to reality, delicacy, and expiation. Most of them did in fact do this while clearly showing the tendency to push outward on the restrictions – trying to include more sexuality than the norms permitted. Under these conditions, it is not believable that the novelists wrote about less illicit sex than was observable in the system. Analysis of an objective sample of the novels of these authors showed that less than ten percent of love couples had illicit sexual intercourse. If adulteries are subtracted, since our focus at this point is on premarital sex,

the tally is substantially further reduced. Lastly, a logical demonstration based on the absence of appealing illicit sexual encounters in the novels also demonstrates that the actual incidence of premarital sexual intercourse was low.

3. Historical events in Britain and America justify the proposition that it would be extremely difficult to make a population more prudish in its reading than in its behavior. The period of the waning of Puritanism, the Restoration of the British monarchy in 1660-1661, the long period between the Restoration and Victoria, the tail end of the Victorian era, the period after the First World War, and the 1960s all show a pattern in which the permissiveness of publishing norms came to correspond to the behavior prevailing in the system. Since the publishing norms in the Victorian era were prudish in the extreme, we can infer that the prevailing moral behavior was correspondingly repressed.
4. The Mosher women revealed zero instances of intercourse before marriage. In the question about their knowledge before marriage of sexual physiology, they had an opportunity – even a request – to affirm such experience if they had had it, but none indicated that she had acquired the knowledge in that way. In the study by Davis of women born somewhat later, when norms were somewhat more permissive, seven percent indicated that they had intercourse before marriage. In the study by Kinsey and his colleagues, fourteen percent gave the same response. The respondents in the Kinsey study were not only born even later but also included working-class women.

I conclude that the level of premarital sexual intercourse in Victorian times – in both England and America – was well under ten percent of relevant women and that the repression model is therefore solidly vindicated in this aspect. Since the prevention of premarital coitus was, under the model, the primary goal of the sexually pertinent socialization of young Victorian women, this result can be considered important. But the prevention of coitus is not the only element in the model. There is also the issue of whether the result on coitus was obtained by virtue of the socialization aimed at achieving it and also the further issue of preventing sexuality below the level of intercourse: thoughts, desire, conversation, and the milder forms of sexual behavior such as touching the breasts, for example, and other parts of the body. For convenience, I will refer to all of the latter as "petting."

The repression model would be supported more fully and more strongly if one could show not only that there was a bare minimum of premarital coitus but that coitus was prevented by internalization of the moral code that the coalition for repression tried so hard to instill. The evidence on intercourse does not speak to that issue in any way. Here, however, is where the letters and diaries of the present chapter can render material assistance.

I noted above, when analyzing the love letters of unmarried women, that they give support to the traditional theory. That is true, but how do they manage to do so? The letters and diaries cannot support the traditional theory of Victorian behavior by showing *statistically* that the majority of unmarried women of the period were chaste. As noted many times previously, the sample is not nearly objective enough to be considered representative; ultimately, it is anecdotal – just individual stories. But the love letters and diaries do support the theory in another important manner. They explain how coitus and other sexual behaviors were often prevented by showing that the code was in force. By this I mean that people in general in the social system believed that young women should be chaste in their deportment and that they should not indulge in risky behaviors – actions by them or to them that might lead too far down the sexual path. "Too far" is imprecise, but no matter; the idea is to stop early in the process and know that going any further is wrong – more and more wrong the further one goes. Not only, according to the model, must these beliefs be ubiquitously held, but individual young women must know this and feel it as restraining pressure on their behavior. This prudish set of beliefs and attitudes constitutes a significant part of the traditional theory; it is perhaps the most important part of what is commonly meant by the stereotype "Victorian" in regard to sexual matters.

I do not propose that the letters and diaries can demonstrate whether the code was in force by treating the letter writers as subjects in a study, to be counted up and put in tables. Rather, I propose that they be considered as *informants* regarding characteristics not of themselves but of the social system, as is common in the discipline of social anthropology. In the case at hand, the informants do not tell the researcher (and the reader) directly what the pertinent characteristics of the social system presumably are. I am not sure that they would be able to do so if asked. We depend instead on their free choice of language that happens to relate to the prevailing beliefs and expectations in the surrounding social milieu, expecting that these choices will enable us to see with a high degree of confidence whether the attributes expected by the traditional model did or did not characterize the true, prevailing norms. Jumping ahead, the letters and diaries show that the code was in force, just as the repression model would maintain, and that although it certainly was not one hundred percent successful, it acted effectively in the direction of sexual restraint.

Returning once again to the method employed previously in this chapter, consider the following short excerpts from the letters and diaries in terms of how the chosen words and phrases reveal the widespread adoption and internalization of the code. For example, in the first excerpt, it is the word "astray" that reveals the accepted, underlying moral prohibition.

- There never was a moment when I felt anything by which you could have drawn me astray.
- He says, if I loved him as he loved me I wouldn't care for the whole world to know that he held me in his arms and kissed me good-night. But I told him it was highly improper.
- There will be lots of things I will tell you 'you mustn't do.'
- I didn't think that you thought me that sort but now you know that I'm not.
- I made up my mind that if I allowed things I knew I should regret that I should not allow you to come out for two weeks as punishment for myself. . . . The only thing we can do . . . is to practice and learn self control & self denial.
- Women so naturally guard such treasures with jealousy & care, that it seems very "strange" to yield them even to the "best loved one."

- I am in *continual* danger of doing wrong – my affections too strongly fix upon things [that] "must perish with their using – ."
- Though I would fain be all loveliness yet while I feel so much of evil rioting in my bosom how *can* I conceal it?
- I woke up the next morning very happy though, & feeling not at all condemned.
- And if I don't behave with great impropriety then it will be for better reasons than I can now foresee. I'll just squeeze her and hug her, and kiss her forehead and eyes.
- I hope there will be a carpet on the floor for it seems you intend to act worse than you ever did before.
- Oh Mi how intensely do I long to see you – to *feel* you . . . My passions are terrible and none but you could master them.
- And took too many liberties with her sweet person and we are going to stop.
- A man can never know the deadening feeling of utter despair that a woman knows at the shadow on her fair name.
- When temptation to wrong suggested itself from natural passions and opportunity, 'twas my mission to have been *fine*, giving you a kind refusal and leading your mind away and beyond. . . . God only knows how I detested myself. . . . We have both done wrong. I having done much the greater because I should have acted the part of a true, noble, Christian woman.

First, note that none of these excerpts is from the letters of married women; those correspondents apparently felt that the code need not apply to their situation, and so they ignored it completely. Over and over in the excerpts from unmarried men and women, however, key words and phrases are used in such a way as to betray the assumption that everybody knows – it goes without saying – that there is a range of universally forbidden behaviors, so that the code is shown to have been in force in the social system.

astray
improper

things I know I should regret
wrong
evil
condemned
impropriety
act worse
liberties
wrong
wrong

When people are aware of what they should not do, the cognition would generally act to restrain their behavior. The pressure toward restraint may be completely successful, as we have seen, but it may also be only partially successful or even not at all, as we have also seen, in which cases there is likely to be a feeling of guilt. The issue is whether the code in force is regarded simply as a collection of the outmoded ideas of old folks or as a living force that acts in the direction of restraining behavior. What we find is a kind of repetitive phraseology in the excerpts showing that the general knowledge of forbidden territory did act, for many women at least, in the direction of restraining sexuality, as would be expected. It is important from the standpoint of tentative generalization that a restraining force was felt even by women who were most likely to be unaffected by such a force – women in love and, even more strongly, women in love who wrote love letters.

- not expect me to stay on the porch alone with him
- things I will tell you "you mustn't do"
- now you know that I'm not [that sort]
- practice and learn self control & self denial
- keep your hands just to hold me to you *nothing* else
- women so naturally guard such treasures with jealousy & care
- none but you could master them
- we are going to stop

- giving you a kind refusal
- how I detested myself

And so we see that the traditional model is valid both in that there was a bare minimum of premarital sexual intercourse and that the code was internalized throughout the system, apparently functioning quite successfully to keep risky sexual behavior in check.

There are remaining aspects of the traditional model, however, that do not fare quite so well given the evidence at hand. The letters and diaries indicate that there may have been a substantial amount both of desire and of petting among middle-class women, whereas there should have been none at all according to the model of repression. As to desire, I believe we must give up the hope of supporting the repression model in this respect. The argument on this subject in Chapter IV showed that the limited amount of desire expressly declared or alluded to in the novels would have been much greater if not for the requirements of necessity and delicacy.

But besides that, over and over again in Victorian novels, young men and women are very passionately in love. Under one definition, being in love automatically would include and convey the idea of sexual desire. The writers could easily get away with portraying intense romantic love because the feelings could readily be interpreted as purely spiritual, which was the way it was supposed to be, and that was enough to pass muster with Mudie and the critics. But a great many readers, especially those with personal experience in the matter, would interpret the feelings as desire, as a yearning of these young bodies toward one another, even if they, especially the women, did not know exactly what this yearning was all about. There was a good deal of desire among unmarried women in the Victorian social system, particularly if and when they fell in love. I submit that the model must be qualified in that regard.

Along these lines, one might think to invoke the novels to claim that the petting in our letters and diaries was highly unusual. The suggestion would be that there actually was little or no petting in the system because there is none in the novels. This use of the novels is unsuccessful, however, because it would have been impossible to depict instances of petting in the fiction of the period; such depictions would grossly have transgressed the requirements for necessity and delicacy. Under the informal rules, it was permissible to allude to episodes of sexual intercourse in one way or another but license to depict petting was apparently limited to approximately one kiss per novel. Since we have a certain amount of evidence of petting, perhaps it was widespread and the repression model must again be considered to be faulty. Perhaps, but there is one condition to be recognized in possible mitigation of this criticism of the theory.

The parties concerned in those letters and diary entries that betray a certain amount of petting were committed couples who intended to be married in the near future. If their experience is generalizable, there may have been more petting than the theory would have predicted for such couples but still little or none for couples who had not fallen deeply in love or progressed very far toward marriage in their plans. If true, this would call only for a qualification of the theory and not an important revision. Crucially, we know that the code was what I have called "in force" and that it tended to restrain sexual behavior. It is eminently reasonable on this basis to infer that, among couples at some stage of acquaintance below the late phases of courtship, sexual exploration beyond the level of kissing was absent or at least rare. The couples did not just "play around." As for couples deeply in love and mutually committed, we have vivid evidence of petting but, given the arbitrary nature of the sample, it cannot be generalized even to the larger population of committed couples. In the matter of petting, therefore, the evidence is simply not strong enough to relieve uncertainty in either direction.

As concerns unmarried women then, the repression model is substantiated in its two most important aspects: the prevention of premarital sexual intercourse and the widespread internalization of a strict moral code that functioned to restrain sexual exploration. There is no solid proof regarding desire, but all indications are that it blossomed commonly once a woman fell in love or even experienced an attraction short of love. As for petting, the evidence suggests that there was a good deal of it among committed couples, perhaps often encumbered by guilt, but the validity of this inference must remain uncertain unless further pertinent documents come to light, such as another, more explicit Mosher survey.

We began with an explanation of two opposing theories of the sexual behavior of middle-class Victorian women, characterizing the potential resolution of this disagreement as a mystery. I now propose that the mystery is solved. With significant reservations regarding desire and petting, the traditional theory is upheld. However, it applies only to unmarried women.

In spite of this last limitation, I would consider the conclusion to be a validation of the major thrust of long-held ideas concerning the sexuality of Victorians. The large collection of nebulous, diverse, and informal evidence previously available did not mislead. The Victorian era was a period of repressed sexuality.

Nevertheless, the Mosher survey and the available relevant letters and diaries unquestionably demand a revision, because the traditional theory has appeared to apply indiscriminately to all middle-class Victorian women. We now see that it fails completely with respect to married women as a class. They do not fit the model of repression. The discoveries of Degler, Lystra, Rothman, Gay, and others constitute a remarkable revelation in that even in a time of the most severe prudery, most middle-class married women were able to enjoy emphatically fulfilling sex lives, agreeably free of guilt.

In my opinion, these results on married women do not change very radically our overall view of Victorianism. Rather, they constitute new information about a hitherto hidden component of Victorianism, and at the same time, much more broadly, they provide important insight into both the role of marriage in the sexual development of individuals and the power of privacy to keep that role fairly constant, even in the most prudish of surrounding circumstances.

The primary implication of the findings is that the sexuality of middle-class Victorian women should no longer be considered as unitary but rather as differing between the unmarried and the married.

Finally, the evidence we have relied on to reach the above conclusions comes very heavily from the American side of the Atlantic. Do these conclusions therefore apply only to American Victorians or to the British as well?

Unfortunately, I cannot say for sure, but let us look separately at the results for married and unmarried women.

On the unmarried side, I summarized the evidence in favor of the traditional model in four points, above, dealing with sexual intercourse. Point number one considers the statistics on prebridal pregnancy, where the data summarized are completely American. British data do exist, but they are too untrustworthy in this context to be used.[67] Skipping around a bit, point number four had to do with the Mosher, Davis, and Kinsey surveys. Again, these were all American and cannot be used in themselves to paint the scene in Great Britain. Point number three, however, which recalls the tight connection between factual behavior and publishing norms, is different. The evidence is equally British and American, indicating that behavior was similar in both geographic areas and similarly repressed in the age of Victoria. Point number two, which relies on an analysis of the Victorian novels, applies most directly to Britain, although America is also represented. It reaches roughly the same quantitative conclusion on repression as the statistical evidence from the United States referenced in points one and four. One would feel more confident with similar statistical data from Britain, but the evidence that we do have suggests that the repression model holds for unmarried women in Britain as well as in America insofar as the central goal of preventing premarital intercourse is concerned.

The evidence on the code's being in force in the system and influencing unmarried women was based primarily on excerpts from American letters and diaries and therefore cannot readily be used to generalize about Britain. We can observe, however, that the training of young women in this regard was stricter in Britain than in the United States, and the historical interests of the coalition for repression were at least as British as American if not more so. Furthermore, the novels are drenched in propriety and the concern of young

67 Smith and Hindus 1975, pp. 569-570. The percentages are based on very few marriages and so may be unreliable. They also come from a few tiny rural districts and so may be largely working class and therefore not strictly pertinent. Lastly, the figures are so very high at over forty percent of births within eight and one half months of the wedding and so constant between 1750 and 1887 as to be anomalous, what are called "outliers," and therefore not reliable for generalization. See Wilson 2007, p.78, as quoted in Chapter II.

women for virtue. It is in fact prominently from the British novels that the prudish image of the Victorian era, and especially its middle-class women, derives. It is reasonable to conclude, therefore, that the Victorian moral code was in force and influencing behavior both in Britain and America.

The potential qualifications on desire and petting were tentative for America and would be similarly tentative for Britain.

Lastly, on the married side, the evidence for revision of the traditional theory comes from the Mosher survey and American (almost entirely) letters and diaries, and so cannot be generalized readily to Great Britain. What can be generalized, however, are the conditions we found in the analysis that allowed the majority of American women to set the code aside and enjoy full and satisfying marital relations. These conditions were the same on both sides of the Atlantic. They were, first of all, sex hormones, their effects enhanced by legal Christian marriage, privacy, and actual sexual experience. Second was the spiritualization of sex by love. When there is true love, which seems frequently to have been the case with married Victorian women, marital sex becomes right – godly – and not base, animal, and wrong. Third was the crucial fact that interest in enforcement of the code by the coalition for repression was both half-hearted and toothless. Married women on both sides of the Atlantic were left on their own to discover and pursue their sexuality in the privacy of their bedrooms. On the basis of these three conditions, then, it seems reasonable to guess that if a Mosher survey for Britain were discovered, its results would be much the same as in the American survey we know.

I conclude that the results of the foregoing exposition and analysis are valid for both America and Britain, except that the conclusion regarding married women in Britain depends only on indirect inference rather than clear, pertinent evidence. We can therefore sum up with confidence regarding America, pulling Britain along only tentatively for the last part of the story: The Victorian stereotype remains in full force – up to the point of marriage. It may be surprising to some, unsurprising to others, but the fact is that marriage was a watershed for the substantial majority of middle-class Victorian women. It both piloted and enabled a fresh, unschooled outlook on women's sex and sexuality.

Appendices

Appendix I
Sampling Frame, Novels

JANE AUSTEN

1. Northanger Abbey
2. Sense and Sensibility
3. Pride and Prejudice
4. Mansfield Park
5. Emma
6. Persuasion

SIR WALTER SCOTT

7. Waverley
8. Guy Mannering
9. The Antiquary
10. The Black Dwarf
11. Old Mortality
12. Rob Roy
13. The Heart of Midlothian
14. The Bride of Lammermoor
15. The Legend of Montrose
16. Ivanhoe
17. The Monastery
18. The Abbot
19. Kenilworth
20. The Pirate
21. The Fortunes of Nigel
22. Peveril of the Peak
23. Quentin Durward
24. St. Ronan's Well
25. Redgauntlet
26. The Betrothed
27. The Talisman
28. Woodstock
29. The Fair Maid of Perth
30. Anne of Geierstein
31. Count Robert of Paris
32. Castle Dangerous

CHARLES DICKENS

33. Pickwick Papers
34. Oliver Twist
35. Nicholas Nickleby
36. Barnaby Rudge
37. The Old Curiosity Shop

38. Martin Chuzzlewit
39. Dombey and Son
40. David Copperfield
41. Bleak House
42. Hard Times
43. Little Dorritt
44. A Tale of Two Cities
45. Great Expectations
46. Our Mutual Friend
47. The Mystery of Edwin Drood

WILLIAM M. THACKERAY

48. Barry Lyndon
49. Vanity Fair
50. Pendennis
51. Henry Esmond
52. The Newcomes
53. The Virginians

ELIZABETH GASKELL

54. Mary Barton
55. Ruth
56. Cranford
57. North and South
58. Sylvia's Lovers
59. Wives and Daughters

WILKIE COLLINS

60. Antonina
61. Basil
62. Hide and Seek
63. The Dead Secret
64. The Woman in White
65. No Name
66. Armadale
67. The Moonstone
68. Man and Wife
69. Poor Miss Finch
70. The New Magdalen
71. The Law and the Lady
72. The Two Destinies
73. Jezebel's Daughter
74. The Black Robe
75. Heart and Science
76. I Say No
77. The Evil Genius
78. The Legacy of Cain
79. Blind Love

CHARLOTTE BRONTË

80. The Professor
81. Jane Eyre
82. Shirley
83. Villette

GEORGE ELIOT

84. Adam Bede
85. The Mill on the Floss
86. Romola
87. Felix Holt, the Radical
88. Middlemarch
89. Daniel Deronda

ANTHONY TROLLOPE

90. The Macdermots of Ballycloran
91. The Kellys and the O'Kellys
92. La Vendee
93. The Warden
94. Barchester Towers
95. The Three Clerks
96. Doctor Thorne
97. The Bertrams
98. Castle Richmond
99. Framley Parsonage

100. Orley Farm
101. The Struggles of Brown, Jones, and Robinson
102. Rachel Ray
103. The Small House at Allington
104. Can You Forgive Her?
105. Miss Mackenzie
106. The Belton Estate
107. The Claverings
108. The Last Chronicle of Barset
109. Phineas Finn
110. He Knew He Was Right
111. The Vicar of Bullhampton
112. Sir Harry Hotspur of Humblethwaite
113. Ralph the Heir
114. The Golden Lion of Granpere
115. The Eustace Diamonds
116. Phineas Redux
117. Lady Anna
118. The Way We Live Now
119. The Prime Minister
120. The American Senator
121. Is He Popenjoy?
122. An Eye for an Eye
123. John Caldigate
124. Cousin Henry
125. The Duke's Children
126. Dr. Wortle's School
127. Ayala's Angel
128. The Fixed Period
129. Marion Fay
130. Kept in the Dark
131. Mr. Scarborough's Family
132. An Old Man's Love

GEORGE MEREDITH

133. The Ordeal of Richard Feverel
134. Evan Harrington
135. Sandra Belloni
136. Rhoda Fleming
137. Vittoria
138. The Adventures of Harry Richmond
139. Beauchamp's Career
140. The Egoist
141. The Tragic Comedians
142. Diana of the Crossways
143. One of our Conquerors
144. Lord Ormont and His Aminta
145. The Amazing Marriage

THOMAS HARDY

146. Desperate Remedies
147. Under the Greenwood Tree
148. A Pair of Blue Eyes
149. Far from the Madding Crowd
150. The Hand of Ethelberta
151. The Return of the Native
152. The Trumpet-Major
153. A Laodicean
154. Two on a Tower
155. The Mayor of Casterbridge
156. The Woodlanders
157. Tess of the d'Urbervilles
158. Jude the Obscure
159. The Well-Beloved

HENRY JAMES

160. Roderick Hudson
161. The American

162. The Europeans
163. Washington Square
164. The Portrait of a Lady
165. The Bostonians
166. The Princess Casamassima
167. The Tragic Muse
168. The Spoils of Poynton
169. What Maisie Knew
170. The Awkward Age
171. The Sacred Fount
172. The Wings of the Dove
173. The Ambassadors
174. The Golden Bowl

WILLIAM DEAN HOWELLS

175. Their Wedding Journey
176. A Chance Acquaintance
177. A Foregone Conclusion
178. The Lady of the Aroostook
179. The Undiscovered Country
180. A Modern Instance
181. The Rise of Silas Lapham
182. Indian Summer
183. The Minister's Charge
184. Annie Kilburn
185. April Hopes
186. A Hazard of New Fortunes
187. The Quality of Mercy
188. A Traveler from Altruria
189. The Landlord at Lion's Head
190. Ragged Lady
191. The Kentons
192. The Son of Royal Langbrith
193. Their Silver Wedding Journey
194. The Leatherwood God
195. The Vacation of the Kelwyns

Appendix II
The Sample of Novels

JANE AUSTEN

1. Persuasion, 1818
2. Pride and Prejudice, 1813

SIR WALTER SCOTT

3. The Talisman, 1825
4. Woodstock, 1826

CHARLES DICKENS

5. Nicholas Nickleby, 1839
6. Hard Times, 1854

WILLIAM M. THACKERAY

7. Pendennis, 1850
8. The Virginians, 1859

ELIZABETH GASKELL

9. Cranford, 1853
10. Wives and Daughters, 1866

WILKIE COLLINS

11. Hide and Seek, 1854
12. I Say No, 1884

CHARLOTTE BRONTË

13. Villette, 1853
14. Shirley, 1849

GEORGE ELIOT

15. The Mill on the Floss, 1860
16. Daniel Deronda, 1876

ANTHONY TROLLOPE

17. The Macdermots of Ballycloran, 1847
18. The Eustace Diamonds, 1871

GEORGE MEREDITH

19. The Adventures of Harry Richmond, 1871
20. Lord Ormont and His Aminta, 1894

THOMAS HARDY

21. Tess of the d'Urbervilles, 1891
22. Far from the Madding Crowd, 1874

HENRY JAMES

23. The Ambassadors, 1903
24. The Golden Bowl, 1904

WILLIAM DEAN HOWELLS

25. April Hopes, 1888
26. The Leatherwood God, 1916

Appendix III-A
Questionnaire for Novels
First Love Couple

Identify the "love couples" in the novel, i.e., a pair of individuals who get married, or, who remain unmarried while at least one of the two is romantically attracted to the other, for love, lust, or convenience, including those who are seen to form a potentially adulterous pair. If information on the couple is scant, leave for the last three sections. Omit those who have little or no interaction and are treated only in passing by the author.

Author:

Title:

Love Couple, number and names:

Social Class

1. What social class is the woman?
    1. Working
    2. Middle
    3. Upper

Feelings

2. In the woman's thoughts about her feelings for the man, is there any sexual connotation – e.g., wanting to touch?
    0. No
    1. Yes
3. If Yes (Q2), describe.
    Incident 1
    Incident 2
    Etc.

Love-Couple Interaction

4. Is it known whether love was expressed?
    0. No
    1. Yes
5. If Yes (Q4), was it?
    0. No
    1. Yes
6. If Yes (Q5), to whom does this apply?
    1. The man only
    2. The woman only
    3. Both
7. Is it known whether physical admiration, attraction, or desire was expressed?
    0. No
    1. Yes
8. If Yes (Q7), was it?
    0. No
    1. Yes
9. If Yes (Q8), in what terms? Describe.
10. If Yes (Q8), to whom does this apply?
    1. The man only
    2. The woman only
    3. Both
11. Aside from being expressed (Q8), is it alluded to by the author?
    0. No
    1. Yes
12. If Yes (Q11), in what terms? Describe.
13. If Yes (Q11), to whom does this apply?
    1. The man only
    2. The woman only
    3. Both

14. Is it known whether or not they kiss?
    0. No
    1. Yes
15. If Yes (Q14), do they?
    0. No
    1. Yes
16. If Yes (Q15), does this include a kiss other than to seal an engagement?
    0. No
    1. Yes
17. Is there explicit erotic touching or nakedness?
    0. No
    1. Yes

Seduction

18. Does the man try to get the woman to have extra-marital sex?
    0. No
    1. Yes
19. If Yes (Q18), how is this event conveyed by the author? Describe.
20. If Yes (Q18), does the woman refuse?
    0. No
    1. Yes
21. If Yes (Q20), in what terms? Describe.
    Incident 1
    Incident 2
    Etc.
22. Do they have extra-marital sex?
    0. No
    1. Yes
23. If Yes (Q22), how do we know they did? Describe.
24. If Yes (Q22), is it adulterous?
    0. No
    1. Yes

25. If Yes (Q24), who is married to someone else?
    1. The man
    2. The woman
    3. Both
26. If Yes (Q22), is it rape?
    0. No
    1. Yes
27. If Yes (Q26), how did it happen? Describe.
28. If Yes (Q26), what eventually happens to the woman? Describe.
29. If they do have extra-marital sex (Yes, Q22), is there any reference to or indication of the quality of the sexual intimacy?
    0. No
    1. Yes
30. If Yes (Q29), describe.
31. If Yes (Q29), is there any reference to the idea of sexual climax?
    0. No
    1. Yes
32. If Yes (Q31), describe.
33. If pregnancy or children result from the extra-marital sex, is there any reference to the love act as a part of producing children, or do the pregnancies or children just occur?
    0. No reference at all. They just occur.
    1. Some reference to the love act is made.
    8. No children result
34. If reference is made (Q33), in what terms is it made? Describe.

Engagement

35. If the love couple gets engaged, what difference in sexual behavior takes place after the engagement? Describe.
    8. They don't get engaged.

36. If engaged, do the characters or author refer in any way to the sex to come after marriage?
    0. No
    1. Yes
37. If Yes (Q 36), how? Describe

Marriage

38. If they marry, is there any reference to or recognition of the consummation?
    0. No
    1. Yes
    8. They don't marry.
39. If they marry, how is the morning or day after the wedding night handled with respect to recognition of the sexual intercourse that might have taken place?
    0. No allusion to it in any way
    1. Recognized in some way.
40. If recognized (Q39), how? Describe.
41. If they marry, is there any reference to or indication of the quality of the marital intimacy?
    0. No
    1. Yes
42. If Yes (Q41), describe.
43. If Yes (Q41), is there any reference to the idea of sexual climax?
    0. No
    1. Yes
44. If Yes (Q43), describe.
45. If they marry, is there any reference to the love act as a part of producing children, or do the pregnancies or children just occur?
    0. No reference at all. They just occur.
    1. Some reference to the love act is made.
46. If reference is made (Q45), in what terms is it made? Describe.

Intercourse

47. Is there any explicit or implied premarital sexual intercourse in the novel other than between named love couples?
    0. No
    1. Yes

If Yes (Q47),

Instance 1

Instance 2

Etc.

48. If Yes (Q47, each instance), is it middle class?
    0. No
    1. Yes
49. If Yes (Q47), how could it have happened? Describe.
50. Is the woman seduced, raped, etc.?
    1. Voluntary
    2. Seduced
    3. Raped
51. What eventually happens to the woman? Describe.

Fallen Women

52. Is there a fallen woman in the novel?
    0. No
    1. Yes

    If Yes (Q52)
    First woman
    Second woman
    Etc.
53. If Yes (Q 52, each woman), is she the woman in a named love couple?
    0. No
    1. Yes
54. If No (Q53), what social class?
    1. Working
    2. Middle
    3. Upper
55. If No (Q53), what happens to her? Describe.
56. If No (Q53), how do we know that she fell? Describe.

Adultery

57. Does a married woman in the novel who is not part of a named love couple commit adultery?
    0. No
    1. Yes
58. If Yes (Q57), what class is she?
    1. Working
    2. Middle
    3. Upper
59. If Yes (Q57), what happens to her? Describe.
60. If Yes (Q57), does the adultery produce a child?
    0. No
    1. Yes

    Missing data = 9 for all questions.
    Not applicable = 8 for all questions.

Appendix III-B
Novelsdata Coding

Open-ended Variables
(Relevant case numbers follow #)

9. **How physical admiration or desire is expressed.**
   1. Comments on loveliness or attractiveness. #17, 18
   2. Expresses desire for physical contact. #91
   3. Both 1 and 2. #12, 14

12. **How the author alludes to physical admiration or desire.**
   1. Refers to "Desire."
   2. Refers to "sensual passion."
   3. Both 1 and 2. #47
   4. Records her blushing at mention of his attractiveness. #44
   5. His physical approach would melt her.
   6. Both 1 and 5. #92

19. **How the author conveys the attempted seduction.**
   1. It emerges that she becomes pregnant or has a child. #43, 65, 66, 88
   2. They run off and live together for a time. #7
   3. Author narrates the attempted persuasion. #12, 14, 19
   4. Author narrates his imposing on her in physical ways. #18, 83

21. **How the woman refuses extra-marital sex.**
   1. She pleads the case for refusal with reasons. #12
   2. She puts up a strong physical resistance.
   3. She seeks help.
   4. Both 1 and 2. #14
   5. Methods 1, 2, and 3. #18
   6. She flees to a sanctuary. #19

23. **How we know that they had extra-marital sex.**
   1. She becomes pregnant. #66
   2. She has one or more children. #43, 65, 88

3. The author describes them as being together in such a way that sex is taken for granted. #7, 80, 91
4. Both 2 and 3. #83, 96
5. Both 3 and the fact that they are said to have been living a lie. #89

27. **How did the rape happen?**
    1. Tess is sleeping. Alec falls on top of her and takes her. #83

28. **What eventually happens to the raped woman?**
    1. She murders Alec and is hanged. #83

40. **How is sex on the wedding night recognized?**
    1. There's a very strong suggestion that Mr. Verver is impotent, at least with Charlotte. #93

49. **How did the premarital sexual intercourse between a non-named love couple happen?**
    1. Not described. Just alluded to as the usual story. #45

51. **What eventually happens to the woman who has premarital sexual intercourse?**
    1. She refuses to marry another man but without telling him it's because of her past. He commits suicide. #45

55. **What happens to the fallen woman in a non-named love couple?**
    1. Her life is pretty much ruined. #45

56. **How do we know that the fallen woman fell?**
    1. 1. She tells the novel's hero. #45

References

Acton, William. 1857. *The Functions and Disorders of the Reproductive Organs in Youth, in Adult Age, and in Advanced Life: Considered in Their Physiological, Social, and Psychological Relations*. London: John Churchill.

American Association of University Women, St. Lawrence County, NY Branch. Undated. Early College Women: Determined to be Educated. A Woman of Courage Profile. http://www.northnet.org/stlawrenceaauw/college.htm.

Anonymous. 1752. *The Works of Aristotle, the Famous Philosopher. Containing I – His Complete Masterpiece, II – His Experienced Midwife, III – His Book of Problems, IV – His Remarks on Physiognomy, V – The Family Physician*. London: Published by the Booksellers. Printed and Published by J. Coker & Co., 208 Shoe Lane, London E. C.4. 25th edition.

Austen, Jane. 2000. *Pride and Prejudice*. New York: Scholastic Inc. (First published in 1813.)

Barker-Benfield, Ben. 1973. The Spermatic Economy: A Nineteenth-Century View of Sexuality. In Michael Gordon (ed.), *The American Family in Social-Historical Perspective*. New York: St. Martin's Press, 1973, pp. 339-372.

Barret-Ducrocq, Francoise. 1991. *Love in the Time of Victoria: Sexuality, Class, and Gender in Nineteenth-Century London.* Translated by John Howe. New York: Verso.

Boyle, Thomas F. 1984. Morbid depression alternating with excitement: Sex in Victorian newspapers. In Don Richard Cox (ed.), *Sexuality and Victorian Literature.* Knoxville: University of Tennessee Press, pp. 212-233.

Branagan, Thomas. 1828. *Excellency of the Female Character Revisited; Being an Investigation Relative to the Cause and Effects of the Encroachments of Men upon the Rights of Women and the Too Frequent Degradation and Consequent Misfortunes of the Fair Sex.* Harrisburg: Francis Wyeth.

Burstyn, Joan N. 1973. Education and sex: The medical case against higher education for women in England, 1870-1900. *Proceedings of the American Philosophical Society.* Vol. 117, No. 2 (April 10), pp. 79-89.

Byatt, A. S. 1991. *Possession: A Romance.* New York: Vintage International.

Canadian Content. 2006. "The London Gin Craze." April 9. http://forums.canadiancontent.net/history/45486-london-gin-craze.html

Chamberlain, Geoffery. 2006. British maternal mortality in the 19th and early 20th centuries. *Journal of the Royal Society of Medicine.* Vol. 99, No. 11, November, pp. 559-563.

Clarke, Eric O. 1998. Review of *Scandal and Scholarship: A Review of Sex Scandal: The Private Parts of Victorian Fiction*, by William A. Cohen. *NOVEL: A Forum on Fiction.* Vol. 31, No. 2, Spring, pp. 260-262.

Cobbe, Frances Power. 1869. *Criminals, Idiots, Women, and Minors. Is the Classification Sound? A Discussion on the Laws concerning the Property of Married Women.* Manchester: A. Ireland & Co., Pall Mall. (Reprinted: Library Electronic Text Resource Service. Bloomington: Indiana University 2005.)

Collins, Wilkie. 1995. *I Say No*. London: Sutton Publishing Ltd. (Pocket Classics).

Cominos, Peter T. 1963. Late Victorian sexual respectability and the social system. *International Review of Social History*, Vol. 8, pp. 18-48, 216-50.

Cominos, Peter T. 1973. Innocent Femina Sensualis in Unconscious Conflict. In Martha Vicinus (ed.), *Suffer and Be Still: Women in the Victorian Age*. Chapter 9. Bloomington: Indiana University Press, pp. 155-172.

Cott, Nancy F. 1978. Passionlessness: An Interpretation of Victorian Sexual Ideology, 1790-1850. *Signs*, Vol. 4, No. 2 (Winter), pp. 219-236.

Cowan, John, MD. 1874. *The Science of a New Life*. New York: Cowan & Company.

Curtis, Simon and Steve Hudson (directors). 2008. *Cranford*. DVD. London: BBC Video.

David, Paul and Warren Sanderson. 1986. Rudimentary Contraceptive Methods and the American Transition to Marital Fertility Control. In Engerman, Stanley L. and Robert E. Gallman (eds.), *Long-Term Factors in American Economic Growth*. Chicago: University of Chicago Press, pp. 307-390.

Davis, Katharine B. 1929. *Factors in the Sex Life of Twenty-Two Hundred Women*. New York and London: Harper and Brothers.

Degler, Carl N. 1974. What ought to be and what was: women's sexuality in the nineteenth century. *The American Historical Review*. Vol. 79, No. 5, December, pp.1467-1490.

Degler, Carl N. 1980. *At Odds: Women and the Family in America from the Revolution to the Present*. New York: Oxford.

D'Emilio, John and Estelle B. Freedman. 1988. *Intimate Matters: A History of Sexuality in America*. New York: Harper and Row.

Dickens, Charles. 2006. *The Life and Adventures of Nicholas Nickleby*. Project Gutenberg EBook #967. First published in 1839.

Dickinson, Robert L. and Laura Beam. 1970. *A Thousand Marriages*. Westport, Connecticut: Greenwod Press. (First published in 1931.)

Fellman, Anita Clair and Michael Fellman. 1981. The Rule of Moderation in Late Nineteenty-Century American Sexual Ideology. *Journal of Sex Research*. Vol. 17, No. 3, *History and Sexuality*, pp. 238-255.

Fordyce, James. 1766. *Sermons to Young Women*. Third edition. London: Millar and Cadell, Dodsley, Payne. (London: William Pickering, 1996.)

Frank, Ellen, Carol Anderson, and Debra Rubinstein. 1978. Frequency of Sexual Dysfunction in "Normal" Couples. *The New England Journal of Medicine*. Vol. 299, Issue 3, pp. 111-115.

Garrison, Dee. 1976. Immoral fiction in the late Victorian library. *American Quarterly*, Vol. 28, No. 1, Spring, pp. 71-89.

Gay, Peter. 1984. *The Bourgeois Experience: Victoria to Freud*. Volume I, *Education of the Senses*. New York: Oxford University Press.

Gay, Peter. 1999. *The Bourgeois Experience: Victoria to Freud*. Volume II, *The Tender Passion*. New York: W. W. Norton.

Gisborne, Thomas. 1797. *An Enquiry into the Duties of the Female Sex*. London: Cadell and Davies. In Janet Todd (ed.), *Female Education in the Age of Enlightenment*. Vol. 2. London: William Pickering, 1996.

Gordon, Michael (ed). 1973. *The American Family in Social-Historical Perspective.* New York: St. Martin's Press.

Grafton, Sue. 2004. *R is for Ricochet.* New York: The Berkley Publishing Group.

Gregory, John. 1774. *A Father's Legacy to His Daughters.* Third edition. Dublin: John Colles.

Howe, Daniel Walker. 1975. American Victorianism as a Culture. *American Quarterly.* Vol. 27, No. 5, Special Issue, *Victorian Culture in America*, pp. 507-532.

Howells, William Dean. 1904. *The Son of Royal Langbrith.* New York: Harper and Brothers.

Jacob, Kathryn Allamong. 1981. The Mosher Report: The sexual habits of American women, examined half a century before Kinsey. http://www.americanheritage.com (*American Heritage Magazine*, Vol. 32, Issue 4, pp. 56-64), pp. 1-7.

James, Henry. 2009. *The Golden Bowl.* Oxford University Press, re-issue edition. First published in 1904.

Jordan, Ellen. 1991. "Making good wives and mothers"? The transformation of middle-class girls' education in nineteenth-century Britain. *History of Education Quarterly.* Vol. 31, No. 4 (Winter), pp. 439-462.

Kinsey, Alfred C., Wardell B. Pomeroy, Clyde E. Martin, and Paul H. Gebhard. 1953. *Sexual Behavior in the Human Female.* Philadelphia: W.B. Saunders.

Lambert, Tim. Life in the Nineteenth Century. Undated. http://www.localhistories.org/19thcent.html

Landale, Nancy S. and Avery M. Guest. 1986. Ideology and Sexuality among Victorian Women. *Social Science History,* Vol. 10, No. 2 (Summer), pp. 147-170.

Landow, George P. 1972. Review of *Mudie's Circulating Library and the Victorian Novel* by Guinevere L. Griest. *Modern Philology,* Vol. 69, No. 4 (May), pp. 367-369.

Lawrence, D. H. 1928. *Lady Chatterley's Lover.* London: Penguin Books.

Lively, Penelope. 2003. *The Photograph.* New York: Viking.

Loudon, Irvine. 2000. Maternal mortality in the past and its relevance to developing countries today. *American Journal of Clinical Nutrition.* Vol. 72 (Supplement), pp. 241S-246S.

Lurie, Alison. 1965. *The Nowhere City.* New York: Henry Holt and Company.

Lystra, Karen. 1992. *Searching the Heart: Women, Men, and Romantic Love in Nineteenth-Century America.* New York: Oxford University Press.

Marcus, Steven. 1966. *The Other Victorians.* New York: Basic Books.

McCall, Laura. 1994. "With all the wild, trembling, rapturous feelings of a lover": Men, women, and sexuality in American literature, 1820-1860. *Journal of the Early Republic. Vol. 14, No. 1 (Spring), pp. 71-89.*

Mohr, Lawrence B. 1990. *Understanding Significance Testing.* Thousand Oaks, CA: Sage Publications.

Mohr, Lawrence B. 1995. *Impact Analysis for Program Evaluation.* (Second ed.). Thousand Oaks, CA: Sage Publications.

Mosher, Clelia Duel. 1980. *The Mosher Survey: sexual attitudes of 45 victorian women.* James Mahood and Kristine Wenburg (eds.). North Stratford, NH: Ayer Company.

Napheys, George H. MD. 1876. *The Physical Life of Woman: Advice to the Maiden, Wife, and Mother.* Revised edition. Philadelphia: H. C. Watts & Company. (First published in 1870.)

Nichols, Thomas Low. 1853. *Esoteric Anthropology (The Mysteries of Man).* United Kingdom: Nichols, Malvern. Revised edition, 1873.

Patmore, Coventry. 1854-1862. *The Angel in the House.* http://www.gutenberg.org/cache/epub/4099/pg4099.html

Roth, Philip. 1963. *Goodbye, Columbus.* New York: Bantam.

Rothman, Ellen K. 1982. Sex and Self-Control: Middle-Class Courtship in America, 1770-1870. *Journal of Social History.* Vol. 15, No. 3, Special Issue on the History of Love. (Spring), pp. 409-425.

Rothman, Ellen K. 1987. *Hands and Hearts: A History of Courtship in America.* Cambridge: Harvard University Press.

Seidman, Steven. 1990. The power of desire and the danger of pleasure: Victorian sexuality reconsidered. *Journal of Social History.* Vol. 24, No. 1, Autumn, pp. 47-67.

Seidman, Steven 1991. *Romantic Longings: Love in America, 1830-1980.* New York: Routledge, Chapman & Hall.

Smith, Daniel Scott and Michael S. Hindus. 1975. Premarital Pregnancy in America 1640-1971: An Overview and Interpretation. *Journal of Interdisciplinary History,* Vol. 5, No. 4, Spring, The History of the Family II., pp. 537-570.

Smith, Daniel Scott. 1973a. Family Limitation, Sexual Control, and Domestic Feminism in Victorian America. *Feminist Studies.* Vol. 1, No. 3/4, Special Double Issue: Women's History. Winter-Spring, pp. 40-57.

Smith, Daniel Scott. 1973b. The Dating of the American Sexual Revolution: Evidence and Interpretation. In Michael Gordon (ed.), *The American Family in Social-Historical Perspective*. New York, St. Martins Press, pp. 321-335.

Smith, F. Barry. 1977. Sexuality in Britain, 1800-1900: Some suggested revisions. In Martha Vicinus (ed.) *Widening Sphere*. Chapter 9. Indiana University Press: Bloomington, pp. 182-198.

Smollett, Tobias. 1748. *Roderick Random*. In *The Complete Works of Tobias Smollett*. Kindle edition.

Stage, Sarah J. 1975. Review: Out of the attic: Studies of Victorian sexuality. *American Quarterly*. Vol. 27, No. 4, October, pp. 480-485.

Stang, Richard. 1959. *The Theory of the Novel in England, 1850-1870*. New York: Columbia University Press.

Stearns, Carol Z. and Peter N. Stearns. 1985. Victorian Sexuality: Can Historians Do It Better? *Journal of Social History*, Vol. 18, No. 4, Summer, pp. 625-634.

Stockham, Alice B., M.D. 1911. *Tokology: A Book for Every Woman*. London: L. N. Fowler & Co. (First published in 1883.)

Taine, Hyppolyte. 1900. *History of English Literature*. New York: Colonial Press.

Thomas, Keith. 1959. The Double Standard. *Journal of the History of Ideas*, Vol 20, No. 2, April, pp. 195-216.

Tillotson, Kathleen. 1954. *Novels of the 1840s*. Oxford: The Clarendon Press.

Tone, Andrea. 2000. Black Market Birth Control: Contraceptive Entrepreneurship and Criminality in the Gilded Age. *Journal of American History,* Vol. 87, No. 2, September, pp. 435-459.

Trudgill, Eric. 1976. *Madonnas and Magdalens: The Origins and Development of Victorian Sexual Attitudes.* New York: Holmes and Meier.

Vicinus, Martha (ed.). 1972. *Suffer and Be Still: Women in the Victorian Age.* Bloomington: Indiana University Press.

Vicinus, Martha (ed.). 1977. *Widening Sphere.* Bloomington: Indiana University Press.

Welter, Barbara. 1966. The cult of True Womanhood: 1820 – 1860. *American Quarterly,* Vol. 18, No. 2, Part 1, Summer, pp. 151-174.

Wikipedia. American Middle Class. Undated. http://en.wikipedia.org/wiki/American_middle_class

Wilson, Ben. 2007. *The Making of Victorian Values: Decency and Dissent in Britain, 1789-1837.* New York: Penguin Press.